25.00
CIIR

P9-CDJ-273

Acceptable Risk?

Acceptable Risk?

Making Decisions in a
Toxic Environment

LEE CLARKE

UNIVERSITY OF CALIFORNIA PRESS
Berkeley   Los Angeles   London

University of California Press
Berkeley and Los Angeles, California

University of California Press, Ltd.
London, England

© 1989 by
The Regents of the University of California

Library of Congress Cataloging-in-Publication Data

Clarke, Lee Ben.
    Acceptable risk? : making decisions in a toxic environment / Lee
Clarke.
        p.   cm.
    ISBN 0–520–06303–1 (alk. paper)
    1. Environmental protection—United States.   2. Risk assessment—
United States.   3. Environmental health—United States.
4. Environmental policy—United States.   I. Title.
TD171.C7 1989
363.1—dc19   88–30640
                                                                              CIP

Printed in the United States of America
1   2   3   4   5   6   7   8   9

For Frances Clarke
and Katherine Harvey

Contents

List of Tables and Figures

Acknowledgments

Other people besides myself share in the responsibility for this work. Robin Karbowski was generous with her time and ideas during the data-gathering stage of the study. Carol Heimer and Dorothy Nelkin carefully criticized the entire manuscript. John Gagnon pushed me to be interesting, while Paul Attewell pushed me to be precise. Judith Tanur caused me to be more sociological than I otherwise would have been, straightened out my confused logic, cleaned up my grammar, and shored up my morale. Michael Schwartz helped me find ways to make clear the sociological importance of this work, and introduced me to my editor, Naomi Schneider. Charles Perrow's support of the study was above and beyond the call of his duty as mentor. This study would be much the poorer without his searching critiques, unflagging friendship, and generosity in letting me borrow his ideas. My greatest debt, both intellectual and personal, is to Patricia Roos, who critiqued the whole manuscript several times and who serves as my reminder of the private significance of scholarly work.

I would not have been able to conduct this research without funding from the Russell Sage Foundation. Some of the editing of the manuscript was carried out while I was a postdoctoral scholar at UCLA (MH 14583 "Services Research Training Program"). Homer and Dolly Hand, forever my friends (and indispensable source of moral fortitude), granted me several summers of unfettered writing.

Finally, I owe a debt of gratitude to the people who allowed me to invade their personal and organizational lives to discover what they had done and why.

To all these people I extend heartfelt thanks.

List of Abbreviations

BCHD	Broome County Health Department
CDC	Centers for Disease Control
CSEA	Civil Service Employees Association
DEC	New York State Department of Environmental Conservation
DOH	New York State Department of Health
DOT	New York State Department of Transportation
EPA	Environmental Protection Agency (U.S.)
NEPCO	New England Pollution Control, Inc.
NIOSH	National Institute of Occupational Safety and Health
NYSEG	New York State Electric and Gas
OGS	New York State Office of General Services
OSHA	Occupational Safety and Health Administration
PBB	Polybrominated biphenyl
PCB	Polychlorinated biphenyl
PCDF	Polychlorinated dibenzofuran
SBA	Small Business Administration (U.S.)
SOB	(Binghamton) State Office Building
TCDD	Tetrachlorinated dibenzo-p-dioxin
TCDF	Tetrachlorinated dibenzofuran
TMI	Three Mile Island

ONE

Creating Risks

We now have a new environmental hazard to
live with. We have a unique event here that
could only happen in the chemical age.
                                  —Local health officer

Consider some grim statistics:

- In 1973 in Michigan, cattle feed was accidentally contaminated with PBB (more toxic than the familiar PCBs), resulting in the poisoning of more than 90 percent of that state's inhabitants (Egginton 1980).
- In 1976 in Seveso, Italy, a chemical plant explosion dispersed a cloud of toxic chemicals, including dioxin, over seven hundred acres and five thousand people, causing birds to drop out of trees and small animals to fall dead in their tracks. People who were outdoors suffered burning sores on their faces, arms, and legs; many developed chloracne, an ailment in which the skin develops hard, black, painful pimples that in some cases never go away (Whiteside 1979).
- In 1977 at Love Canal in Niagara Falls, New York, multicolored toxic sludge surfaced in residents' backyards, leading to complete disruption of a community, possible birth defects and cancer, and a bad reputation for the state of New York (Brown 1979; Levine 1982).
- In 1979 near Harrisburg, Pennsylvania, the near meltdown of a nuclear power plant at Three Mile Island (TMI) led to documented mental disturbances among young mothers (Bromet and Dunn 1981), arguably an increased cancer risk for nearby residents, and certain stress for the social fabric there. The accident at TMI also damaged the reputations of the nuclear industry and the Nuclear Regulatory Commission.

1

- In 1983 in Missouri, the entire town of Times Beach had to be bought by the federal government because high levels of dioxin were found in the soil. Adverse health effects have yet to be documented there, but, like Love Canal, the town suffered devastating social disruption.
- In 1984 a toxic chemical leak killed at least twenty-six hundred people in Bhopal, India.
- In 1986 in the Soviet Union, a near meltdown at the Chernobyl nuclear power station claimed an untold number of lives through radiation poisoning and cancer.

The common threads running through these cases are also the reasons they are sociologically interesting. At the most basic level, these tragedies are public health threats from substances and technologies over which victims have little control. Although it is not clear that such events are becoming more common, many of our newer technologies portend that they will (Perrow 1984). More important, in each of these incidents and others like them, *organizations* played central roles as agents of harm and rescue, and also as victims. This is not a trivial observation. People have always worried about threats over which they have little or no control—the Black Death, the diseases that decimated colonial populations, and floods, earthquakes, and famines. Today, organizations can create events or products at least as threatening as those created by the natural environment. At the same time, we depend on organizations to mitigate untoward consequences of risky technologies.

Over the past twenty years questions of risk have been increasingly debated in overtly political terms. Some argue that these risks are not so different from the threats people have worried about for centuries. Douglas and Wildavsky (1982, 10–11), for example, see similarities between the way people made sense of threats from Satan and "the evil world" and modern perceptions of insidious environmental hazards. Clark (1980) places popular concern over nuclear-power risks in the same category as superstitious fears of the evil eye, the environmental movement in the same category as witch hunts, and Rachel Carson's *Silent Spring* (1962) in the same category as the *Malleus*

Maleficarum.[1] These comparisons are certainly overdrawn, for there have been important changes in the way we think about, tolerate, and struggle over risks to life, community, and property.

One explanation for increased social conflict over questions of risk is that technological advances allow substances to be measured in ever-smaller quantities. Dioxins, for example, simply could not be studied twenty years ago, even though they were undoubtedly as dangerous then as they are now. But changes in measurement technology do not account for a heightened concern with risks, because there is nothing inherent in the risks themselves that necessarily leads to conflict. Rather, both the form and the content of political debate over hazards are socially defined, and it is those definitions that have changed.

The early 1960s were a watershed. Carson's book marked the beginning of an upsurge in the creation of formal organizations and voluntary associations designed to advance the causes of environmental and consumer protection, public health, and worker safety in the United States. The activities of these groups were not new simply because they challenged existing institutional arrangements. They differed from previous conflicts—class warfare during industrialization, mass protests during the Depression, and demonstrations against the United States' entry into World War I—in that, to be credible, laypeople had to understand highly specialized languages, technical details, tort law, resource mobilization, and bureaucratic organization.

As Carson's work spurred popular concern about toxic chemicals, Ralph Nader's *Unsafe at Any Speed* (1965), and its widespread acceptance, signaled important changes in conceptions of corporate responsibility. The first million-dollar award for product liability in 1962 symbolized a shift toward using the legal system to hold corporations responsible for hazards they create. (In 1962 there was only 1 million-dollar award; there

---

1. The *Malleus Maleficarum* (The Hammer of the Witches), published in 1486, was sanctioned by the Catholic church and was used to excuse witch hunting.

were 8 in 1970, 26 in 1975, 134 in 1980, and 360 in 1983 [*New York Times* 1985].)

One significant organizational response to this change in the social, economic, and political environments of corporations was the institutionalization of explicit, formal risk assessment as a method for balancing benefits and costs. Used in this form, risk assessment is an addition to the array of tools bureaucracies use to resolve competing demands. One of the more celebrated examples was the Ford Motor Company's use of formal risk analyses in its decision to produce the defective Pinto (Dowie 1977).

These social changes—pressure and increasing sophistication from below and the organizational response from above— suggest the importance of the role organizations play in defining acceptable risk (Heimer 1985). Yet we have few sociological studies of the processes through which organizations respond to technological risks. The premise of this book is that organizations are central actors in assessing, mitigating, and accepting risks. Moreover, it is usually the case that several or many organizations play key roles in situations involving risks. For each of the cases listed at the beginning of this chapter, corporations, voluntary associations, and federal, state, and local agencies determined the definitions of either the problems or the solutions. This suggests that differences in how collections of organizations are configured can affect policy regarding risk. In the pages to follow I examine in detail how a group of organizations responded to demands that risks be assessed and mitigated. I begin with a general description of the case.

The Binghamton State Office Building

Lois Whittemore is afraid to have children. She was twenty-three years old when the accident happened and, up to that point, always assumed she would settle down some day and help raise a family. But now Whittemore belongs to the growing list of victims of exposure to toxic materials, and her plans are more uncertain:

> You know, I want to get married and have children, but how will I know my babies will be okay? Someone told me not to worry be-

cause they now have good detection techniques and you can abort. But what about the next one? I can't do that too many times. (Whittemore interview, August 11, 1981)

Whittemore used to guard the Binghamton State Office Building, known sardonically in Binghamton as the SOB. Binghamton, New York, and the surrounding area, has a population of about 215,000 and lies about ten miles north of the Pennsylvania border and some two hundred miles northwest of New York City. Though hardly a metropolitan area, Binghamton is not rural. Broome County boasts seventeen corporations with more than five hundred employees, including branches of IBM, Savin, and Singer. In addition, the former New York senate majority leader is from Binghamton, and the Security Mutual Insurance Company is based there, as is a major university in the New York State system (SUNY, Binghamton). Binghamton also has four large hospitals (totaling 1,120 beds) and two newspapers.

The seat of government for Broome County, Binghamton had an office complex composed of three buildings, until the accident. Two of these buildings are used by both the city of Binghamton and Broome County. Each is six stories tall, with two additional stories underground. These two office buildings sit on either side of a third building, the Binghamton State Office Building (eighteen stories, the tallest in town), which housed thirty-three agencies and approximately seven hundred New York State employees.

The office complex is fairly new (construction was completed in 1966 at a cost of $17 million) and thus was built with many conveniences and technologies commonly available in modern workplaces. Among those technologies were the latest fire-protection systems, inasmuch as fires in large buildings can be so catastrophic. Hatches atop the stairwells, for example, automatically opened to the sky when the fire alarm was activated so that smoke would not get trapped in the escape routes. Another important fire-prevention feature was the use of a solution of 65 percent polychlorinated biphenyls (PCBs) and 35 percent chlorinated benzenes to cool the SOB's electrical transformers, located in the mechanical room in the basement. PCB solutions replaced mineral oil as transformer coolants because the former burn only at very high temperatures. But because PCBs cause cancer, liver disease, and other ailments, Congress banned their manufacture for "nonenclosed systems" in 1976 (Toxic Substances Control Act 1976).[2] Nevertheless, PCB solutions are still widely used—New York State alone has forty-five hundred PCB-containing transformers in public buildings. Approximately 95 percent of the electrical capacitors produced in the United States contain PCBs, although only an estimated 5 percent of electrical transformers contain the compound (NIOSH 1977, 26).

In addition to adverse health effects, other risks are also associated with PCB-containing transformer solutions. Many of these mixtures contain dibenzofurans and naphthalenes, both considered highly toxic (NIOSH 1977, 23–24). These mixtures, when burned at very high temperatures, can yield chemically separate compounds of dioxins (including 2,3,7,8 tetrachlorinated dibenzo-p-dioxin [TCDD], considered by many scientists to be our most deadly synthetic chemical), among other, generally less toxic, chemicals.[3]

At 5:33 A.M. on February 5, 1981, a switch gear (which functions much as a fuse box or circuit breaker does) in the SOB's mechanical room failed, causing an electrical arc that lasted twenty to thirty minutes. The heat in the room rose to an estimated 2,000 degrees Fahrenheit, causing a ceramic bushing on one of two nearby transformers to crack. About 180 gallons of the transformer's PCB-containing coolant were released by the accident. Fortunately, only two people were in the building that early in the morning, a guard and an engineer. It was no ordinary fire. The night guard on duty recalled: "Around five-thirty I heard this big noise that sounded like thunder. I thought an elevator had fallen, so I was on my way to the base-

2. The ban did not apply to PCB transformers already in use. Christoffer Rappe, a professor of organic chemistry in Sweden, reports ten similar fires in Sweden between 1981 and 1983. Rappe estimates there are 1.8 million capacitors and 200,000 PCB-containing transformers in the United States (Boffey 1983).

3. For information on the toxicological and other properties of these chemicals, see the entire issue of *Environmental Health Perspectives* (1973), NIOSH (1977), Esposito, Tiernan, and Dryden (1980), and Silbergeld (1983).

ment when the fire alarm went off. I talked to the engineer, and he was white as a ghost. He said there was a red glow coming from under and around a door that you normally could not see under" (Whittemore interview, August 11, 1981). The fire alarm summoned the graveyard shift of firefighters, and the guard directed them to the mechanical room. Crawling through the thick, black smoke, the assistant fire chief cracked the door and peeked in:

> First there would be this intense rumbling and then a large explosion. There were probably eight to ten electrical-arc explosions which sounded like a giant beast. There was oil all over the floor, and the stuff went through our gloves like they were made of gauze—it even went through our OSHA-approved boots, and *nothing* is supposed to go through those boots. I only looked in for about a second. It looked like an electrical storm in there; it looked just like a Frankenstein movie with all that electricity popping. When I looked at the electrical panel the next day it looked like a bullet the size of a cannon had gone through it. (Faughnan interview, August 13, 1981)

When the transformer coolant breached containment, it was vaporized by the intense heat, and the vapor mixed with soot that was produced when insulated wires (the only combustible materials present) caught fire. The fire alarm triggered the automatic hatches on the roof, which opened just as designed. But it gets cold in Binghamton in February (the temperature was below freezing), and heat rises. When firefighters opened the door to the mechanical room, the State Office Building became an eighteen-story chimney, drawing the contaminated soot up the stairwells, into the building's ventilation system, throughout the building, and out to downtown Binghamton. The SOB was completely contaminated with the oily, toxin-laden soot; even closed file cabinets and locked desk drawers did not escape the soot. Later, investigators realized that the spaces between each floor, used as plena for normal air circulation, helped distribute the poisons between walls, ruining insulation and ductwork. Unfortunately, one of the by-products of the burning transformer coolant was dioxin, which was also among the contaminants in the soot. The accident presented state and local agencies with a number of monumental, and very dangerous, tasks.

The cause of the accident is unknown. Only one of the two transformers leaked its coolant, and the switch gear that malfunctioned was not charged with electricity at the time. The electrical explosions wrought such damage to the switch gear that an intensive investigation was probably not possible. In any case, the State of New York removed both transformers shortly after the fire and buried them at a toxic waste dump in Niagara Falls in the summer of 1983, so explanations for why that particular transformer cracked, or indeed why there was a failure at all, will remain a mystery. Had the accident occurred in a building owned by a private company, it is likely that the spread of toxic chemicals would have been limited to the mechanical room. A private organization would have had to adhere to the fire codes of New York State, one of which is that a building's ventilation shafts must be sealed if they are located near a mechanical room. But New York State exempted itself from these requirements in public buildings.

At the time, the accident at the Binghamton State Office Building was unprecedented, although accidents involving dioxin were not new. In 1963 a chemical explosion contaminated a factory in Amsterdam, which was subsequently disassembled piece by piece, encased in concrete, and dumped in the Atlantic Ocean near the Azores. In 1976 residents of Seveso, Italy, were contaminated with dioxin as a result of an industrial accident (described at the beginning of this chapter). Other incidents occurred in West Germany in 1953, Czechoslovakia in the mid-1960s, and England in 1968 (Whiteside 1979, 26–27). None of these accidents, however, was in an office building—a seemingly unexceptional fact with quite exceptional implications, as we shall see.

Since the Binghamton accident, several similar incidents have been reported, although none has been as serious or extensive. Only a week after the Binghamton incident a transformer leak occurred in an office building in Albany, New York. On May 15, 1983, a transformer fire caused the evacuation of a large office building in San Francisco; 150 people are now included in a medical surveillance program as a result of that fire (Wegars 1983). In December of 1983 an office building in downtown Syracuse, New York, had to be closed in a similar incident (*New York Times* 1983). But in each of those cases the transformers were located outside the buildings; the toxic chemicals were thus spewed into the air or onto city streets rather than distributed throughout the buildings. New York State officials claim to have defined an acceptable level of exposure to the contaminants that remain in the SOB, though the building remained completely closed for seven and a half years. But even after several extensive cleanups, it is still appropriate to ask, Is this acceptable risk?

Organizational Anarchy and Personal Jeopardy

The accident at the Binghamton State Office Building had several adverse consequences. One immediate misfortune was that seven hundred hapless workers suddenly had to be relocated to crowded, ill-equipped offices throughout Binghamton. An official at the New York State Department of Labor, whose office had been in the SOB, remarked from his new office:

> At the State Office Building, we had a rotating phone line, so if one line was busy, the phone would automatically trip the call over to the next line. Now, the call gets tripped over to the next line at the [State] Office Building, but we can't answer it. So it just rings and rings. People get angry because they think we're not answering our phone. (McCullough 1981b)

Worse than the loss of sophisticated telephone systems was the loss of files, which gave new meaning to the term "bureaucratic nightmare." As if to confirm Max Weber's analysis of the centrality of written files to the functioning of bureaucratic organizations, employees complained: "Our normal working habits are based on working around files. Those files are one of a kind. Now they're unavailable" (McCullough 1981b). Another employee told a reporter: "All our records and files are locked in the tower. Geez, all our brains are in there" (*Binghamton Evening Press* 1981a). An estimated eighty thousand files were lost because of the tainted soot, delaying bridge and highway construction, complicating lawsuits and criminal trials, postponing worker-compensation hearings, and slowing distribution of checks to the disabled. Thousands of tax returns and refunds were lost. These adverse effects of the accident were eventually overcome, however, as agencies found new homes in different locations throughout the city. Indeed, according to state workers, the New York agencies displaced from their offices in the State Office Building are now functioning as well as they did before the accident.

But the accident involved more serious consequences. First was the problem of what to do with the toxic tower. The puzzle of cleaning up the SOB is an intriguing one, and, indeed, many of the pieces are still missing. The building has gone through several cleanups to date, and although the State of New York has declared acceptable levels of chemical exposure for people who will again work in the building, it is still not clear that levels of toxic chemicals can be reached that all will agree are safe. Previous cleanup technologies—such as buying entire communities (Love Canal) and towns (Times Beach) and closing them off to people, perhaps forever—were not options in Binghamton. Two weeks after the accident, the commissioner of the New York Health Department, Dr. David Axelrod, said: "Right now we are learning to walk. This [decontamination] has never been done before, and we are working to discover what levels are safe" (Fecteau 1981d).

State agencies have worked assiduously to define acceptable levels of risk from the toxic chemicals, and some of their efforts have been pioneering. There are no standards for acceptable levels of exposure to PCBs on surfaces (although the Occupational Safety and Health Administration [OSHA] has set an acceptable level for airborne PCBs), and no standards whatsoever exist for exposure to dioxins and furans. Although state officials have been determined to clean the building and put it back into service, scientists agree there is no threshold level below which dioxins pose no risk to human health. Thus, cleanups progressed in Binghamton without the benefit of knowing when it was appropriate to stop.

The second important problem was what to do with the people who were exposed to the toxic chemicals. The New York State Department of Health is conducting medical surveillance on 482 exposed people, but there are important uncertainties in the project, ranging from the definition of the exposed population, to the number of people who should be tested, to the value of medical surveillance itself. There is, after all, no cure for exposure to toxic substances. Later in this book I examine the surveillance program in detail, seeking to understand the process that created it and its underlying assumptions. As an organizational response to a highly ambiguous task, the medical surveillance program furnishes an interesting opportunity to observe the interplay among organizational interests, politics, and science.

Science and experts, as one would expect, have played crucial roles in the Binghamton story, but they have failed to provide the answers some might expect of them. "High-tech accidents" involve state-of-the-art science in the process that produced the accident itself (such as in nuclear and chemical plants), in recovery from ill-effects (such as medical treatment and detection of maladies), or in solutions designed to insulate populations from hostile agents (such as decontamination technologies and protective measures). Because science and technology figure so prominently in accidents such as those in Binghamton, Three Mile Island, and Bhopal, solutions tend to be framed in technical terms. Although technical issues are certainly important, they have neither posed the most important dilemmas facing decision makers in Binghamton nor provided solutions to them. Science and experts have failed to provide either clear definitions of acceptable risk or ways to make trade-offs between organizational health and public health. Although we almost instinctively turn to science for answers to problems such as those produced by the SOB, science is rarely able to solve such social problems.

The reactions to the State Office Building accident provide a valuable opportunity to examine how "tragic choices"—to borrow an apt phrase from Calabresi and Bobbitt (1978)—are assessed and ameliorated. Organizational theory, along with some ideas from the literature on risk analysis, furnish the main clues to understanding those reactions. I draw on loose-coupling theories of decision making to explain the processes through which risks were defined and accepted. The analysis departs from previous work in two basic ways. First, by extending the ideas of decision-making theory to the interorganizational (as opposed to intraorganizational) level of analysis, we gain a useful analytic tool for understanding how organizations behave under ambiguous conditions involving multiple actors. Second, by placing problems of risk analysis within their organizational contexts, we gain a realistic understanding of the important social factors and interests that shape definitions of acceptable risk.

· · ·

This is a detailed study of organizations and publics interacting in a very uncertain environment, trying to solve some perplexing social and technical problems. The general process developed thus: The State Office Building accident drew together more than a score of actors—including legislative bodies, health agencies, unions, government executives, hospitals, the media, private firms, universities, and a grass-roots association—to form a crowd of organizations. This early phase after the accident was characterized by pervasive ambiguities as the actors struggled to define both the problem and their response. Over time, the organizational crowd configured itself so that three agencies were left with the responsibility for the exposed people and the polluted building. As this structuring process proceeded, policies that were designed to solve those puzzles underwent radical change.

The next chapter describes initial medical surveillance and cleanup efforts, thus introducing the major topics addressed in the later chapters. Chapter 3 examines why the many organizations from local, state, and federal levels of government—organizations that *could* have been more involved in the controversies over the State Office Building—were *not*. A form of counterfactual inquiry, chapter 3 traces the contours of the social, political, and organizational environments of the agencies described in the succeeding chapters. Chapter 4 departs from the main story line to explore how the county government assessed and resolved the risk of the contaminated garage under the State Office Building (a task jurisdictionally separate from decontamination of the SOB). In many ways, the solutions and problems attached to the garage mirrored those of the SOB. One important difference, however, is that the garage was fairly quickly declared safe and reopened for use.

In chapters 5 and 6 I return to medical surveillance and decontamination, respectively, to analyze the specific solutions that were devised to deal with the poisoned people and the poisoned building. Chapter 7 examines the reactions and perceptions of those without direct connections to organizational authority: exposed workers and a grass-roots association that formed to protest definitions of acceptable risk developed by New York State. In the final chapter I draw some conclusions about risk analysis and recent developments in organization theory.

TWO

Organizational Chaos: Beginning Decontamination and Medical Surveillance

I think it's crazy that the scientists don't know
what they created and don't know what to
do about it.

—Office worker

The [estimates of] months and years are a
little far-fetched; I think we're looking at
a month.

—Cleanup engineer

The State Office Building accident provoked responses from
many organizations. Because the building was out of service,
New York's Office of General Services (OGS), which is responsible for maintaining state buildings, initiated a cleanup effort.
Because the soot was contaminated with dangerous chemicals,
the local and state health departments also became involved.
Because the accident received a great deal of media attention,
local and state politicians frequently commented. The actual
content of these apparently reasonable responses made little
sense, however—at least from the standpoint of social theory.
There was no obvious connection between organizational com-
petence and participation (or the lack of participation) in key
decisions regarding medical surveillance and decontamination.
Solutions were constructed that were not obviously relevant to
the problems at hand. Pronouncements from officials served
mainly to polarize positions rather than to inform. Decontamination and medical surveillance programs were set in motion,
but agencies and officials could not agree on the basic parameters of the problems. The situation, in short, was highly ambiguous. In this chapter I describe this organizational chaos.

Decontamination

Two days after the fire, on February 7, 1981, OGS set about to rehabilitate the State Office Building. Although one of the two transformers was undamaged, and therefore presumably still usable, both were removed from the mechanical room and carted away to a landfill. Engineers worked to prevent possible damage to water pipes in the unheated building (temperatures outside were in the teens), and so used a large extension cord to connect the SOB to the electrical system of the nearby Broome County office building. "We have a serious problem," said OGS's senior public building manager. "If we don't get in there tonight, we'll have no building" (Geimann 1981a). OGS officials in Albany, where OGS is headquartered, also recruited janitors from its offices in Binghamton and other locations around the state for an initial cleanup effort. Twenty-two janitors spent almost three weeks working in the building, until it was closed on February 26, 1981, by state officials.

This cleanup was by most accounts a disaster in itself. Privately, officials described the janitorial cleanup as "chaotic," "unfortunate," or "bungled." The two local newspapers reported that workers were passing from the SOB to the adjacent city building to change from their protective suits into their street clothes and to use restrooms. Photographs were published showing janitors working without face masks, and there were reports that protective gear was used only sporadically. Later, it was discovered that some cash and lottery tickets, all contaminated with toxic chemicals, had been stolen from a newsstand in the building and that food and cigarettes from the building's cafeteria had been consumed by the janitors. To make matters worse, the building's entrances and exits were not closely supervised, so that by the time the building was closed (three weeks after the fire) nearly five hundred people had been directly exposed to the toxic soot; those indirectly exposed through leakage from the building and from materials that were removed remain uncounted.

Between the day of the fire and the day decontamination was halted, state officials aroused anger and distrust among Binghamton's citizens, the media, the county medical society, the

Binghamton city council, and the Broome County Health Department (BCHD) by belittling possible dangers. Citizens' suspicions that the state was minimizing the SOB's hazards were seemingly confirmed when Governor Hugh L. Carey insisted:

> Somebody went amok in the Binghamton condition. I offer here and now to walk into Binghamton, to any part of that building, and swallow an entire glass of PCB and then run a mile afterwards. . . . I'd like to meet that local health officer who put that building in that [*sic*]. . . . If I had a couple of willing hands and a few vacuum cleaners I'd clean that building myself.[1] (portion of transcript from Carey's press conference, March 17, 1981)

Charges of maleficence and deception were published in the local papers almost daily. Within a month after the fire, lawsuits totaling $1 billion were pending against the State of New York.

On February 26, the commissioner of the Office of General Services, along with the state health department, stopped the janitorial cleanup and officially closed the building. This action was ostensibly prompted by the discovery that highly toxic dioxins and furans, in addition to PCBs, were among the contaminants in the soot. The commissioner of OGS announced:

> Last night, Dr. Axelrod [commissioner of the New York Health Department] and I discussed the most recent test results as well as the valuable information we obtained from our cleaning operation to date. Our conclusion was that in light of this more detailed information, the most productive action is to suspend the present cleaning operations. . . . While the indefinite suspension of cleaning activities in the building is a conservative step, I believe it is the most realistic one at this time. (OGS, February 26, 1981)

Before analyzing this first decontamination, let us outline the initial medical surveillance effort.

Medical Surveillance

In a sense, medical surveillance of people exposed to the toxins began when Binghamton's assistant fire chief sent his fire-

---

1. Four years later Carey conceded that his comment had been "reckless," the product of a "moment of frustration" (Lynn 1985).

fighters to Binghamton General Hospital for physical examinations. He had looked into the mechanical room, where he saw a label on one of the transformers warning of PCBs. After the fire was extinguished, he consulted Chemtrec, an emergency information service maintained by the Chemical Manufacturers Association, and a slim "emergency response guidebook" entitled *Hazardous Materials* (1980). While the firefighters waited for Chemtrec to return their calls, they read precautions from the guidebook. Warnings such as "keep unnecessary people away" and "isolate hazard area and deny entry" seemed sensible enough, but they were puzzled to read at the top of the single page devoted to PCBs that there was "little immediate health hazard," and then at the bottom that firefighters should "remove and isolate clothing and shoes."

Several firefighters had sustained burns and rashes while extinguishing the fire, so the fire chief called Binghamton General's chief executive officer, Dr. Jason Moyer, at eight-thirty on the morning of the accident to relay what he knew of the chemicals and to let him know that the firefighters were being sent over for examinations. The hospital was the poison-control center for the Binghamton area, but until that morning, hospital officials had not even been aware of a test for PCB levels in the body. It is not the sort of information that one needs on a daily basis.

Dr. Moyer first called the local utility company, New York State Electric and Gas (NYSEG), for information on the chemicals but was told that because the transformer did not belong to the utility, NYSEG was not responsible. He then called General Electric (G.E.) in Syracuse and obtained information on the chemical properties of PCBs; he also found out that Monsanto had manufactured the transformer's coolant. Moyer talked to Monsanto's medical director, who told him that PCBs can cause chloracne, a very serious, sometimes permanent skin disorder. He also learned that exposure to PCBs is associated with liver damage.

In the meantime, Dr. Arnold Schecter, director of the Broome County Health Department, was called to the State Office Building, where firefighters warned him of the PCBs and advised him to call the hospital. Moyer then relayed what he now knew, prompting Schecter to call G.E. himself, whereupon he learned the coolant mixture was 65 percent PCB and 35 percent chlorinated benzenes. Because BCHD was responsible for monitoring some wells contaminated with benzenes (among other toxic chemicals) in a nearby town, Schecter was familiar with the dangers of those chemical compounds. He told reporters it was unlikely that the building was much of a health hazard but nevertheless reckoned that extensive medical examinations were in order.

In view of the OGS's assumption of fiscal responsibility for the building, Schecter sought authorization from an OGS official to order medical tests. Receiving that authority on the day of the accident (February 5), Binghamton General began conducting physical exams and drawing blood for testing. Several employees at BCHD were charged with coordinating the voluminous paperwork that would be generated by such an effort. Schecter also began contacting experts around the world for advice on proper testing procedures and for toxicological information.

Although the New York State Department of Health (DOH) eventually came to play an important role in the Binghamton incident, its initial response was less than might have been expected. Commissioner Axelrod flew to Binghamton the day after the fire, held a press conference where he announced that an OGS engineer would direct the cleanup, assigned two DOH officials to advise the engineer, appointed Schecter as his on-site representative—a decision he would soon regret—and then returned to Albany. The two DOH advisors Axelrod appointed had worked on problems associated with Love Canal; indeed, the SOB's first "safety plan" was, according to the engineer in charge, the Love Canal plan reworked for the special conditions at the State Office Building.

By the time the DOH advisors arrived in Binghamton, the laboratory at Binghamton General was performing physical examinations on some of the exposed people and drawing blood for tests. Three test tubes of blood were taken from each of the 479 exposed people, and the sera extracted for later analysis. The head of Binghamton General's labs knew little about blood tests for PCBs and therefore called several commercial laboratories to check on their capabilities and prices—an important consideration with so many samples to test. Chemlab, a firm in New Jersey, offered to do the tests for $30 each. Three hundred of the frozen samples were carefully packed and mailed to New Jersey.[2] Chemlab discovered no PCBs in the samples.

After test results began flowing into BCHD, the next step was to transmit them to the patients' physicians. The records had to be organized, patients had to be notified, and patients' written consent to release the documents had to be obtained. Because Schecter was the physician of record, he was responsible for seeing that those tasks were accomplished. BCHD personnel, of course, were already committed to other projects, so BCHD asked DOH for assistance and OGS for resources to hire a nurse. Although OGS had approved funding for the blood tests, it refused this request for assistance, as well as subsequent ones. As one official put it: "Schecter asked me if he could do PCB bloods. He was my consultant, and I knew nothing about that stuff. So I said, 'Arnie, if you think you need that, go ahead.' Now I guess I was wrong" (Seiffert interview, October 8, 1981).

Although, officially, Schecter represented the state department of health, DOH, like the Office of General Services, soon expressed dissatisfaction with the policies his organization was instituting. DOH officials, who had started out as advisors to the county, soon began to question the county's role in medical surveillance and especially challenged BCHD's control of the test results.

Schecter's program called for testing everyone who was exposed, including people in buildings close to the State Office Building and members of the general public who had ventured near it. But DOH disagreed not only with this broad definition of exposure but also with the need for a large-scale study in the first place. Some state scientists claimed Chemlab's failure to detect PCBs indicated the lab had inadequate facilities; nearly everyone, they argued, should show at least some levels of it in their bodies (because of the ubiquity of PCBs in the environ-

2. Two tubes of sera were to be kept in the hospital's freezers for later use. Only three hundred samples were sent to "Chemlab" (not the lab's real name), because DOH intervened and halted the testing.

ment). Moreover, DOH officials blamed Schecter himself for this apparent bad judgment. One of the advisors appointed by Axelrod, for example, was convinced that the data from the initial medical surveillance were useless. He argued that because the subjects had not fasted before the blood samples were taken, the data were "dirty" and that Schecter was exacerbating, rather than helping to alleviate, a difficult situation. This official claimed that Schecter sent the blood samples "to some laboratory that basically didn't know a hole in the ground from PCB analysis, and as a result we have . . . blood analyses for PCB that cost $30 a sample that are totally worthless" (Taylor interview, July 8, 1981).

These initial conflicts between the county and state health departments (as well as the Office of General Services) were the beginning of a tumultuous process of negotiation over what roles these organizations would play in solving the problems created by the State Office Building accident. Later, we will examine the outcome of those negotiations in detail. For the present, we need to analyze the general disorganization among organizations in the wake of the accident.

Interpreting Organizational Anarchy

The Binghamton State Office Building accident drew together an assortment of organizations to deal with some difficult problems. Cleanup and medical surveillance were the focal points for their interactions. Their initial efforts raise two vexing issues about these focal points. Why would the Office of General Services send untrained and relatively unsupervised janitors into an eighteen-story toxic-disaster site without informing them that their work environment contained dioxins?[3] One tempting explanation is that it is somehow inherent in bureaucratic organizations to conceal their mistakes and to ignore the negative consequences of their actions. This reasoning is found in popular accounts of Union Carbide's response to the chemical carnage in Bhopal, Hooker Chemical's (and the New York

3. Had a private corporation done this, the state's Right-to-Know law probably would have been violated.

Health Department's) response to health threats from Love Canal, and General Public Utilities' response to the accident at Three Mile Island. This view, which might be labeled the "callous-bureaucracy theory," is attractive because it establishes a clear connection between the intent of those who run organizations and organizational action, thereby permitting ready assessment of responsibility and comprehension of otherwise baffling behavior. Fortunately, the data from Binghamton, unlike comparable data from Bhopal, Love Canal, and TMI, allow us to take a detailed look at exactly why officials instituted a project that seems so clearly imprudent.

The callous-bureaucracy theory would hold that decision makers should have known from the start that using janitors for the initial cleanup was ill advised. Even common sense would suggest the folly of using nonexperts for such dangerous work. State officials rejected this charge, claiming that the janitors' lack of experience and training was irrelevant and that, had the cleanup crew followed instructions, no problems would have ensued. The OGS deputy commissioner, for example, believed the janitorial cleanup was basically a sound idea, "but not with that group." This defense is not very convincing, however; these same officials would not have used bookkeepers, however well trained, to perform the tasks of OGS's accountants preparing an annual budget.

Moreover, there is some evidence to support the charge that OGS tried to conceal its mistake. OGS's deputy commissioner, when asked what OGS would have done had it known about dioxins earlier, replied: "We closed the building on the twenty-sixth, the day after the evening we found out dioxins were there, so obviously if we had known, we probably would have closed it much sooner" (Hudacs interview, October 8, 1981). But the presence of dioxins and furans in the building might not have been as unexpected as these officials suggest. The New York State Department of Health employs some of the leading toxicologists, chemists, and health experts in the world, and its scientists and technicians are widely respected in the scientific community. Many of them have done extensive and pioneering work on dioxins and PCBs (and worked on the Love Canal case, which involved some of the same chemicals). It is difficult to believe these scientists did not suspect chemicals more toxic than PCBs were also in the soot.

There are additional reasons to believe that officials suspected these highly toxic chemicals were present very soon after the accident. On February 11, 1981, for example (six days after the accident, fifteen days before the SOB was closed), a DOH official wrote a memorandum to the OGS engineer in charge of the cleanup; attached to the memorandum was the first written "safety plan." That document describes the accident and concludes that "other hazardous pyrolysis products are probably present," although those products are not identified (Huffaker to Seiffert, February 11, 1981). In another early intra-agency document, a DOH scientist describes the procedures used for detecting dioxins and furans in the soot samples, concluding that "the concentration of CDFs [chlorinated dibenzofurans] increased approximately 1,000-fold from pyrolysis of PCBs in the fire" (O'Keefe, February 8, 1981). Additionally, in a description of work performed at the behest of the state, a private cleanup firm called to the disaster site on the day of the accident notes the "possible levels of dioxin released by fire" (Briganti interview, July 17, 1981). This report was signed by the cleanup firm's president and a representative of the New York State Department of Transportation, with whom it had its original contract. Discoveries such as these lend support to the charge that state bureaucracies deliberately misled workers and the public about their early knowledge of these deadly chemicals.

At the same time, there are good organizational reasons to doubt that state officials plotted a pernicious cover-up. It is unlikely that OGS would deliberately pursue a course of action that would be certain to bring bad publicity; nor is it likely that decision makers would knowingly subject workers to unnecessary toxic-chemical exposure. Furthermore, the decision to use a crew of janitors was not a bungled attempt to deny there was an important problem in the building. It was clear from interviews with OGS employees that they possess an almost reverent regard for their role in keeping state organizations operating. As one high-level official in Albany said: "This is the first time in eighteen years that I haven't opened a state building. Even during the blizzard of 1977, Watertown and Buffalo were open. We've never had anything like this before" (Fecteau 1981a). The loss of the building greatly disrupted operations for many organizations, and in beginning remediation for the SOB, the Office of General Services was performing its major responsibility: to keep state agencies operating.

There is also evidence that it was simply inconceivable that an eighteen-story building could be so completely poisoned with dioxins, furans, and PCBs. The soot was obviously distributed throughout the building, including file cabinets and hidden spaces, but there was no reason to think *the soot itself* was contaminated with toxic chemicals. As the engineer in charge of the cleanup remarked, "It wasn't until Saturday [more than two days after the fire] that we realized chemicals were in the soot" (Seiffert interview, October 8, 1981). Similarly, the OGS official who ordered the formation of the cleanup crew said: "We had no reason to think that PCBs were in the soot. We just thought we had a soot problem to be cleaned up. We certainly didn't know dioxins were there" (Beaudoin interview, October 6, 1981).

For these officials, the most logical definition of the problem was that the State Office Building was "dirty." "We had a cleanup job," said the cleanup supervisor. "So it was a job for janitors; it seemed like a great idea to send the workers in at the time" (Seiffert interview, October 8, 1981). In fact, it was not until a week after the fire that OGS officials began to comprehend the task ahead of them. "I had high hopes in the beginning," said the supervisor of the cleanup, "that it would just be a janitorial thing, not contamination, but it's a whole other thing, the extent of it" (Fecteau 1981c).

In 99 percent of the cases that might require these types of actions (e.g., organizing workers, sanitizing a building), OGS's response would have been exemplary. The crew was swiftly organized, and cleanup was efficiently begun. Moreover, the written warning from the cleanup company president probably never reached important decision makers in the Office of General Services. It was a long organizational road from the chaos in Binghamton to the local Department of Transportation office to the highest offices in the state health department and then over to OGS, and the report probably never moved beyond a file cabinet in a relatively low-level office.[4]

OGS's decision to send in the vacuum brigade can also be considered in another way: Imagine OGS engineers, the day after the accident, announcing to the press that they were closing down the State Office Building because they suspected it was permeated with an oily soot containing polychlorinated biphenyls, polychlorinated dibenzo-p-dioxins, and polychlorinated dibenzofurans. Charges of bureaucratic bungling and foot-dragging would have been both immediate and scathing. Health experts had given no indication that there was much to be concerned about, and nearly seven hundred people suddenly had no place to work. The director of the Broome County Health Department told reporters: "With PCBs you have a built-in safety factor in that it has a characteristic odor. If you can smell it, you can just get away from it. Almost no one should have anything other than a short-term problem" (Fecteau 1981a). The director also said, referring to the cleanup, "It's not too much of a health hazard" (Fecteau 1981a), and: "We've got an inconsequential problem. The people who were exposed seem to be in good shape" (Geimann 1981a).

Looking closely at the decision-making process, we learn that the procedure for proper decontamination was not at all obvious. OGS's decisions were based on certain premises about the nature of the problem they confronted, premises that were no doubt developed in response to situations the organization had faced in the past. That these premises were inappropriate for the State Office Building situation and led to decisions with adverse consequences should not lead us to neglect the fact that, *given the assumptions and constraints under which officials were working, the decision to send in the untrained janitors made reasonable organizational sense.*

This analysis suggests that the callous-bureaucracy theory, as applied to Binghamton as well as to other incidents (e.g., TMI, Bhopal, Chernobyl), fails to take into account social constraints

---

4. Repeated attempts to obtain a copy of this report, through Freedom of Information Act requests, were unsuccessful. All officials who might have known of the document were interviewed, but none knew its whereabouts.

on official behavior in ambiguous situations. This is an important issue because if organizational reform is based on assumptions that bureaucracies are inherently callous—when in fact other factors are at work in decision making—then the reforms will be ineffective and possibly even dangerous.

Turning to medical surveillance, why was there acrimonious conflict between the state and county health departments? Both organizations had identical mandates to protect public health, and they each had special and complementary competencies. DOH possessed superior resources (more personnel, more funds, etc.), while BCHD commanded the knowledge necessary to negotiate the local political environment.

Again the callous-bureaucracy theory offers one explanation for this clash: that is, the state health department was only marginally concerned with the risks to public health posed by the SOB, whereas the county health department was virtuously fulfilling its responsibility to protect public health. Again, too, there is some evidence to support this theory. It is certainly true that DOH tended to deny the potential significance of the incident, a tendency it had exhibited regarding Love Canal several years before (Levine 1982). It is also true that BCHD took its responsibility to protect Binghamton's population very seriously, even to the point of alienating important state officials such as the governor. And, yet, we miss some important features of the conflict by focusing on official motivations or organizational missions. After all, it is doubtful that DOH officials were conspiring to harm the public, and there is no reason to impute any particular heroism to BCHD officials just because they were doing their jobs.

The county and state health departments had similar goals but could not agree on the appropriate means for ensuring public health. Beyond this obvious fact, though, it is not clear why these organizations disagreed so strongly over the need for and design of medical surveillance. To understand this conflict, we need to analyze the interorganizational context in which these problems emerged.

The state health department held the view that the initial medical surveillance was badly designed, lacked a systematic protocol, and was therefore fruitless. DOH officials also argued that the PCB blood analyses were scientifically and medically worthless, partly because the subjects had not fasted, and that sending the blood samples to Chemlab was a bad decision.

From the view of BCHD, however, the experts could not specify what should be done both medically and epidemiologically for the exposed people. Few available experts, including those from DOH, knew much about detecting symptoms of PCB exposure (the presence of dioxins would have aggravated the medical and epidemiological problems posed by the accident had their presence been widely acknowledged). Schecter, after some inquiries, found out that PCBs can adversely affect the liver, and because the liver helps purify blood, the blood seemed a likely place to detect them. Moreover, the lack of a detailed protocol made data interpretation difficult, but not impossible. Indeed, without BCHD's initial actions, DOH would have had no data for the analyses it later conducted. When the blood was drawn for the PCB analyses, three test tubes were taken from each person and then frozen. (Most of one set was sent to Chemlab; the rest were subsequently forwarded to the state health department.) This foresight provided the state an opportunity to have the extra samples analyzed at a later date, perhaps permitting measurements of change over time. True, the samples were collected under less than perfect conditions (e.g., the subjects had not fasted), but this is not unusual in epidemiological research. Most important, the state health commissioner had explicitly assigned responsibility for public health to BCHD but did not grant sufficient access to scientific and political resources that might facilitate that task. Acrimonious and unproductive conflict between the organizations was structured into their relations.

•   •   •

The immediate aftermath of the accident constituted what might be termed an "interorganizational garbage can." Briefly, "garbage can" theory seeks to explain how decisions are made within organizations when conditions are unclear (Cohen, March, and Olsen 1972; March and Olsen 1979). It holds that in some organizations (e.g., universities) the connections between problems and solutions, between decision makers and choices, and between intentions and outcomes are loosely coupled and, indeed, may vary in an almost random fashion. The accident at the SOB created similar ambiguities, but *among* rather than within organizations. Normal relations between organizations were disrupted as routines of conducting business changed rapidly and in unpredictable ways. An assembly of loosely coupled organizations was drawn together with few established rules to govern their behavior. Because no agency possessed an obvious obligation or right to deal with the effects of the accident, it was surprisingly easy for organizations to become involved with, or to avoid, the problems of the contaminated building and the exposed people. One consequence of this lack of structure was that participation in key decisions and policies was more fluid than might be expected.

Another important ambiguity affected the medical and scientific responses. Although the accident raised a number of scientific problems (detecting chemicals, measuring exposure), the appropriate response was not obvious. There *were* methods for detecting levels of toxic chemicals in the human body. Schecter and coauthors, for example, report high levels of furans and dioxins in subjects' fatty tissue (cited in Fox 1983). It is not clear, however, what these results signify. Dioxin-induced illnesses are nebulous, including chloracne, liver necrosis, hyperpigmentation, myocardial damage, cancer, muscle pains and cramps, irritation, diminished libido and mental capacity, and depression (Baughman 1974). Specifying the etiology of these illnesses, moreover, requires holding many variables constant, making it very difficult to directly relate amount and duration of exposure to specific medical maladies. Nevertheless, it was important to implement a medical monitoring program for two reasons: (1) its findings might be used in lawsuits to apportion blame for unnecessary exposure; and (2) it might help to detect cancers in their early stages.

The organizational behavior chronicled in this chapter contradicts usual views about how organizations act. Theories of rational choice stress the extent to which the search for alternatives is clearly related to some goal or problem. From this standpoint, we might judge that OGS's decision to use janitors as decontamination workers was the result of insufficient consideration of the seriousness of the situation, in addition to being organizationally and politically foolish. But, as the evidence shows, such a view of the decision-making process would be inaccurate. For the rational model to be useful, decision makers must clearly define the problem or goal toward which action is directed. Yet the goals for both cleanup and medical surveillance for the Binghamton accident were quite vague in this early period: It was difficult to define the extent and nature of contamination within and outside of the building, and there was considerable disagreement among organizations concerning the possible dangers of exposure. Indeed, as I document in chapters 5 and 6, it was not until these organizational problems moved toward resolution that a medical surveillance protocol was constructed and acceptable risk defined.

Rational models of decision making also posit that decision makers will consider a wide range of competing solutions before choosing one that will maximize some utility. In this case, the utility would be protecting public health and cleaning the building so that state organizations could use it again. If, as I argued above, the goals in Binghamton were not well defined, how could such a menu of choices exist? Clearly, no such array of solutions was presented to decision makers, nor was there a wide-ranging search for options. For example, rather than create new solutions to the contamination problem, OGS picked a solution with which it was proficient—sweeping and vacuuming—rather than a solution more appropriate for toxic-chemical contamination.

Similarly, concerning medical surveillance, a rational model predicts that when a set of organizations is confronted with a new problem, the organizations will arrange themselves in accordance with the principle of comparative advantage so that agencies divide tasks and assume responsibilities for which each is best suited. Thus, because the Broome County Health Department was closest to the scene of the accident, it was functionally necessary for it to be assigned the responsibility of overseeing medical monitoring, while the New York State Department of Health could best serve public health by providing advice and expertise and otherwise supporting the efforts of the local health department. But the facts of the case argue for a different interpretation. BCHD was not designated the state's representative because of functional necessity but because the state health department did not, initially at least, perceive the State Office Building to be an important threat to public health. In addition, DOH, aside from a small measure of advice, did not support Broome County's medical surveillance plan—another departure from the rational model.

In chapters 5 and 6 I return to the problems of medical surveillance and decontamination, respectively, for a more detailed treatment of the development of the policies to mitigate the risks posed by the State Office Building. As I lay the empirical groundwork for understanding that process, I will more explicitly develop the interorganizational "garbage can" theory, which provides another way to view decision making. At this point, it suffices to note that neither the callous-bureaucracy theory nor the functional, rationalist theory is conceptually equipped to explain how decisions about the SOB emerged from the interactions of many organizations. At the end of the most important of those processes—the one that structured relationships among agencies—three main organizations assumed the major responsibility for the SOB and the exposed people. This situation, however, was not inevitable. We therefore need to examine other organizations that might have played more important roles in the Binghamton case. That is the topic of the next chapter.

THREE

Constricting the Field of Organizations

They can't just be part of the problem. They
have to be part of the solution as well.
—State health commissioner,
on the EPA

To understand modern horror stories such as Chernobyl, the
Challenger disaster, and the "poisoning of Michigan" (Egginton
1980), one needs to take the larger context into account. For
sociologists, this means broadening our scope of vision so that
decisions can be understood within the context of organizational environments. I argued earlier that it is impossible to
explain key decisions in Binghamton without examining the
multiorganizational settings from which they emerged. I will
now expand the analysis to address the plethora of organizations that made up the remote environment in which those decisions were made.

Ultimately, three agencies—the Broome County Health Department, the New York State Health Department, and the
New York State Office of General Services—assumed responsibility for developing and implementing programs to rehabilitate the building, monitor the exposed people, and define acceptable levels of risk. This particular arrangement of agencies
was not foreordained but, rather, emerged from an eight-
month-long process during which many organizations flowed
into and out of policy domains.

The members of this larger set of agencies were not centrally
involved in devising solutions to the problems of cleanup and
medical monitoring. Nevertheless, there are good theoretic
reasons to analyze their behavior. "Garbage can" theory implies
that organizations are repositories for solutions to a range of
problems. It follows that the more organizations involved in a

policy domain, the higher the likelihood that alternative solutions will be proposed and considered. Soon after the accident at the State Office Building, many organizations had the potential to affect definitions of acceptable risk by posing alternative policies or solutions. With time, the field of possible contributors dwindled, creating one of the conditions necessary for defining and legitimating an acceptable level of risk.

In this chapter the chief ambiguity we see resolved is that of the distribution of authority among organizations. Although there certainly were no formal connections among most of these actors, there was remarkably little variation in the range of responses they offered. The collective effect of those responses, not planned in any meaningful sense, was both a decrease in public debate over questions of risk and a rearrangement of authority among organizations, the more powerful of which were state government agencies.

Local Agencies

City Government

Problems of toxic contamination went beyond the SOB into Binghamton's city building (where the mayor, fire and police departments, courts, and city council all had offices). The city building's ventilation system, it turned out, was connected to that of the State Office Building. Parts of the building were closed for nine months because of unusually high levels of PCBs. Worse, state janitors had tracked contaminated soot from the state building into the city building. The cleanup workers, like their supervisors, acted as if the only danger was in the SOB itself.

City employees were alarmed that the janitors were using city building restrooms to change from "bunny suits" (i.e., protective suits) into street clothes, that contaminated gloves were dropped in the hallways, and that toxic rugs were stored on the building's loading dock. Binghamton's personnel and safety director recounted that "the janitors apparently used the wrong doors when they were coming out of the State Office Build-

ing. . . . The state thought the doors were locked that led to the
city building and assumed that there was only one way to get
out. But there are crash bars on the doors and so they could
get out any way they wanted" (Byrne interview, August 13,
1981).

Workers in the county building, which is on the other side of
the SOB, had fears of their own; two weeks after the accident
some of them petitioned the governor: "This letter is being
written to inform the powers that be that since the fire and
explosion . . . we the undersigned have come in contact with the
so-called PCB fallout. This has occurred either by use of county
vehicles which were deemed safe after the mishap or by going
to the basement to obtain vehicles" (Broome County Employees
to Carey, February 18, 1981). The director of DOH's Office of
Public Health, who later became a principal policymaker in that
department, responded to the petition two weeks later: "This
letter is to confirm receipt of your petition. This letter, however,
should not be construed as concurrence of [*sic*] any elements in
the petition" (Haughie to County Employees, March 4, 1981).

As the media reported lax security and unnecessary hazards,
local citizens, and especially city and county workers, became
increasingly concerned about risks to their health. Many agreed
with the Binghamton mayor, who complained that "there were
inadequate precautions taken after [the janitors] came out of
the building. . . . It was like letting a wild dog run loose and
start taking a bite out of everyone on the leg" (Libous interview,
November 30, 1981). Local politicians called for more stringent
discipline at the SOB and asked the state to test and decontaminate the city building. The president of the city council raised
questions about potential health threats after OGS and DOH
acknowledged that dioxins were in the soot. She wrote a letter
to the mayor, with copies sent to, among others, the commissioner of the state health department:

> I am extremely concerned, given the recent disclosure of the pres-
> ence of lethal [dioxin] in the State Office Building. . . . I am ap-
> palled at what appears to be a deliberate minimizing of the dangers
> to avoid panic, and the apparent lack of concern and knowledge
> involving the ramifications to the residents and employees of our
> community. (Eggleston to Libous, March 2, 1981)

Dr. Arnold Schecter, director of the county health department, shared these reservations and issued a Commissioner's Order on March 4, 1981 (partly in response to reports that contaminated vehicles were still being used), stipulating that anything taken from the building must be returned. Although this order should have had the force of law, no one paid much attention to it.[1] BCHD received complaints about automobiles that had been taken out of the garage even after the order was issued. The state took no subsequent action concerning the contaminated vehicles, and only a few files were returned as a result of the order.

The lack of adequate controls on the egress of toxic chemicals from the State Office Building clearly frightened employees, customers, and citizens. Along with reporting the events, the media also helped to frame the problem by using other disasters for comparison. Geographically, Binghamton is about midway between Love Canal and Three Mile Island, a fact that rendered the comparisons even more apposite. Unfortunately, Governor Carey confused public alarm with public hysteria, dismissing the possibility that the public may have had some cause for grievance:

> You've got to take PCBs in quantities, steadily, over long periods of time, and probably be pregnant, which I don't intend to become. It gets into your fatty tissue, and then you get a PCB contamination. I'm not dismissing it, because I've spent too much time on Love Canal to [think] that there aren't serious conditions [in Binghamton] that need our help. . . . But I'm telling you, these things become overblown. (unpublished portion of transcript from Carey's press conference, March 17, 1981)

Two pregnant workers in the city building thought they might indeed have "serious conditions"—one requested a transfer to a job in another building. The other woman, on her physician's advice, quit her job and filed suit against New York State for $310 million. (She filed for $40 million, her husband for $10

---

1. One member of the State Senate, whose office was in the SOB, arranged to have a piece of Steuben crystal taken from his contaminated office. "I have it in my office in Albany," said the senator. "If you cannot clean up glass, I don't know what you can clean up" (Anderson interview, August 20, 1981).

million, and $80 million was claimed on behalf of the fetus; the lawsuit also demanded $60 million in punitive damages for each of the three. The child was born healthy.)

After the local newspapers reported that the janitors were flushing toilets in the SOB (violating a directive from the New York State Department of Environmental Conservation), thus breaking the seals of their protective gear and sending toxic chemicals to Binghamton's sewer system, the chairperson of the city's Municipal and Public Affairs Committee issued a press release in which he claimed he felt compelled

> to seek out the answers to questions that have been posed concerning the direct effect of this situation upon all who must use City Hall. . . . I also feel that questions concerning the environmental impact of this disaster on the City of Binghamton as a whole must be answered. . . . The concerns of the citizens, City workers, City shoppers and City businesspersons are important to each and every member of City Council. (Testani, March 2, 1981)

The same day, this official sent a letter to Dr. Schecter asking about chemical testing and the risks of toxic chemicals:

> It seems as though a day does not pass without more bad news being revealed about the chemicals released in the New York State Office Building. As Chairman of Binghamton City Council's Municipal and Public Affairs Committee and as a resident of the City of Binghamton, I am deeply concerned about the apparent deterioration of events at the Governmental Plaza. With the priority being given these events in the news media, the inquiries to City Council from our constituents, City employees, and other employees of downtown Binghamton are increasing by leaps and bounds. (Testani to Schecter, March 2, 1981)

These statements are especially notable because they show that the city council was pressed by its constituents and others to take a stronger role in what had become a highly politicized controversy. As is often the case in politics, however, words were not followed by action. Once the state health department assured city officials that toxic levels within the municipal building were safe and claimed the chemical releases to the sewer system were unimportant, city government agencies showed little further interest. Although the president of the city council believed the state had treated workers and the public as "guinea pigs," the city council did no more than write a few letters to health officials and the media. One member of the city council remarked that they did not usually shy away from political battles but felt "they were almost thankful not to have to stick their noses into this one." Some initial concern was expressed over what the SOB accident might cost the city. But the mayor remarked: "The cost to the city will be zero. As far as I'm concerned, the state will pick it up" (East 1981). For the most part, city agencies, despite pressure from the media and workers, were able to define the problems created by the State Office Building as outside their proper mandate.

Local Business

There is a qualification to the conclusion that the city was unresponsive, for local businesses fell within the city government's definition of its responsibilities. Owners of downtown businesses claimed that fear of the contaminated building was preventing many customers from shopping downtown, causing a precipitous drop in revenues. A score of downtown merchants, led by store owner Bruce Drazen, sought relief for their economic problems.[2]

Drazen contacted the governor's office to request that a state of emergency be declared in the downtown area, which might have qualified Binghamton for federal assistance. Acting on behalf of worried business owners, Drazen wrote to the governor's

2. The data on Binghamton's business community come from interviews with key city officials; letters and memoranda exchanged between government officials at all levels; and two lengthy interviews with Bruce Drazen, a leader in Binghamton's business community. I conducted one of these interviews, and an informant in Binghamton, who had a greater rapport with Drazen than I did, conducted the second. (I found a general distrust among businesspersons of anyone seeking information on the SOB.) I sent a list of pertinent questions to the informant, who taped the interview. Drazen also provided some of the correspondence I cite. I interviewed other businesspersons, all of whom would speak only on guarantee of anonymity. These interviews substantiated Drazen's account of both the reaction of the business community to the accident and the attempts to obtain financial aid.

office in June: "The PCB dioxin disaster which struck our cen-
ter-city [in] February, 1981 has caused a reduction in retail business which has clearly reached massive proportions" (Drazen to
Burns, June 5, 1981). Drazen explained that he had surveyed a
cross-section of retail businesses downtown, provided figures of
revenue declines ranging from 11 percent to 60 percent (most
were more than 25 percent), and concluded that there was an
"immediate danger of losing the entire downtown retail community." The letter ended with a dramatic appeal: "TIME IS OF
THE ESSENCE. We are crippled and operating on a day-to-day
basis. WE NEED HELP." In addition to the survey, Drazen collected a large set of statistics that in his view conclusively tied
profit losses to the accident: "I had a substantial file on the economic effect of the PCB thing on business downtown. I got the
thing together and took it to a lawyer in New York [City] in
consideration of a class-action suit against the State of New
York, and they lost the file" (Drazen interview, February 15,
1983).[3]

Without a detailed study of business revenues, it is difficult
to ascertain that the business losses were indeed caused by the
contamination of the State Office Building, as business owners
claimed. (All of the firms were or are privately owned and varied in size from corner delicatessens to Binghamton's largest department store, Fowler's, whose downtown store subsequently went out of business.) Further complicating the issue is
the fact that a large shopping mall outside the city limits had
been drawing customers away from the central business district.
In addition, a large urban-renewal project in the downtown
area had restricted the flow of traffic, so downtown businesses
were already in a recession. It is therefore likely that the downtown business community would have experienced a bad fiscal
year even without the problems caused by the SOB.

There is some evidence, however, that the SOB accident did

3. The possibility of a class-action suit was not pursued. Drazen argued:
"We could try . . . but it would be hard to find a law firm to do it. You have to
have massive dollars up front, and nobody [i.e., the business owners] is willing
to do that, and no law firm is going to take it on a contingency basis." Neither
Drazen nor anyone else I spoke with had retained copies of the raw data they
collected.

hurt local business. After the business community's initial requests for assistance, the New York State Department of Commerce conducted its own cross-sectional survey of the principal retail stores in downtown Binghamton. It compared the volume of business from March to May 1981 (the first three months after the accident) with the same period in 1980. Most of the businesses reported revenue losses of between $25,000 and $90,000; one attributed a loss of $308,000 to the State Office Building. Furthermore, the mall had been built nearly ten years before the accident, and although customers were indeed drawn to it, the lost business did not seriously threaten downtown Binghamton.[4]

Binghamton's business leaders enlisted the support of the governor's secretary, who wrote to the acting regional administrator of the Small Business Administration (SBA) in New York City. Citing the large drop in the volume of business (and noting that the declines had been verified by the state Department of Commerce), the governor's secretary asked the SBA to "provide assistance to enable these businesses to return to their former levels of operation." The businesses were requesting low-interest loans to allow them to bolster their dwindling profit margins. One method of qualifying for disaster loans under the provisions of the Small Business Act is for a governor to certify to the administrator of the SBA that a troubled area has "suffered economic injury" (United States Commerce and Trade Code 1982).

Binghamton's mayor requested the governor's support on July 10, 1981. The governor then wrote a letter to both the regional office of the Small Business Administration and SBA's national director in Washington, D.C. To qualify Binghamton for the loans, the governor asked that the city be accorded an "economic dislocation designation." The business owners and the mayor were sent the following information quoted from the Small Business Act:

4. It should be noted that the entire country was in a recession at the time; the business owners did not attribute *all* their troubles to the SOB. They did, however, see it as critical in causing the loss of some establishments and reduced revenues for those that remained.

> Such loans are to be made available to small concerns suffering
> substantial economic injury as a result of situations such as severe
> weather when a physical disaster declaration has not been made
> and SBA's economic injury disaster loan program is not available;
> examples are the lack of snow affecting ski resorts and the Mexican
> currency devaluation which . . . reduced the purchasing power of
> Mexican residents at U.S. businesses.

Members of Binghamton's business community did not simply rely on regional administrators or depend on state government to pursue their interests. Some traveled to Washington,
D.C., to lobby for support. Their conversations with Senator Alfonse D'Amato (R.-N.Y.) resulted in the senator's request
that the SBA administrator meet with the Binghamton delega-
tion. At the bottom of his letter, the senator appended, in
script: "Mike, this is a critical situation deserving of your support. I'm counting on you to help!" (D'Amato to Cardenas, July
13, 1981).

The owners of these businesses thought they had an obviously valid case to present to the Small Business Administration. Some had received low-interest, long-term SBA loans in
the past, and their present calamity was clearly real. Drazen
himself said he had once received a thirty-year loan at 1 percent
interest, simply because one of his stores had been flooded by
heavy rains. (As he declared, "*That's* a bailout for an emergency!") With firm statistics and toxic chemicals, it seemed in-
credible they would be turned away. Said Drazen: "We had all
the tangible evidence we needed. We had a study by the state
Department of Commerce, and we had a request by Governor
Carey for a state of emergency. But it was to no avail. The [fed-
eral] government's position was, 'if we help you, we are liable to
be responsible for these kinds of things all over the country'"
(Drazen interview, February 15, 1983). The group was told they
would have to take their troubles to Congress. But the Binghamton case was not receiving media attention comparable to
that accorded, say, the Love Canal disaster, so Congress was not
likely to be much help.

In the end, the lobby was unsuccessful. Even though SBA
officials acknowledged that the fiscal losses were caused by the

SOB, they apparently did not judge the accident at the State Office Building a genuine disaster. On August 4, 1981, SBA's Office of Disaster Policy responded to the governor's request with the following telegram:

> Please be advised that on July 31, 1981, Administrator Cardenas of the Small Business Administration declined your request for an economic dislocation designation for businesses in the city of Binghamton, New York, which are suffering substantial economic injury *as a result of the contamination of the state office building.* . . . The situation . . . did not appear to meet the criteria of the economic dislocation loan program. (Jennings telegram to Carey, August 4, 1981; emphasis added)

Business leaders felt abandoned. One of them felt the SBA "would not touch us with a ten-foot pole." It was clear to them that the State Office Building accident had cost jobs, profits, and emotional stress. Twenty-nine businesses were prepared to ask for low-interest loans that, if granted, would have totaled $3.35 million. But they were not offered the loans they requested. Instead, they were offered loans at going interest rates—rates available from a commercial bank. Drazen wryly remarked: "They offered money, but they offered it at 16 percent and a six-year payback. And they wouldn't lend it to anybody unless they put up their house, their wives, their children, and had other collateral. That's loan sharking, not emergency loans" (Drazen interview, February 15, 1983). Only one store took a $100,000 loan at a 17 percent interest rate. That store and several other businesses have since gone bankrupt or had to sell their assets.

It is interesting that the Small Business Administration did not consider the State Office Building situation serious enough to qualify for disaster loans. If the local businesses could have claimed that their losses were caused by a riot, or civil disobedience, or toxic contamination of their products, they might have been able to secure SBA's disaster loans (United States Commerce and Trade Code 1982). It is hard to imagine that the lack of snow at a ski resort would be considered disastrous but that contamination of the magnitude that occurred at the SOB would not be so defined. There is one difference, however, for our purposes, between an afflicted ski resort and business losses caused by a contaminated office building. In the latter case, public health is threatened by exposure to noxious materials. But this consideration is irrelevant to the SBA. Neither the Small Business Administration nor the SBA legislation was designed to mitigate health threats.

The downtown businesses were unable to get their loans because they could not find an appropriate bureaucratic label for the contingencies posed by the toxic accident. Customer fear is not considered a cause for "economic dislocation"; to have considered it thus would have required the creation of a new rule. The only other possibility was to ask that Binghamton be formally declared a disaster area. The bureaucratic distinction between an "emergency" and a "disaster" is not very meaningful in terms of qualifying for low-interest loans. But business owners in Binghamton perceived that a formally announced federal declaration that the downtown area was a disaster area (possibly conjuring up images of Love Canal) might scare away those customers still willing to shop there. The SBA seems to have taken advantage of the ambiguity inherent in the situation to avoid the negative economic effects of the SOB.

Despite the fact that the mayor went to Washington to ask for help, and despite the governor's appeal to the SBA, business leaders eventually concluded that government officials were neither much help nor overly concerned about their problems. After the group met with assistants in Senator D'Amato's office, and D'Amato helped to arrange the meeting with the SBA administrator, the senator asked the business owners to direct any further correspondence to his regional representative in Syracuse. Binghamton's mayor had no further alternatives for action, and the governor apparently did no more than send his letter of support to the SBA.

Binghamton's various government agencies limited their definition of unacceptable risk to that which threatened local business. Other risks, such as health risks posed by the chemicals, were considered the responsibility of the more powerful state-level organizations. Before drawing more conclusions concerning the inaction of the city government, let us examine the responses of other agencies to similar demands.

County Agencies

Unlike the city government building, Broome County's government building was not contaminated. An important set of demands nevertheless required the county government's time and attention. Although two committees of the county legislature (in addition to the legislature more generally) might have responded to the health threats posed by the SOB, what these actors in fact debated were the actions of the Broome County Health Department.

Broome County is mainly Republican, and the legislature is therefore generally dominated by Republicans. As in most legislative bodies, the important decisions are made in committees. The chairperson of the legislature, elected by majority vote among the legislators, assigns members to committees. Almost all committees in the county legislature are controlled by Republicans. Two committees might have been expected to assume central roles following the accident: the Finance Committee and the Public Health Committee. Because the former controlled appropriations, it was widely regarded as the most powerful committee in the legislature. It was chaired by the Republican majority leader, a conservative considered "well connected" with the business elite in the Binghamton area; he was also considered the political patron of the county executive. Except for a power struggle with the county health department over contamination of the office complex's garage, the Finance Committee basically ignored the SOB. An unusual consensus developed in the legislature between Republicans and Democrats that the SOB was outside their bailiwick. One legislator tried to explain the Democrats' failure to act:

> Broome County is heavily Republican. They can do anything they want. There are also limits on the minority. For the most part, the Democrats are not willing to speak out because of the nature of their employment. There used to be a couple of other mavericks (like me), but they were both self-employed. You don't buck the Binghamton club here. (Svoboda interview, December 3, 1981)

The Finance Committee will resurface, however, when we turn to the problem of the contaminated garage in chapter 4.

The Public Health Committee was the other actor in the legislature that might have taken a stronger role in devising policies toward the State Office Building situation. But it, too, considered the SOB accident the problem of other agencies. A Democrat serving on the Public Health Committee said the committee members relied on the county health department to guard public health. Like many other officials, members of this committee felt they lacked the expertise or resources to respond. And yet, the committee was in fact familiar with the difficult issues of public health and toxic chemicals. A year or so before the accident, several wells near Binghamton had been contaminated with chemicals, and the committee played a central role in finding a remedy for that situation. But the accident at the State Office Building was not seen to require a similar response. "It is obviously a state problem" was the repeated reply from legislators, both Democrat and Republican, when asked why the legislature was so passive. It seems odd that in the midst of widespread political controversy both political parties would come to such undisputed agreement. That was not normally the case. In fact, many legislators expressed to me their surprise at the high level of consensus on the question of what to do in the wake of the disaster.

The real problem here was political, not technical; it was a no-win situation for politicians. "The Republican makeup of the legislature," I was told, "would indicate 'hands off' on this problem." The problem of assessing and managing this hazardous situation was therefore determined by the demands of partisan politics.

Looking at the legislature as a whole, rather than at the committees, it is clear that the Finance and Public Health committees' perceptions of risk reflected the political consensus in the legislature. It would have been perfectly reasonable to have witnessed disagreement and debate over the idea that the State Office Building was *not* simply the state's problem. Like city agencies, the legislature prevented its resources from being diverted from the usual routines to the more troublesome problem at the SOB. By proclaiming that the building was the exclusive problem of New York State, the county legislature absolved itself of responsibility for a potentially risky situation. The running battle that developed between BCHD and the county executive over the county's appropriate role in protecting public health provided the legislature an opportunity to let that (often public) disagreement be the main attraction. With no strong demands issuing from any group or organization outside the legislature, the legislators were able to define the contaminated building as outside their proper policy domain. The county legislature was therefore able to continue to function, for the most part, as if the calamity had never occurred.

State Agencies

The State of New York ultimately bore the largest fiscal, medical, and legal responsibility for the State Office Building. But New York State is composed of many organizations, each of which performs myriad functions. Two of those functions— protecting public health and maintaining state buildings—are primarily the responsibility of the Department of Health and the Office of General Services, respectively. But formal mandates for health and building maintenance do not exclude the involvement of other organizations. In this section I describe the activities of some of these other state organizations. What is important is not necessarily what they did, but what they could have done (yet did not do) about problems associated with the State Office Building.

Department of Transportation

New York's Department of Transportation (DOT) was the first state agency called to the scene of the accident. DOT is responsible for emergency oil spills in New York, and the leak of transformer oil was akin to that category. DOT had an emergency contract with the New England Pollution Control company (NEPCO), which was experienced with PCBs, so NEPCO was called in as soon as it was known that these toxins were involved. The local oil-spill engineer responsible for calling NEPCO was at first unable to ascertain exactly what had happened at the State Office Building. He was in a meeting in Albany at the time and tried to call his Binghamton office, located in the SOB, but no one answered:

> I tried to call the Department of Environmental Conservation, po-
> sitioned on the eighth floor [of the SOB], and I kept ringing and
> nobody answered, and I said "That is pretty strange, 'cause there
> is always somebody there." My supervisor here gave me a number
> to call, and I finally [got through], and they told me that all three
> buildings had been closed. Then I called out the contractor. Then
> I talked to a couple of people from OGS, but they were getting bits
> and pieces of information, too. . . . You know, what was going on
> just really was all confused. (Peterson interview, July 27, 1981)

The oil-spill engineer and his supervisor in Albany decided that
because DOT had initially called NEPCO, they would keep the
company there until the oil in the mechanical room was cleaned
up, and that "OGS would handle any other cleanup. So Sunday
morning [four days after the fire] we were all cleaned up at the
transformer room and the whole shot went over to them" (Peterson interview, July 27, 1981). The Department of Transportation also helped to find a certified landfill for the contaminated oil.

But DOT, presaging the actions of other agencies, did not
expand its role beyond these initial efforts: "If it is only a trace
amount [of PCBs], we will handle it. But when the facts started
coming out about the amount of PCBs and the other stuff that
was associated with it, we got out" (Peterson interview, July 27,
1981). Although it may have been surprising that the various
agents in city government did not become actively involved in
the SOB situation, it is not surprising that DOT did not become
a central player in Binghamton. Its responsibilities, after all,
were quite remote from toxic-chemical decontamination and
medical surveillance. Discussing DOT's role is nevertheless important because it illustrates how even organizations whose
functions were only distantly related to the demands of the
State Office Building accident were drawn into this loosely connected network of agencies.

Department of Environmental Conservation

In spite of what its name might lead one to expect, the Department of Environmental Conservation (DEC) managed, as did
so many other organizations, to distance itself from the SOB

disaster. Some local officials, seeing that DEC was not performing its usual function of regulator, tried to elicit more participation from the agency when OGS announced plans to vent
the SOB to the atmosphere in the summer of 1981. In May,
Broome County Health Director Schecter wrote to DEC that he
was "very surprised to learn two weeks ago when the Binghamton City Hall was polluted with PCBs and we applied to
your agency . . . in order to vent, that DEC still had no standards for venting PCBs, etc., to the atmosphere" (Schecter to
Mullins, May 14, 1981).[5] Schecter pointed out the seriousness
and unknown qualities of the chemicals, asking the department
to set standards for venting toxic effluents. But the director's
requests were to no avail. The building, incidentally, was not
vented that summer, and DEC did not develop any standards.

According to one of its top officials, the Department of Environmental Conservation normally functions as a regulatory
agency.[6] If the accident had happened in a private firm, the
firm would have had to clean up the site and prove to DEC that
it was safe to reopen. DEC usually issues permits for a specific
site or substance. According to DEC officials, the Office of General Services needed no permit and no oversight for the SOB
because the situation was originally an emergency.

Like workers who stage a work slowdown by strict adherence
to rules when they cannot legally strike, DEC kept the SOB
problems at arm's length by sticking to the letter of the law. "We
have no authority in something like this," said a DEC official,
"because it happened in an office building. [For us to be more
involved] you would have to redefine the environment." Again,
had a private corporation been responsible for the decontamination, DEC would have been integrally involved, as indeed it
was at Love Canal. One official said DEC's only concern was
with problems concerning the release of chemicals to the environment, but DEC decided there were none (although this
same official admitted that "there are inevitable leaks from the

5. This incident was unrelated to the SOB. A small electrical capacitor,
like those in fluorescent lights, broke and spilled about a cup of PCB-
containing oil on the floor. The oil was wiped up and discarded.
6. I interviewed several DEC officials, although the commissioner declined to be interviewed. Most officials requested anonymity.

building"). DEC's main interest was to ensure that its local officers not raise too many troubling questions: "Some of our site engineers had qualms [in the early days], and we went down to ensure that we were only making contributions in our areas of expertise." Thus did DEC constrict its boundaries and narrow the definition of its responsibilities.

As with most other organizations, the department's decision was not dictated by a formal mandate. There was, in fact, a nearly constant release of the SOB's air to what DEC considers the real environment. First, the building could not be made airtight. High-level officials and engineers said the air in the building was completely exchanging with outside air every twenty-four to thirty-six hours. Furthermore, the janitors tracked contaminants outside the building fairly regularly for about three weeks, as I described earlier. Finally, at least one fire alarm went off in the building after it was officially closed, and the same rooftop venting hatches, which had initially drawn the toxic smoke through the building during the fire, opened again. Venting the air was, it seems, a fairly regular occurrence at the SOB following the disaster.

There was one other opportunity for the Department of Environmental Conservation to act in its usual capacity as regulator. In the summer of 1981, when OGS announced plans to initiate a second cleanup, it was required by law to prove to DEC that its activities would not endanger the environment. This requirement could be fulfilled in two ways. One was to construct an Environmental Impact Statement, and the other was to file a Negative Declaration. An Environmental Impact Statement means, as a DEC official said, "going the whole nine yards" with hearings so that the public can evaluate whether or not its interests are reflected in policy. Filing a Negative Declaration is very different: "You present plans to the public that say there will be no impact," said a DEC official, "and then if there are no significant public comments, that is the end of the process." "Presenting plans to the public," however, means little more than filing a formal statement with the Department of Environmental Conservation claiming that the cleanup activities do not, or cannot, pose any kind of health threat. The OGS avoided public hearings and opted for the Negative Declaration.

DEC faced an interesting dilemma. On the one hand, it could pursue a regulatory policy, as it would if the organization responsible for cleanup had been a private firm. But that would require the department to act as watchdog over other state agencies—a difficult position if it found itself in fundamental disagreement with those organizations. On the other hand, it could interpret its mandate in a more restricted fashion, leaving OGS (and the state health department) to regulate itself. DEC chose the latter option. "Look," a DEC official said in an interview, "the environment is just not an issue now."

State Legislature

The New York state legislature, normally a lively group of politicians, was remarkably subdued when it came to the issue of the State Office Building. Even the two legislators from the Binghamton area decided there was little that interested them about the SOB. The state senate majority leader said: "We have appropriated funds—that is the interest we have. In other words, we had an interest . . . in getting [the building] rehabilitated and back in use" (Anderson interview, August 20, 1981). The chairperson of the Health Committee also saw no point in involving his committee: "The Health Committee really doesn't have the resources to deal with something like this, and it's not really the committee's responsibility" (Tallon interview, August 10, 1981).

Yet, the usual ideas about what constituted responsibility were not binding constraints on all legislators. One member of the assembly, whose constituency was in New York City, took at least a peripheral interest, summoning several firefighters to Albany to testify before his Committee on Governmental Employees. One of his assistants tried to explain the lack of interest: "That's being handled by several government agencies now, and . . . they want to retain control, and we don't want to tell them how to do their job" (Thompson interview, October 28, 1981). Thus, state agencies that might have assumed much stronger roles in responding to the Binghamton accident chose to define those problems as outside their areas of expertise or responsibility. Even the state's Department of Labor, charged with protecting the interests of New York workers by enforcing the state's Right-to-Know law (which stipulates that all workers in private firms be fully informed of the dangers of their jobs), chose to ignore the plight of SOB workers.

Federal Agencies

Several agencies of the federal government could have affected policy in Binghamton: the Occupational Health and Safety Administration (OSHA), the National Institute of Occupational Safety and Health (NIOSH), and the Environmental Protection Agency (EPA). Each of these agencies could legitimately have claimed a larger interest in the SOB accident on the grounds that toxic chemicals and threats to worker safety and health were involved. Their inaction contributed to the final configuration of agencies responsible for managing the situation and therefore to the final definition of acceptable risk.

OSHA

Workers and management frequently perceive that they have contradictory interests in health issues, and in such instances the Occupational Safety and Health Administration bears some responsibility for protecting workers' interests. In Binghamton, many workers thought their health had been jeopardized. For example, one member of the original janitorial cleanup crew recounted:

> There were rumors going around that if employees did not work, they would get in trouble, and it would reflect on employees' evaluation and job security. I [worked on] the fourth floor with a protective suit and respirator, gloves, and boots. Nobody instructed me how to put the suit on or how to use the respirator. There were no safety checks made. My job was to tear down draperies on the fourth floor. I got a face full of soot. There were no goggles. The boots I was wearing kept coming off and ripping because they were made of paper. The sleeves of the suit would ride down when I

reached over my head. My arms were covered with soot. The last few days I experienced nausea, headaches, and [had] trouble swallowing. Since I have been out of the building, I have experienced lack of coordination, disorientation, extreme irritability, faint[ness], fatigue, insomnia, and cold sweating at night.

Other workers involved in later cleanups also complained of inadequate protection. I talked with about a dozen people who worked in the building before it was closed. Each of them expressed great dissatisfaction with what, in their view, was a disregard for their health and safety. Whether or not that distrust was founded on actual threats to their health is not the point. The point is that many workers considered themselves unprotected.

New York's Right-to-Know law was designed to ensure that people who work around toxic chemicals are apprised of the potential health hazards. None of the janitorial cleanup workers, however, was informed about the presence of dioxins. But state officials claimed that emergency conditions relaxed usual standards of safety. These workers were also in the unusual position of not having an agency to which they could report hazardous conditions. When private firms, such as chemical manufacturers, develop toxic contaminations, OSHA must provide such a protective mechanism for workers. The official explanation for OSHA's noninvolvement in this case was that the SOB was, after all, an accident involving state workers, who are not the responsibility of the federal government. As was the case with the New York Department of Environmental Conservation, there was no bureaucratic category that made OSHA responsible for the workers' problems. Nor was there any category requiring OSHA to become involved.

NIOSH

The prestigious National Institute of Occupational Safety and Health occupied an interesting position in the Binghamton situation. NIOSH's role following the accident could have been defined in several ways. Although its major function is to advise OSHA, NIOSH can intervene in dangerous situations if intervention seems warranted. The institute's director of the Division of Surveillance, Hazard Evaluations, and Field Studies said:

> Usually we prefer to be asked by either a union, or a management group, or a state government, but we can go in on our own if it's important that we do so. . . . I suppose we could have developed a plan. . . . We could have written the whole plan. We could have had people up there full-time. We could have had doctors up there on a continuous basis, actually doing physical exams on people. (Landrigan interview, September 1, 1981)

Both the county and state health departments sought advice from NIOSH on medical surveillance, although some in county government thought the institute would actually regulate the state health department. The county health department, for example, often asked NIOSH officials both to develop and to administer a medical monitoring program. On May 15, 1981, Dr. Schecter wrote to NIOSH asking for a clarification of its role. He was troubled that nearly four months after the fire there appeared to be no medical surveillance program (beyond that which had already begun). The doctor was disappointed with NIOSH's response, which stated:

> The central point is that the Protocol for medical surveillance of exposed persons is to be a NIOSH document. . . . The document is being prepared conjointly by Dr. Phil Taylor, our man in Albany, and by members of my staff in Cincinnati. When it has been approved, the provisions of the Protocol will be implemented by New York State Health Department personnel with close . . . supervision and consultation by members of my staff. (Landrigan to Schecter, May 20, 1981)

No one supported BCHD's attempts to enlist further resources from NIOSH. The deputy county executive wrote to Schecter in August 1981 in response to one of the doctor's requests that the county hire an expert consultant:[7] "NIOSH has

7. Schecter requested county funds to hire Irving Selikoff, the renowned specialist in environmental sciences at Mt. Sinai Hospital in New York City, to run a medical surveillance program. Selikoff gave verbal assurance that he would design and run such a program, but the request for funding was denied.

indicated that it will act [in the role of environmental and medical advisor], and the county executive is satisfied that NIOSH will perform this role" (Lee to Schecter, August 5, 1981). But NIOSH would be of little help to the county health department. A NIOSH official explained that one reason the agency saw no potential conflict of interest in New York State's role as polluter and protector of health is that "we try not to step on each other's toes" (Mesite interview, June 14, 1981).

NIOSH furnished advice and legitimated the decisions of the New York Department of Health, and NIOSH scientists reviewed research designs through various stages of the medical surveillance study. But, as a high-level scientist explained, the institute concluded that, rather than being involved with "the nuts and bolts" of the study, it was "more important that we should review it—that we should lend our credibility to it if the project looked good" (Landrigan interview, September 1, 1981).

New York State has been criticized about conflict of interest throughout the Binghamton episode. The state is responsible for alleviating adverse effects from the pollution in the State Office Building, but it is also responsible for any legal liability that may arise from the exposure of individuals to lethal toxins. Suspicion might have been dispelled if the state had an independent agency to lend its credibility to the medical surveillance program.

EPA

The Environmental Protection Agency has often been controversial, playing important parts in several of the United States' toxic tragedies (e.g., Times Beach, PBB in Michigan, Love Canal). In contrast to some of EPA's more well-known ventures, in Binghamton it weighed the dilemma of political commitment and public health and disclaimed jurisdiction.

A 1980 pamphlet published by EPA warns that toxic chemicals are "everybody's problem." Because the EPA is the federal government's toxic expert, one would have expected the agency to take a strong interest in the Binghamton case. In fact, EPA had even devised a formal structure for dealing with the risks of dioxins. The Dioxins Work Group, a policy-making body within this formal EPA structure, more or less supervised the Dioxin Task Force, a study group. These groups were composed of respected experts on dioxin, risk assessment, and decontamination. The EPA was thus well equipped to respond to the accident in Binghamton. Soon after the fire at the State Office Building, the BCHD asked members of the Dioxins Work Group for help. An EPA memorandum explained those requests to EPA's Superfund program manager: "Among other services, Dr. Schecter requested that a sampling and analysis program be planned and carried out to assure that the environment in downtown Binghamton was not contaminated . . . and that it does not become contaminated during the building clean-up" (Lafornara to Stoller, March 20, 1981). But Broome County Health Director Schecter was the only actor in Binghamton who wanted EPA on the stage.

Befitting the circumstances in Binghamton, EPA's involvement was caused by a mixture of chance and politics. Senator Daniel Patrick Moynihan (D.-N.Y.) happened to be on two Senate committees then reviewing EPA's budget. He also happened to be in Binghamton on Saturday, March 14, 1981, and he met with Schecter. The senator told a reporter: "I've got to get the EPA up here right away to see what has happened. They'll be involved Monday morning. If I tell them to get up here, they'll get up here because they want to" (Geimann 1981e). Schecter impressed on the senator that the SOB posed a grave danger to the community and that the state was not handling the situation very well. Moynihan called EPA directly to see what could be done. EPA responded with what one of its officers called "senatorial courtesy" and sent a couple of specialists to Binghamton.

One way EPA could have become more involved in Binghamton was through the federal Superfund law, which taxes chemical companies and provides a mechanism whereby EPA can arrange for a cleanup of chemically contaminated locations. The Superfund was designed to protect public health in the event of irresponsible dumping of toxic waste by private firms. EPA's authority, however, is not strictly limited to waste dumps. It can also intervene in any cleanup situation where it decides public health would benefit. It was Superfund resources that Senator Moynihan was requesting.

Moynihan wrote to EPA's acting administrator in April 1981, inquiring about "the extent to which financial assistance would be available through your agency under [Superfund]" (Moynihan to Barber, April 14, 1981). Moynihan quoted relevant sections of the Superfund Act that gave EPA the legal authority to conduct medical surveillance, cleanup, and epidemiological studies and closed his letter by expressing his belief that "the task of the federal government is to learn as much as it can from the Binghamton experience." EPA responded to Moynihan in early May, explaining that "we believe the State and local officials are handling the Binghamton incident as well as the situation permits and should maintain their lead role" (Barber to Moynihan, May 7, 1981).

Here, then, was a situation in which EPA had the authority to intervene and, publicly at least, also had an official invitation. Dr. Axelrod, commissioner of the state health department, remarked: "We are prepared to turn over to EPA all environmental sampling. . . . If they are prepared to handle testing, we would be more than happy to have them do it. . . . We welcome any expense they are willing [to assume] and any resource anyone has to give us" (Fecteau 1981h). Closer inspection, however, reveals that only BCHD pressed EPA to assume a stronger role. A cochairperson of the Dioxins Work Group admitted, after Schecter lost his position as county health director, "Since Dr. Schecter is out of the picture, my phone has stopped ringing." The same scientist contradicted Axelrod's statement that New York State would welcome any and all assistance, saying: "Basically, we weren't invited [by the state]. We were invited by the county health department."

It might be argued that EPA's reluctance reflected an efficient division of labor among organizations. EPA scientists concurred with most other scientists that the laboratories of the New York State Health Department were among the best in the nation. But efficient allocation of resources was not the driving force behind EPA's refusal to become involved. Rather, the agency was driven by the politics of prestige.

First was the political battle between officials in the New York

State Health Department and OGS, on the one hand, and the Broome County Health Department, on the other. Schecter, as the county health official, was criticizing state actions often and openly, arguing that the county should have, at the very least, veto power over the state's decisions about medical surveillance and cleanup. Unquestionably, the situation was highly politicized. And EPA, understandably, was none too eager to get involved in politicized situations. As one EPA official explained: "Somebody here has made a policy decision that we respond to states rather than counties. And if the county has a problem with the state, that remains their problem; we don't act as a referee between Democrat-controlled counties and Republican-controlled states."[8]

And, of course, the newly installed Reagan administration was proclaiming states' rights in nearly all matters. A cochairperson of the Dioxins Work Group tried to explain the dilemma:

> To do otherwise [i.e., to go in without the state's invitation] is to say, "Hey, state, you are not doing your job of protecting the health of your people; therefore the feds have to come in and show you how to do it." I don't think this administration is up to making statements like that, whether they are justified or not. . . . [Under the Reagan administration] we [no] longer get excited at risks at the same level as we used to. (Brown interview, May 3, 1982)

Finally, EPA had been embarrassed in New York before. The agency had moved quickly into Love Canal in 1979 and 1980 and conducted a study on chromosome breakage and health hazards that many scientists considered flawed and unsystematic.[9] EPA's actions at Love Canal helped to politicize *that* situation, embarrassed the New York State Health Department, and brought a good deal of ridicule to the agency from scientific and political communities. A high-level official in New York's Department of Environmental Conservation said: "We begged EPA to let us handle Love Canal, thinking it was a state

8. Actually, Republicans held the majority in county government and Democrats held the majority in state government.

9. For evidence to the contrary, see Brown's *Laying Waste* (1979) and Levine's *Love Canal: Science, Politics, and People* (1982).

problem and not a federal one. But they wanted to look good, so they went in." I asked a Dioxins Work Group cochairperson if it were true, as I had heard, that EPA had to be asked in by a state before it can assume a role: "Pretty much that's true, especially in the State of New York. . . . We have not had the best of relations in the past [over] Love Canal and [that] made us a little shy of working with each other. So pretty much, in the State of New York especially, we wait until we are asked—and the 'new federalism' has something to do with it, too" (Brown interview, May 3, 1982).

It was not that EPA scientists were uninterested in the Binghamton case. On the contrary, every scientist and expert there was very interested. A member of the Dioxins Work Group offered this anecdote:

> The thing that was most telling to me is that some of our scientists coming back from trips . . . [said] that the building had been there for six months or so undisturbed, and yet there was no evidence of rodent or insect infestation of the building, which was incredible. There are cockroaches everywhere, unless there are toxic chemicals. If something is bad enough to wipe out a cockroach population, it is pretty bad. (Brown interview, May 3, 1982)

EPA's lack of meaningful involvement is explained by the possibility of political recriminations from both New York State and the Reagan administration. Another constraint on the agency's behavior was that, to use Superfund money, EPA is required to attempt to locate the polluting party to obtain partial reimbursement. Such an effort would require attributions of responsibility to New York State.

Given the precedent of Love Canal, it is not surprising that EPA was hesitant to invest resources in such an uncertain and politically dangerous venture. By the time the Reagan administration took office, it was clear that EPA should avoid a situation involving high political and fiscal risks. Nevertheless, it is not inconceivable that the agency might have become one of the core organizations that responded to the SOB accident. It could have provided a great deal of technical direction. It could have implemented a medical surveillance program. It could have performed chemical and biological tests, and it could have supervised the cleanup. Constraints at EPA, however, tended to define such lines of action as unwise. EPA officials accurately perceived that its intervention would be anathema to the new administration's policies. Most important, however, was that Love Canal was a bitter memory for EPA. It is clear that the Environmental Protection Agency was not, and is not, eager to repeat the jurisdictional battles that took place there.

·   ·   ·

The larger process illustrated in this chapter is one in which centripetal forces initially assembled a fairly large number of organizations to address the dangers posed by the State Office Building accident. Centrifugal forces then pushed them away. As a result, a hierarchical division of labor emerged among agencies—a precondition for the legitimation of definitions of acceptable risk. The process moved in fits and starts rather than in a smooth progression; ill-defined tasks, unsettled mechanisms of control, and multiple uses for policies lent a measure of unpredictability to the case—for both participants and organization theory. Each agency had its particular reasons for avoiding the SOB, although there are similarities (table 1).

Obviously, the two most frequently cited "mechanisms of exit" were the lack of expertise and the absence of a bureaucratic category that would classify the accident and its aftermath as relevant to a particular agency. Interviews and documents show that formal mandates did not prevent these agencies from becoming involved in the Binghamton controversy. In other cases—such as contaminated wells in Broome County and at Love Canal—the Broome County legislature and the EPA, respectively, were quite active in constructing solutions and helping to define acceptable risk. These agencies avoided the Binghamton case not because of intraorganizational forces but because of organizational *environments*. The theme that runs through each agency's demurral is that there was little or no outside pressure demanding that it assert authority.

Drawing attention to what *could* have happened, but did not, might seem like ghost-chasing. But consider the entire collection of organizations in Binghamton, those discussed in this

Table 1. Mechanisms of Exit from Problem Areas:
City, County, State, and Federal Agencies

Agency	*Claim*
City	
Executive	Lack of expertise
Council	Lack of expertise
County	
Executive	Lack of expertise
Legislature and committees	Lack of expertise
State	
Department of Environmental Conservation	Not an "environmental" issue
Legislature	Lack of jurisdiction
Department of Transportation	Lack of jurisdiction
Federal	
Small Business Administration	Problem is not a "disaster"
OSHA	State workers are not a federal responsibility
NIOSH	Not a federal problem
EPA	Lack of authority (Reagan federalism; conflict with DOH over Love Canal)

chapter as well as the county health department, the state health department, and the Office of General Services. Each could have pursued several courses of action. Certainly, constraints limited the number and kinds of alternatives. But it is just as certain that some flexibility nevertheless existed within those constraints—so that what happened did not have to happen.

Organizations, as I argued previously, are (among other things) repositories for alternative solutions that are sometimes applied, sometimes not. Therefore, as organizations estranged themselves from the controversies swirling around the SOB, the number and types of solutions to those problems declined. For example, although EPA's (possible) blunders at Love Canal brought it widespread criticism, its participation helped to create one of the conditions that made decision making a more

open process: Several social actors began negotiating definitions of appropriate behavior, which are important variables
in organizational conflict over acceptable risk. In the case of
Three Mile Island, local, state, and federal agencies, as well as
corporations, all influenced decisions about what to do with the
nearly destroyed reactor and the surrounding community. At
Bhopal the range of organizations was broadened to include
international actors.

It is not likely that any single organization, by becoming
more involved in Binghamton, would have radically changed
the solutions eventually proposed to deal with the contaminated building, the exposed people, or Binghamton's environment. Yet, the combined effect of these organizational exits
meant that some solutions would be considered legitimate to
pursue, and others would not.[10] As organizations left, or were
pushed out of, the organizational field, three organizations—
the county health department, the state health department,
and the state Office of General Services—were left to negotiate
solutions to the problems in Binghamton.

10. Ideally, we would have data on the process through which each organization decided to exit the organizational field. To do so would require an
understanding of the environments of each organization, as well as extensive
interviewing within each agency. Resource limitations prevented such a data-
collection effort. This deficiency is not terribly important here, because I am
mainly interested in the *consequences* rather than the *causes* of the exits.

FOUR

An Excursus on Resolving Organizational Dilemmas: The County Government's Risk

> Whatever risks there are are balanced out by
> the good.
>
> —Risk consultant

After the electricity to the State Office Building's damaged transformers was shut off on the morning of the accident, some twenty minutes after the alarm, firefighters opened the doors to the mechanical room to inspect the damage and to extinguish the flaming electrical wires. As the doors opened, toxic smoke billowed out, contaminating the garage. For the next ten months local experts and decision makers made the same types of judgments about the garage that eventually would be made about the building itself. But there were several notable differences. First, contamination levels were much lower in the garage, although it contained most of the same chemicals as those present in the SOB. Second, a medical surveillance program was *not* devised for those whose primary source of exposure was the garage. Third, county, rather than state, officials were responsible for deciding what to do about the garage. Finally, unlike the dilemmas associated with the State Office Building, the difficulties in this case were resolved so that conditions in the garage returned nearly to normal: The garage was declared safe and reopened for use relatively quickly.

The case of the contaminated parking garage is sociologically interesting because of the unusually rich detail on how organizations manage and accept risk. This chapter thus addresses the sociology of risk analysis more than the sociology of organizations. The series of events and decisions concerning the polluted garage, contrary to much of the risk assessment literature, does not confirm the notion that risk evaluation is fundamentally a rational, scientific enterprise. Rather, the solution depended on outcomes of interorganizational struggles. Risks were assessed and accepted in a way that was determined by organizational interests, which coincided only to some extent with the public interest. There are five steps in the process of accepting risk: defining the problem, assessing consequences, ordering alternatives, constructing acceptable risk assessments, and accepting the risk.

Phase One: Defining the Problem

It was not evident at first that the garage was contaminated: People were still trying to make sense of the news that oily soot was distributed throughout the eighteen-story building. On February 7, two days after the explosion, a BCHD officer went to the government complex to survey the damage. His inspection of the garage revealed nothing remarkable:

> Upon opening the door to the main parking area at the basement level, we [noticed] a slight odor, but this was not noticeable inside the lobby. On the grate opening immediately adjacent to the parking area there was some cobwebbing material which appears very much like ordinary dust, *not at all similar to the ash found in the State Building.* (Austin to Schecter, February 9, 1981; emphasis added)

The officer discovered a similar light dust and odor in the sub-basement (also used for parking), but they, too, bore no resemblance to damage in the state building. Thus, officials initially thought these lower levels had escaped the toxic fate of the building. According to Schecter, "the garage stayed open . . . for about two weeks—maybe one. People were going in and out with their cars" (Schecter interview, August 10, 1981).

But the visual inspection was insufficient to detect contaminants. The county therefore used an independent laboratory, Galson Technical Services, to test the garage. Galson reported PCB concentrations in the garage ranging from 2,500 to 4,700 micrograms per square meter (1 microgram = one millionth of a gram); results from the state health department's labs showed PCB concentrations ranging from 0 to 240 micrograms per square meter on automobiles parked in the garage. For comparative purposes, DOH took samples from various places in

Binghamton (the local press building and a bank building, including the bank's garage). All of those surface samples showed PCB levels of less than .1 microgram per square meter.

The PCB levels in the garage were too high to be simple background contaminants and, so, must have resulted from the fire and explosion on February 5 in the mechanical room. The high levels suggested yet another hazard and a new set of ambiguities. The current federal standard, set by the Occupational Safety and Health Administration for PCB *air* levels in a workplace, was 500 micrograms per cubic meter (NIOSH recommends 1 microgram per cubic meter per 40-hour workweek). The OSHA and NIOSH standards could not be used for surface-level contamination, and no others were available. The lack of clear guidelines for determining safety levels made it difficult to solve the problem of the polluted garage by appeal to scientific expertise.

Although county officials claimed responsibility for the disposition of the garage, the Office of General Services assumed the task of providing security for the building as a whole. During the first week or so after the fire, everyone's attention was riveted on the state building; the garage was relatively accessible. Some automobiles in the garage at the time of the fire were used by state and county employees. A city mailroom worker said: "We've had people in and out [of the garage]. The door was kept open with a wedge" (Fecteau 1981e). Stories on security problems were published almost daily in the Binghamton newspapers, helping to politicize the issue.

After the New York Department of Health confirmed Galson's findings, OGS added the garage to its list of places requiring decontamination. The loss of parking space soon led to crowding in the streets of downtown Binghamton, and OGS immediately began cleanup of the garage with soap and water. Hundreds of drums of this toxic cleanup water were stored and eventually hauled away to a landfill in Niagara Falls (near Love Canal).

After this initial cleaning, Schecter inspected the garage and evaluated DOH test data. As the county's health representative, he was charged with recommending to the county executive whether or not the garage was safe to open. The decision was important because county legislators, having defined the garage as their responsibility, were pressing both BCHD and the county executive for action. It was also an important professional decision for the county health director. Schecter had been appointed not by the current county executive, Carl Young, but by Young's predecessor, and his contract with the county would soon expire. By this time, journalists were turning to Dr. Schecter for a lot of their information, some of which was critical of the state, and he was developing a popular reputation as a concerned public protector. But Schecter's posture put the county executive, as well as powerful members of the legislature, in a difficult position. On the one hand, county legislators did not wish to challenge state decisions regarding the contaminated building. On the other hand, if they openly criticized their county health director, the public might view them as siding with the polluter—New York State—against the public's representative. Arnold Schecter thus became a risk.

Schecter's judgments on the garage were subjected to intense scrutiny, and the types of risks he had to balance were not limited to those of safety and health. Each of the several audiences for his decisions had its own idea of what constituted "reasoned judgment." The director was aware that the county executive and legislature both wanted to avoid political turmoil, that DOH disagreed with BCHD's scientific procedures, and that the media expected complete and honest information—all this on top of his responsibility for the health of Broome County's citizens. These constraints were reflected in his decisions.

Dr. Schecter sent a letter to County Executive Young in March, responding to expectations that the time was at hand for a positive decision on the garage. "I have carefully considered the data available to me about the State Office Building," wrote the health director, "and have concluded that it will be reasonable to open the basement garage as soon as all overhead pipes have been cleaned or recleaned" (Schecter to Young, March 24, 1981a). In a memo to the executive of the same date, the health director released Broome County automobiles that had been impounded in the basement (Schecter to Young, March 24, 1981b).

In explaining his actions, Dr. Schecter noted that the highest surface level of PCBs in the garage was 1.5 µg/m², according to DOH data. Multiplying this amount by the garage's surface area (9,300 square meters), the director estimated an upper limit of "the total estimated residue of PCBs" to be 13,950 µg, or nearly 14 milligrams, roughly equivalent, he explained, to "¹⁄₂,₀₀₀ of a tablespoon—less than a grain of salt." To ensure that he had not underestimated the amount of contaminants in the garage, Schecter multiplied this estimate by 100. "It is possible," he wrote to Young, "that total remaining residue may be as much as 1.4 grams, which would be something like ¹⁄₁₀ teaspoon." Schecter was concerned not only with PCBs but also with furans and dioxins—especially the 2,3,7,8 TCDD isomer, which many scientists consider our most deadly synthetic chemical.[1] But the test results did not include data on dioxin and furan levels, so Schecter used the DOH's earlier data that showed TCDD at 3 and 4 parts per million (ppm) in the soot from the State Office Building. Because PCBs had been measured in the soot from 5 percent to 20 percent of the soot by weight, he multiplied 5 by 3, and 4 by 200 (presumably for the sake of caution), arriving at the "estimate that TCDD constitutes on the order of 15 to 800 ppm of the PCBs" (all quotations above in Schecter to Young, March 24, 1981a).

This estimate was based on two questionable assumptions, however. First, it assumed the highest surface level of PCBs in the garage after cleaning was 1.5 µg/m². Second, it assumed the measure of 3 or 4 ppm TCDD in the soot was representative of all samples in which PCBs were found. In fact, no scientific basis existed for either assumption. The samples were neither random nor numerous (there were five), so there was no way of knowing with confidence if the 1.5 µg/m² figure was representative of *any* level of PCBs in the garage. Similarly, with no

1. An isomer is a particular compound of a type of chemical. For example, there is a class of chemicals known as dioxins. Within this class there is one isomer called 2,3,7,8 tetrachlorinated dibenzo-p-dioxin (TCDD). This is the dioxin isomer scientists have dubbed the most dangerous synthetic chemical yet produced. In addition to 2,3,7,8 TCDD there are twenty-one other "tetra" isomers; there are also other classes of isomers, such as octa, and penta, chlorinated dibenzo-p-dioxin. These categories also apply to the furans, PCBs, and other chemicals in and around the SOB. Obviously, it is impossible to test for all isomers.

tests for either dioxins or furans, literally nothing was known about these substances. Yet assuming a known correlation between PCB and dioxin (or furan) content, as well as discounting the sampling problems, seemed necessary and therefore reasonable, given the demands on the county health department. The assumptions were obviously a way to manage some of those demands and helped form the conclusion that the garage represented a negligible risk to public health.

After Schecter decided, on March 24, to allow the garage to reopen, the state health department announced that an "expert blue-ribbon panel," composed of internationally renowned scientists, would meet in New York City on April 3 to assess the Binghamton situation. One of their tasks would be to define "How safe is safe?" During the ten days that elapsed between his decision and the first meeting of the expert panel, Schecter recanted his pronouncement on the garage. On April 1, 1981, he urged the county executive to await the opinions of the "blue-ribbon" scientists before reopening the garage. He also made an interesting admission:

> Because I am *not* an expert in these specific types of chemical contamination, e.g., the dioxins, furans and PCBs, polychlorinated benzenes, etc., and because of the significant potential health and legal implications of this very difficult decision, I believe the interests of Broome County would best be served by Broome County attorneys and health officials consulting with the six *real* experts who will be in town tomorrow prior to our opening the garage. . . . After reflecting on the over twenty international experts who will be advising Dr. Axelrod . . . it seems to me extremely unwise for Broome County to not take advantage of a portion of this same expertise to make certain which of our assumptions regarding the safety of the garage might be or not be simply unwarranted speculations rather than hard reality. (Schecter to Young, April 1, 1981; emphasis added)

Before the formation of the blue-ribbon panel, Schecter had considered himself expert enough to determine if the garage represented a health risk. But now he was telling the county executive—who would bear the political brunt of potentially adverse consequences of opening the garage—that he was not a "real expert" and that the assumptions that underlay his risk assessment might be "unwarranted speculations."

Although many interpreted this equivocation as evidence of a cautious rethinking of the problem, Schecter's detractors used it to label him unreliable. The Republican majority leader in the Broome County legislature, for example, held the opinion that Dr. Schecter "flipflopped a lot and has made no positive decisions. . . . He has aggravated the crisis and raised more questions than answers" (Barber interview, August 12, 1981). Accurate or not, these perceptions were shared by many.

Dr. Schecter's denial that he was expert enough to decide the relative safety of the garage presented County Executive Young with a dilemma. On the one hand, Young had to depend on his county health director for a great deal of scientific advice. By becoming the major critic of state organizations, Schecter had staked a claim as an expert evaluator. On the other hand, Young was now being told that "expert" decisions that would be expected from the county health department might not be valid and that Schecter's judgments could not be trusted. The latter message, not the former, was what Broome County politicians heard, and it eventually cost Schecter his job.

The first phase of the story of the contaminated garage is the same as the first stage in any story about reaching a decision: defining the problem. Notice that if we were to analyze this phase in terms of a probability distribution of hazardous amounts of toxic chemicals (an approach taken by many studies of risk), we would learn very little of the *process* of that decision. Organizational issues, not issues of risk, were the key to understanding that process. The significance of this fact will become clear as we proceed.

Phase Two: Assessing Consequences

After the expert panel met on April 3, several of its members journeyed to Binghamton, where Schecter consulted them about the garage. OGS had cleaned it several times by then, and new tests revealed a substantial reduction of PCBs. Up to this point, the notion that PCB levels were a valid, though indirect, indicator of dioxin and furan contamination had not been challenged. But some members of the panel suggested that testing for these more dangerous chemicals was appropriate. The county health director was also demanding, via the press and memoranda to the county executive, that the state do extensive testing outside the SOB proper in order to construct a map of possibly contaminated areas. Privately, Schecter was also asking the state department of health for assurances that the garage presented no health hazard to the public. But DOH personnel had already provided them. As one DOH official expressed it: "We told them in February [1981] that we thought it was safe to use, and now they want us to say it again. We keep telling them we already did that" (Huffaker interview, October 6, 1981). But Schecter gave their assurances little credence, now believing the garage to be more dangerous than he had originally supposed.

Unfortunately for BCHD, the rest of the county government was more aligned with state judgments than with its own health department. Carl Young, the county executive, believed Schecter's openness with the media was causing unnecessary alarm, and he was also convinced the garage was not a health threat. Following are parts of a transcript of a conversation the executive had with a reporter:

> *Young:* If you wanted my opinion, we could all go down there and have lunch in the garage and nobody is going to get sick. But unfortunately, there is the element which would take you to court to sue you for their fortune over any circumstances; people who get a hangnail will be attributing it to PCBs unless you have gone the last mile and can document . . . exactly what the level of PCB and furans and dioxin are.
>
> *Reporter:* Why are you testing when there are no standards?
>
> *Young:* . . . This is liability protection rather than health protection. . . .
>
> *Reporter:* What's the difference between your comment about going down there and eating lunch in the garage and the governor's offer to drink a glass of PCBs?
>
> *Young:* I'd do it. . . . I've been in the garage at least a dozen times since the fire. (Young interview, by Geimann, May 20, 1981)

The county executive thus agreed to further tests, although his use for them differed from BCHD's.

Meanwhile, the state health department had established a new communications policy regarding BCHD, which had initially been the official representative of the state. A DOH scientist explained: "After about a month, we realized that Schecter and us were working at cross-purposes and decided not to give him information. Instead, all information would be given to [DOH's director of public health], and he would be the only one that would talk with Schecter. . . . There was a general feeling that [Schecter] wasn't helping" (Huffaker interview, October 6, 1981). A consensus developed between DOH and the county executive that Schecter's discussions with the media were damaging their credibility. A local paper ran a full-page feature on Schecter (headlined "He's Taken On Polluted Wells, Contaminated Office Building, and Now He's Taking On the Heat"), in which he maintained the media were "the most efficient, least expensive public health educators" (McCullough 1981a)—not a very popular opinion in the state capitol. One scientist at DOH commented:

> The gist of it was, he thinks the media is the cheapest form of public health education, and that is how he justifies it. [And he said] if the media is inaccurate in reporting something, his emphasis would be to sort of try to change them and get them to be accurate. . . . The crazy thing is that 99 percent of the information they were getting was coming from him to begin with, so if it is inaccurate there are two ways you can point your finger. (Taylor interview, July 8, 1981)

The county executive concurred with the general point and in late April tried to mute his director of health with the following order: "No test results are to be publicized, distributed, etc., from any source other than the office of county executive" (Young to Schecter, February 24, 1981). Young was unable to enforce the order, however, and Schecter continued to use the media to educate the public.

In early May Schecter wrote to the DOH deputy director of public health, Glenn Haughie, to request testing of the garage. In his letter, he expressed the hope that "the Office of General

Services . . . would authorize payment for these tests to be performed, at a laboratory acceptable to us (and you), which could give us a relatively rapid response enabling us to open the garage. . . . The precedent of asking the polluter to pay is well established" (Schecter to Haughie, May 5, 1981). Interestingly, Schecter also suggested to Haughie that direct testing was not necessary and that if DOH sent Schecter the data from twenty to thirty samples from the SOB itself, he "could almost certainly extrapolate from these values to the garage." Although Haughie did not acknowledge that New York State was the polluter, he did agree to continue work on the samples, replying: "We expect this task to require a few months to complete" (Haughie to Schecter, May 12, 1981).

The Broome County Health Department could not wait that long. There was intense political pressure to make a decision, and the question of Schecter's continued tenure as health director was to be settled the following month, at the end of June. Schecter thus appealed to the county executive and the county legislature for funds to have the county do the testing itself. A reluctant Broome County legislature authorized furan and dioxin testing at the county's expense.

Granting BCHD's request for these tests constituted an implicit affirmation that the garage was the county's responsibility. According to members of the legislature, Schecter promised to render a definitive judgment on the garage once the test results were in. Finally, out of the confusing barrage of questions posed by the SOB, the legislators thought a solution would be fashioned within constraints they created. The Republican majority leader remarked with irritation:

> We thought it was worth $7,200 to get Schecter to make a decision. When he was asking for money to test the garage, the legislature asked him aggressively and forcefully if he could make a decision if he got the tests he wanted. He couldn't answer at first and started double-talking, then he finally said yes, but now he can't give us the decision he said he would. (Barber interview, August 12, 1981)

Schecter claimed this view was not altogether accurate. The legislators, he said, tried to get me to say that I would absolutely give them a result when the tests were in. That is not true. I didn't agree to that. I agreed that when we got them that we could be able to give them an answer. . . . But I think that since the values are low but not extremely low, no one has come up with a safe level yet—and there is over a billion [dollars] in threatened litigation—. . . it would be bad medicine not to have expert consultants giving their view. After all, if [the garage] were opened, pregnant women would use it, and everyone else. . . . There would most certainly be lawsuits, and I would have to defend that in court some day. (Schecter interview, August 10, 1981)

Whether or not a promise was made, it is easy to understand how the legislature and the executive thought a decision was forthcoming. The county executive's office received a copy of a letter from the health director to the DOH director of public health that stated: "If the amounts of furans and dioxins [on the garage floor] are within an order of magnitude up to 100 times greater than . . . your . . . figures, in my opinion after consultation with experts in the field the garage is safe for use" (Schecter to Haughie, May 15, 1981). Schecter assured the county executive that "the opening of our garage is a fairly straightforward issue. Once we have hard data, not calculations, extrapolations or speculation, we can almost certainly document relative safety or, although not probable, lack of safety" (Schecter to Young and Lee, May 18, 1981).

But a positive decision was not, in fact, forthcoming. Instead, Schecter sought extensive expert advice. By mid-July 1981, two months after the legislature approved the appropriation, the test results had been received by BCHD. (On June 24, the county executive had announced that he would not reappoint Schecter as county health director but would retain him as consultant on the SOB; this special appointment was not long-lived.) On August 6, Schecter sent the test results to various scientists, asking them to review the data. At least six experts responded. The deputy director of the National Toxicology Program at the U.S. Department of Health and Human Services said he did not have enough time to review the data. The chief chemist of the Fish and Wildlife Service, U.S. Department of the Interior, wrote that he was "uncomfortable with opening these contaminated paved areas [to the public] without making one more attempt to reduce . . . these residues" (Stalling to Schecter, August 18, 1981). The chairperson of the Institute of Environmental Medicine at New York University Medical Center was "not able to arrive at a confident opinion concerning the magnitude of risks" posed by the garage, adding that "in view of the economic and psychosocial ramifications of the problem, an in-depth assessment of this type [i.e., consulting experts] would seem to be warranted" (Upton to Schecter, August 21, 1981). The director of NIOSH's Division of Surveillance, Hazard Evaluations, and Field Studies concluded that, although "no definitive judgments" could be made on the basis of the data, "we are of the opinion that, in the areas tested, the concentrations of [PCBs, furans, and dioxins] do not appear to be at levels that would be of significant concern" (Landrigan to Schecter, August 24, 1981). The executive director of the Board on Toxicology and Environmental Health Hazards of the National Research Council offered mixed advice:

> The data on the furans indicate that substantial contamination of several isomers could remain on the basement floor but little else remains elsewhere. . . . These data would suggest a strong possibility of risks to humans occupying the area. However, the nature and extent of potential risks . . . cannot be characterized at this time. The data on dioxins do not indicate much of a risk to human health. (Tardiff to Schecter, September 8, 1981)

Finally, the director of the Centers for Disease Control (CDC) in Atlanta, along with the CDC's director of the Chronic Diseases Division, concluded that "we find no evidence in the material presented that levels of chemicals exist in the garage at levels above what we would consider negligible with respect to human health risk" (Heath to Schecter, October 7, 1981).

The experts were not much use to Schecter. The variation in their opinion reflected the uncertainty inherent in the situation: The sampling was not sufficiently systematic to warrant confidence, and even flawless methodology would not solve the problem because there were many other (chemical and/or biological) tests that could be performed. The more important problem of safety was a foregone nonconclusion.

From one point of view, there was no final determination of the extent and meaning of the garage's contamination. In the end, however, the former health director did indeed decide— the garage would not be opened. In gathering expert opinion, Schecter's actions were no different from those of the state health department. But the county health department, particularly its director, did not enjoy the same amount of power as DOH. Thus, it was not prepared to defend unpopular decisions before the county executive and the county legislature. Assessing the consequences of risky problems, then, is partially a function of the relative power of organizations to influence agendas of debate and to control important resources.

Phase Three: Ordering Alternatives

The problem of the contaminated parking garage moved toward resolution around the middle of June in 1981. More than four months had elapsed since the accident at the State Office Building. The question of what to do with the building and the people who had been exposed because of the accident there caused many resources to be drawn away from numerous organizations' routines. One of those resources was the time and attention of BCHD's director. By all accounts—those of Schecter, his successor, the county executive, informants in the county health department, and the press—Schecter's deputy health officer, Kathleen Gaffney, had been attending to the more mundane tasks of running the health agency. Most of the department's functions (e.g., home health care and its Women, Infants, and Children program) were of a more traditional nature than the political problems that were attracting so much media attention.

Some interpreted Schecter's high visibility as an indication that he was devoting all of his time to the SOB, thus jeopardizing the effectiveness of the health department. Only those outside the Broome County Health Department, however, argued that the department was suffering. Schecter defended himself against allegations of managerial neglect:

That is absolutely a phony issue, because I was assigned the job [of the SOB] by the county executive. Our WIC [Women, Infants, and Children] program went from zero clients when I came here, to five hundred, and then on up to two thousand, in a two-year period under my leadership. Home health visits rose markedly, and I was able to talk the legislature into giving us enough money to help us provide many more home health care visits. The first year I was here, I wasn't able to get the environmental health division to do water inspections, and this year they all will have been done. We were ordered to do fire inspections for the first time by the state of New York's Health Department on all motels and hotels. We had to start training our staff in January 1980 when the new law was passed, but we didn't have an increase in staff. We had a crisis in the Vestal [a nearby town] water with organics in the water supply. I brought a deputy commissioner here—which in retrospect was a political bad move—to delegate a lot of the day-to-day work. We have an excellent budget department and are searching for a new head nurse. I think the accomplishments for under two years for a department, which was considered by everyone to be moribund, were remarkable. Besides, I didn't devote exclusive time [to the SOB]. I think it would have been impossible to do much more than I did in a two-year period. (Schecter interview, August 10, 1981)

Dr. Kathleen Gaffney, who succeeded Schecter, asserted that her predecessor had indeed helped the department by improving its public image, and she agreed, in a wry sort of way, that the department had not suffered because of his attention to the State Office Building: "Before Arnie came here, the nurses were ashamed to say that they worked for the health department, but Schecter has added visibility to the department and brought some salaries up, so they are not ashamed anymore. The other programs haven't been hurt because of the SOB. They have even thrived because his attention has been diverted elsewhere" (Gaffney interview, August 12, 1981). During the several months Schecter was involved with the State Office Building (and the garage), Gaffney's supervision of the daily tasks of a small bureaucracy was intensified. She shared the view of most politicians that Schecter had led the BCHD in an alarmist direction. When queried about a rumor that she had lobbied for Schecter's job, Gaffney replied: "No, but I have been lobbying for his dismissal since September" (five months *before* the accident) (Gaffney interview, August 12, 1981).

In early June, Young, the county executive, said he was likely to renew Schecter's contract as director of the health department. But as the legislature's increasingly negative view of Schecter became clear, Young began to reconsider the appointment. Still, the county executive was under political pressure not to fire Schecter and thus argued in the press, and to the legislature, that the county should retain him specifically as a consultant on the SOB. At the time of the official announcement that Schecter would not be reappointed, June 24, 1981, Young told reporters: "I'm not saying [Schecter] hasn't done the job. I don't think it's realistic to think someone can do two-and-a-half jobs. I'm not critical of his performance at all" (Fairbanks 1981). Privately, however, he expressed a different view:

> Arnie wasn't a good administrator. I didn't say it publicly because when I made the decision not to continue him as commissioner, the rationale I offered was that to be a full-time professor, run the department, and to oversee this whole SOB thing was more than one person could do and do all three competently. I saw no point in criticizing the job he has done. . . . If we were going to have him as our consultant, that would have been detrimental to his credibility. (Young interview, December 2, 1981)

In avoiding open criticism of Schecter, Young was trying to maintain Schecter's status with the public, a status that was a political asset to the county government: "I felt we needed to maintain, from the standpoint of reassuring the community, some continuity. Arnie had achieved a status, he was a focal point in the community. [There] are those who are skeptical about the state's efforts, and with Arnie present there was a higher . . . likelihood that the public would accept the state's actions" (Young interview, December 2, 1981). Schecter stepped down as health director in mid-September 1981; Gaffney became acting commissioner.

Observers thought it curious that the Republican legislature would differ so radically with a Republican county executive, and some accused the executive of shirking responsibility by letting legislators fire Schecter for him. Young nevertheless

persisted with the proposal that Schecter be retained as SOB
consultant. It was a losing proposition:

> I spent a couple of hours with [the leading Republicans] one day,
> trying to persuade them that if they couldn't agree to a two-year
> contract . . . [then to] make it a year, or even six months. Schecter's
> credibility in the legislature had been suffering a precipitous de-
> cline since about June. He was perceived as being very indecisive.
> He made them very upset when he went to them [in May] and said,
> "We need $7,000 for tests." Their feeling was, "How the hell many
> tests do we have to do here?" The question was put directly to him:
> "If these tests are done, when the results come back, will you be
> able to make a decision?" He hedged, but they kept asking him
> until they got a yes or no answer. Finally he said, "Yes, I will." We
> got the results in the first or second week of July, and he felt un-
> qualified to evaluate the data, so he sent the data to it seemed like
> everybody in the world. We said, "Suppose you get conflicting re-
> sponses?" He compared it to getting second opinions if you were
> going to have your gall bladder out. But from July to August
> through September [there was] no decision. . . . His credibility just
> sank and sank. Decisions by default in this business are not well
> regarded. He wouldn't say "No, we shouldn't open it." That would
> have been okay, I think. He always said "Give me another week."
> You are dealing with human beings, and they got pissed off.
> (Young interview, December 2, 1981)

In October the legislature voted 11–7 against continuing
Schecter's appointment as the county's consultant. The vote was
divided strictly along party lines, but with an unusual twist for
Broome County: All the Republicans voted against the Republican executive's proposal, and all the Democrats voted for it.
The Republicans were not rejecting the idea that the county
needed a consultant (another was soon found). Rather, their
vote was a rejection of Schecter himself. The Democrats, in
spite of their unanimous vote, were no great supporters of
Schecter either. Thus, their vote was a vote against the Republicans, rather than a vote of confidence for their county health
director. In this way, Schecter was caught in a vacuum, without
political support.

Before decisions can be made, alternative courses of action
must be eliminated from consideration. Mutually exclusive al-

ternatives, such as whether or not to reopen the garage, demand a method whereby some solutions can be discarded. Many of our decision-making models hold that once the consequences of the available choices have been evaluated, one choice should stand out as more reasonable than others. By withdrawing the organizational basis for Dr. Schecter's authority, the county government effectively excluded him from decision-making arenas. Firing the county health director was one way to eliminate some alternative courses of action.

Phase Four: Constructing Acceptable Risk Assessments

The legislature risked its credibility by firing the county health director in that a strong public outcry against political leaders might obstruct consensus building, even more so than keeping Schecter around. Thus, to maintain a symbolic measure of distance from the interests of the state, the county executive persisted with the proposal that the county hire a consultant on the basis that "it's important that we act quickly to assure people that we're not turning our back on the problem" (Cohen 1981).

The executive's choice for the job, John Buckley, had been a research director for EPA and was the chairperson of Broome County's Environmental Management Council. Much more conservative than Schecter, Buckley was not as accessible to the media and was considerably less critical of state policies. Partly because of this, local officials welcomed Buckley as the county's consultant. Dr. Gaffney, now head of the county health department, found him easier to work with and thought he would be a credible check on any abuses that might occur on the part of the state. Buckley reassured the public that he would not hesitate to "blow the whistle" on the state if necessary and advised the county executive that it was vital to successful risk assessment to be frank and open with the public. "I am not anxious to keep things to myself," said Buckley, "[and] there is no way we can deal with this without absolute honesty" (Broome County Public Health Committee minutes, October 15, 1981).

The county legislature questioned Buckley about his ability to make decisions. The chairperson of the Public Health Committee (a Republican) asked: "You know of our difficulties with the garage, and how we have hired experts and received test results and information. Would you be in a position to give us advice as to a particular direction we might proceed in?" (Broome County Public Health Committee minutes, October 15, 1981). Buckley responded that his role would simply be to advise decision makers. He told the committee he "would not make decisions [but would] just tell people what the alternatives are—the advantages and the disadvantages, and what may be done."

There were noteworthy similarities in the way Buckley and Schecter presented the problem of assessing the risk of the contaminated garage. Like Schecter, Buckley stressed that questions of safety were difficult to answer and that information would have to be garnered from many sources. Like Schecter, Buckley told the county legislature that he would need to consult experts and that he would work hard to ensure that the county was getting reliable information from the state. But these similarities were trivial when compared to the major difference between these two experts: Unlike Schecter, Buckley agreed with the legislators' perceptions of who was, and who was not, qualified to make explicit judgments regarding safety:

> [I] do not want to dodge anything, but it will always be a fuzzy gray in which there are risks, and whatever risks there are are balanced out by the good. We are in the hands of people who are experts, and we have to take it on faith, because we can't smell it, or taste it, or make decisions ourselves. We should do this as publicly as we can. If the decision is wrong, well, the decision is a political action. If whoever makes the decision is wrong, the process will take care of it. There is not any magic. . . . I think we should be able to make up our minds about the garage within the next few weeks. (Broome County Public Health Committee minutes, October 15, 1981)

Buckley was someone the legislature could label credible. "I tend to be low key and I hope I can be that way. . . . I really don't want any authority" (Fecteau 1981o). Assured that Buckley shared its conservative definition of appropriate behavior, the committee approved Buckley's appointment without dissent. When the full legislature voted on the contract the next day, there was only one objection.

Once Schecter was fired, interorganizational dissension over the issue of the contaminated garage (as well as the SOB) abated. As a result, official assessments of risk gradually became accepted. Fewer and fewer articles quoting Schecter appeared in the local papers, and OGS and DOH were less beleaguered now that their actions were not subjected to intense critical scrutiny. The county executive, too, was not put on the spot as often.[2] Local governments could once again concentrate on administering the city of Binghamton and the county of Broome. In hindsight, the county executive believes his fears of losing legitimacy by losing Schecter were not well founded. "In retrospect," he said in an interview, "I have not suffered at all" (Young interview, December 2, 1981).

Accepting a decision as legitimate implies some measure of consensus. Buckley redefined important parameters of debate by accepting the legislature's views on who should play what roles and how they should be played. A necessary condition for defining acceptable risk is the lack of competing definitions.

Phase Five: Accepting Risk

The final phase in managing the risk of the contaminated garage was the decision to determine the hazards were negligible, thus eliminating any rational reason to keep it closed. On November 25, 1981, the county executive announced: "I have concluded that we should be able to open the basement level of the parking garage in the very near future. . . . We would like to invite all employees to a meeting on Monday, November 30, 1981, . . . to respond to any questions or concerns you may have relative to the opening of the garage" (Young to county employees, November 25, 1981). About seventy or eighty people attended the meeting, probably fifteen of whom were from the media, as well as members of a grass-roots association, the Citizens' Committee on the Binghamton State Office Building.[3]

2. The local Red Cross rescinded its decision not to accept blood from those who were exposed in the SOB.
3. My notes on this meeting are taken from a verbatim tape transcription.

The executive was finally able to follow through on a decision he had reached months before. His decision to reopen the garage was legitimated by a formal risk assessment constructed by his new consultant. In a letter to Young, the consultant explained: "Based on my examination of the available data and my discussions with [experts], I believe the risk to health of persons who might use the BSOB garage area to be very small" (Buckley to Young, November 23, 1981). The county executive was certain the garage was safe: "I am convinced that the most dangerous period of time will be about 5:15 [in the afternoon] Monday through Friday when there will be carbon monoxide in far greater quantities than any other toxic substances there" (Broome County Public Meeting, November 30, 1981). Buckley's formal assessment precisely met the needs of the executive and the legislature, providing an apparently rational justification to reopen the garage. It is therefore worth considering in some detail.

The computations in the formal analysis of the garage were based on what Buckley considered a "worst-case analysis."[4] To calculate the overall risk, he first needed to estimate the total amount of dioxins and furans in the garage (PCBs were not used in the assessment). Buckley used four garage samples as a base for his decision (table 2; the data have been verified from the originals).[5] The highest available number—130 (rounded from the fourth sample) nanograms per square meter—was treated as the average amount of extant contaminants; the presumption was that this would assure a conservative estimate. Buckley then assumed the 130 ng/m² applied to 2,3,7,8 TCDD,

4. Actually, he calculated the risk of exposure for four scenarios: (1) a worst-case inhalation exposure; (2) a more "realistic" inhalation exposure; (3) exposure that would occur if an adult were to fall on the floor of the garage; and (4) the exposure that would occur if a child were to drop a lollipop on the garage floor and then eat the total contaminants on a square meter. It is not necessary for our purposes to examine each of these calculations, because the major assumptions of the worst-case scenario were common to the others.

5. Recall there were actually five, not four, samples taken from the garage. I do not know why Buckley used only these four. The original data show that the fifth sample was a piece of concrete taken from the garage floor. The toxic levels on this sample were lower than those detected on the other four. Because Buckley used the highest value as an average, inclusion of the fifth sample would have been inconsequential for the analysis.

Table 2. Dioxin and Furan Levels in the
State Office Building Garage

Location of Samples	Dioxins (ng/m²)	Furans (ng/m²)	Total (ng/m²)
Sub-basement	1.41	2.5	13.9
	0.8	.25	1.1
Basement	3.3	5.6	8.6
	2.1	127.2	129.3

SOURCE: Data from Tiernan et al. 1981.

NOTE: Measured in nanograms per square meter. One nanogram is equal to one billionth of a gram.

the most toxic chemical found in the SOB (this isomer was not found in the garage samples) and multiplied this number times the total surface area in the garage (about 86,000 square meters), yielding an estimate of 11,200,000 nanograms of furans and dioxins.[6] This is equal to 11.2 milligrams, or "about one-sixth of a grain of rice," as Buckley put it. Buckley's "worst case" was a situation in which half the surface contaminants become airborne, remaining in the garage atmosphere for one year (at a constant rate). His conclusion was that if someone of average weight were exposed to this environment for half an hour, he or she would be exposed to $\frac{1}{10,000}$ of a nanogram of toxic chemicals; an employee working full-time for two years would be exposed to $\frac{16}{10,000}$ nanograms. Although the U.S. government had no established safety standards for dioxin intake, Buckley claimed the Food and Drug Administration (FDA) had a standard of 1 nanogram per kilogram per day as the "no-effect" level for 2,3,7,8 TCDD.[7] Buckley reasoned that even the hypothetical worker would be exposed to only $\frac{2}{1,000}$ of the FDA's standard; it would be $\frac{1}{10,000}$ of that standard for those who simply used the facility for parking. The formal analysis also

6. I am unable to account for the discrepancy between Buckley's and Schecter's estimates of the garage's surface area.

7. A search of the *Federal Register* and the *Code of Federal Regulations*, both of which report federal regulations concerning toxic chemicals, reveals no record of a "no effect" level for TCDD.

tried "to put these risks in perspective": "The lifetime risk of being killed by lightning or dying from a hurricane, flood, tornado, or earthquake is about 10 times as great as the risk of cancer from using the garage for parking" (Buckley to Young, November 23, 1981).

These conclusions required three questionable assumptions, the first of which was that PCBs posed no risk. Because dioxins and furans are more poisonous than PCBs, the assumption was that inclusion of PCBs would hardly have made the garage appear more dangerous. This assumption, like most assumptions, is reasonable. But it cannot be known with much certainty the extent to which the assumption is valid. Research on dioxins and furans is relatively new, and each chemical has many isomers about which virtually nothing is known. There also is no consensus in toxicology on the potential additive, or synergistic, properties of these chemicals.

Second, the analysis assumed that at least one of the four, or five, samples had captured the highest level of contaminants in the garage. When this assumption was later challenged, the consultant argued that the four samples were gathered in a deliberate attempt to identify toxic "hot spots." Recall that those tests were ordered by Schecter, who conceded that when he chose the samples he was indeed searching for chemical hot spots. But, as Schecter later admitted, "We made pure guesses." The point is that no one could know whether "hot spots" had actually been sampled or the extent to which the four samples were representative of the whole garage.

Finally, Buckley provided what he assumed were appropriate comparisons for toxic chemical risk by referring to natural disasters such as earthquakes and hurricanes—misleading and irrelevant comparisons in that the risk of one event, an earthquake, for example, cannot be traded for the risk of the other, toxic chemical poisoning. A more useful comparison would have been between the risk of entering the contaminated garage and the risk of never doing so—a comparison that would have made the garage appear much more dangerous. Or the garage's risk could have been compared to that posed by a garage that had never been contaminated with these chemicals.

This comparison, too, would have made the garage appear more dangerous. The point is not that Buckley's assessment was unreasonable, but that his construction of a context for evaluating hazards was designed to make those hazards seem reasonable.

Before it was possible to make that judgment, the county's expert consultant had to discard a whole set of uncertainties, which, if considered, would have undermined the appearance of objectivity that a formal assessment provides. Formal risk assessment is a way to reduce the number of variables that must be considered, a way to include risks and to exclude ambiguities, thus simplifying decision making. By so doing, it creates the context for the types of risks that will be considered. Formal risk assessment tends to sanctify decisions regarding risk, thus legitimating them. Formal assessments also have the paradoxical consequence of allowing the assumptions of the assessment to be debated. Whether or not that debate materializes, or is consequential, depends on other factors.

.   .   .

In this instance, there was some debate over the formal risk analysis and the decision to reopen the garage. We need to address the terms of that debate, while considering more explicitly the political assumptions that underlay the assessment and acceptance of the garage's risks. The analysis of how Binghamton's political and organizational dilemmas were balanced has implications that are not limited to the SOB garage. The most important implication is that understanding how decisions about controversial risks are made requires understanding the organizational and political contexts of those decisions. In particular, *organizational and political interests, and not public welfare or scientific protocol, drive decisions regarding acceptable risk.*

Acceptable risk is an issue that scholars recognize as inherently political. The very term "acceptable" implies a political, not a scientific, judgment. Thus, another way to frame the question of the acceptability of the risk posed by the garage is in terms of political influence and power. Viewed in this light, the scientific assumptions embedded in the consultant's risk analysis, questionable though they may have been, may not be the appropriate standard against which to measure the adequacy of the risk assessment.

The context that makes a danger seem reasonable is influenced by organizational processes. One of those processes is to defeat alternative solutions. For example, Alexander (1979, 391–92) argues that a key factor in the escalation of the Vietnam War was that alternatives were structured so that "military establishment interests and domestic political considerations" would not be threatened. With risk assessment, the defeat of alternative definitions of acceptability is, by definition, necessary to the creation of a political consensus. In the story of the contaminated garage, there were two major aspects to this process.

First, Schecter, the director of the county's health department, defined acceptable risk in a way that was not consonant with that of powerful agents (the county executive, the county legislature, state organizations). He did not construct a formal risk assessment, but his failure to endorse a reopening of the garage ("decision by default," the county executive called it) was tantamount to defining *any* hazard posed by the garage as unacceptable. Intended or not, the effect of Schecter's ouster was to defeat unfavorable definitions of acceptable risks.

Second, it was possible that a popular outcry might emerge, acting as a constraint on the county executive's definition of risk. If the outcry had occurred while the decision was being made, it might have become a factor. But the premises of the debate were already set, so that the (limited) outcry occurred *after* the decision was made, thus rendering public protest ineffective. Rather than consulting with groups that had an interest in the issue of acceptable risk, the decision was made to reopen, and then the public was "educated." The public meetings therefore served only a "cooling out" function, rather than an advisory one—as one might expect in an openly political process.

The process whereby the county's definition of reasonable risk was accepted did not result from a deliberate conspiracy to force that definition on the public. Understanding this process in which contesting alternatives are defeated requires examining the structural context of decision makers. From the view of organizational decision makers, there was great pressure to resolve some debilitating ambiguities. It therefore seemed most reasonable to consider the garage safe unless proven otherwise. At one of the public meetings, the county executive admitted that one reason for opening the garage was the shortage of parking space in downtown Binghamton. He added: "If there is no reason for keeping it closed, why keep it closed?" (public meeting transcript, December 2, 1981).

In some ways, it might be argued that all we have really learned in this chapter is that low levels of toxic chemicals were found in the garage and that officials reopened it. Had high levels been discovered, the garage probably would have remained closed. Yet, the process through which the definitions of "high" and "low" were constructed is what determined the appropriate time to reopen the garage. Looking closely at that process highlights the political and organizational forces that define acceptable risk. The seemingly trivial story of the contaminated garage thus affords us a detailed picture of issues that are central to the sociology of risk.

It may be that the garage posed a negligible risk to public health. If that is the case, it is because testing and consulting were undertaken by the county executive and the director of the health department. One of the major reasons those actions were taken, according to county officials, was to provide protection against potential lawsuits. Thus, structural constraints on decision makers, along with the threat of lawsuits, helped to produce a coincidence of public and organizational health.

FIVE

Organizing Medical Surveillance

I have one child. I'd like to have one more.
Who's to say twenty years from now what
my kid would come down with because I was
exposed to PCBs?

—Office worker

Organizations are the major arenas within which struggles over risk are conducted. They are not, however, value-neutral entities. Instead, they are often very active parties, pursuing their own interests and shaping both the form and the content of controversies over what constitutes acceptable risk. Indeed, after examining cases such as Binghamton, it is clear that assessment and acceptability of risk are, at bottom, the results of bargaining *among organizations.*

This argument—that organizations are the crucial risk assessors in modern society—contradicts the usual social-scientific way of thinking about risk, which emphasizes instead the assessments of isolated members of the public. But, even if one accepts this notion that organizations are the appropriate starting point for analyzing decisions about risks, it still is no simple matter to trace the connections between organizational interests and decisions. To accomplish that task in convincing fashion, one must delineate both the mechanisms through which organizational actors define policies and programs for ameliorating risk and the process through which organizations structure relations among themselves in such situations. Unfortunately, most of organizational sociology is not very useful here, at least as regards Binghamton. A modified "garbage can" decision theory, however, helps make some sense of the medical surveillance program devised for individuals exposed to the State Office Building after the fire.

The proper response to the nearly five hundred exposed individuals turned on two main problems. First was the technical problem of defining what "appropriate medical surveillance" (also known as "medical monitoring") would entail. Second was the lack of a clear structure of authority that would legitimate decisions and control of organizational resources. Interestingly, and unexpectedly, the technical challenges posed by medical monitoring could not be mastered without a definite arrangement of authority among organizations. In this chapter I examine how that necessary structure emerged and the consequences it had for solving the technical problems in medical surveillance. Although my conclusions are based on the Binghamton case, the analysis also illuminates other cases involving health hazards (e.g., Love Canal, Times Beach, TMI).

Assessing the Problem

At least 479 employees from nearly a score of organizations were exposed to toxins in the SOB. (This number is derived from the New York State Health Department's medical surveillance study, wherein those who volunteered for surveillance were defined as exposed. It thus does not necessarily include all those who were, in fact, exposed.) Of those at risk, 208 were exposed within the SOB itself, 99 were exposed in the adjacent city or county buildings, 43 were exposed in the garage or basements of the SOB, 28 came in contact with contaminated materials (such as files) taken from the building, and 21 used cars that had been in the garage. The route of exposure for the rest (80 people) was unknown.[1]

Although test results have been inconclusive, it is possible that exposure to the noxious chemicals increased the risk of adverse health effects for these people. These adverse effects include neurological damage, mental disturbances, chloracne, liver damage, birth defects, immune deficiency, spontaneous abortion, and cancer. One tool for estimating the likelihood of these outcomes was a medical surveillance program. The con-

1. I.e., eighty people did not relay to DOH how their exposure occurred. Note that, over time, the total number of people included in the study increased to 482 (Fitzgerald et al., November/December 1986). The inclusion of the three additional people does not affect the discussion that follows.

duct of such a program is ostensibly dictated by the logic of experimental design: Researchers try to determine the degree to which a change in an individual, sample, or population can be attributed to a particular stimulus—in this instance, toxic chemicals. What follows describes the negotiations over the implementation of this deceptively simple principle.

A Smooth Beginning

The fire chief began medical surveillance, in a sense, on the morning of the fire when he sent his firefighters to Binghamton General for examinations. Later that day, after learning of the firefighters' complaints, Schecter requested and was granted authority from OGS to expand the range of the tested group to include anyone who had entered the building. (Recall that Schecter had been designated the state's representative by DOH Commissioner Axelrod.)

Schecter arranged for three tubes of blood to be taken from each person, two of which were used in two types of tests. One set involved standard biochemistry tests, designed to assess a broad array of medical conditions.[2] According to the director of Binghamton General Hospital's labs, who oversaw the operation: "That was done the same day they brought the firemen in. We drew them, and then somebody started reading up and said, 'Look, we better get something on everybody else,' because they started drawing at least something on everybody who had ever come in contact with the place. We didn't [know what to look for], so we looked for everything" (Slaunwhite interview, December 24, 1981).

The second set of tests was intended to assess the extent of toxic exposure by directly measuring the level of PCBs in blood, rather than trying to detect abnormal functioning of

---

2. There were two sets of these tests. The first, called SMAC-20 (Sequential Multiple Analysis; "C" means chemical), assays blood sera for a variety of conditions. It measures, for example, cholesterol and glucose levels, which can then be used to infer ab/normal physiological conditions. The second, called CBC (Complete Blood Count), is used to measure the amount of red and white cells in blood and can also be used to infer ab/normal physiological conditions. I refer to both sets as "the biochemical tests."

parts of the body, as the other tests did. Binghamton General did not have the capability to test for PCBs, so the lab director assumed the responsibility for finding someone who did:

> What happened was that when the bloods came in, we started looking around for someone who could do PCB levels. You couldn't find anybody. Very few labs can do it. None of the big commercial labs do them because [they are too time-consuming]. . . . So Chemlab called us up and assured us they were licensed by the EPA and certified by New York, that they had a Ph.D. on board who was an expert in the field, and we spoke. So I said: "Are you ready to go to court?" They said, "No problem. We have done this before"— the whole nine yards. (Slaunwhite interview, December 24, 1981)

The lab director, David Slaunwhite, considered Chemlab's call a stroke of luck, because the firm promised both a quick turnaround on the samples and a good price: "Chemlab called up with a price of . . . I think they normally did them for $90, and like any good businessman I said, 'Well, look, we have a lot of samples here,' so they gave them to me for $30 a crack" (Slaunwhite interview, December 24, 1981). Of 1,400 blood samples, nearly 300 were analyzed by Chemlab, and another 460 were used for tests conducted by Binghamton General; roughly 650 samples were left in the freezers at the hospital, later to be retrieved by the state health department.

After DOH officials in Albany learned of these efforts, a comptroller and John Eadie, a DOH administrator, were sent to Binghamton, where they met Slaunwhite and the hospital's chief executive officer, Jason Moyer, who were trying to coordinate the testing with BCHD. Slaunwhite described the result of the meetings:

> We were discussing [things] with Mr. Eadie—Dr. Schecter and Dr. Moyer, and myself—and we were trying to find a place to send [the samples]. . . . At first we had 300 PCB samples. Actually, we had 467, but they wanted to get some of them off and get this whole thing rolling. Everybody was interested in getting back the levels. I say *everybody* was interested, including Mr. Eadie, because he sat right in my office and said he would like to have those bloods taken and tested. He gave me approval before I sent them. He also knew

we were going to send them to Chemlab. (Slaunwhite interview, December 24, 1981)

Chemlab began sending results back to Binghamton General within two weeks after the fire. In an early report on sixty of those samples, "N.D."—none detected—was noted beside every name. Obviously this was good news to health officials and administrators because it suggested that exposure to the SOB might not be an important health threat, confirming what many health experts already believed. BCHD's Schecter, for example, asserted that they "averted a panic situation by being able to say that the laboratory . . . found that all the readings were below 20 parts per billion.[3] That was good news for the [exposed] people" (Schecter interview, January 21, 1982).

With this complicated program under way, BCHD had to be reorganized, to some extent, to continue the program. Several nurses were asked to help, one of whom (referred to here as Nurse Lee) had training in medical records.[4] Although medical surveillance is an elaborate and extensive data-collection effort, if the data are well organized from the start, analysis proceeds efficiently and effectively, thus increasing confidence in the results. Nurse Lee was responsible for organizing the records.

In these early efforts, there seemed to be little disagreement over how surveillance would proceed. DOH and BCHD had apparently agreed on the way in which authority would be distributed among agencies, and there was at least a rudimentary outline for a policy. Eight days after the accident DOH official Philip Taylor wrote to the commissioner of DOH:

> The surveillance that has been initiated on workers calls for the drawing of three tubes of blood on each worker involved in cleanup prior to initial entry into the building. It is recognized that

3. One part per billion by weight is roughly equal to one microgram per liter by volume; Chemlab's level of detection was 20 micrograms per liter.
4. In several places I depend, in one way or another, on testimony from this nurse. For some of what follows I quote the nurse directly; in other places, the nurse provided vital leads to data I might not have otherwise discovered. The alias "Lee" disguises the nurse's name and sex. Four nurses were affiliated with the project, one of whom was denied "clearance" by superiors to speak to me but was able to confirm some facts nevertheless. The nurses I was able to interview asked that I not use their names.

many workers had entered the building before this surveillance was established. For these workers, blood should be drawn as soon as possible after initial entry into the building. In addition to entrance screening, exit screening will also be required. The same test will be repeated as soon as possible after each worker has terminated all activities related to clean-up of the building. (Taylor to Axelrod, February 13, 1981)

In another memo of the same date, Taylor added: "At least one nurse to coordinate worker surveillance activities at the PCB fire site will be needed as long as clean-up continues. Following my discussions with Dr. Schecter today I feel it would be best to have nurses providing on-site coverage 12 hours per day, 7 days a week for the next 7 days as a minimum" (Taylor to Axelrod, February 13, 1981).

In some respects, these early efforts were very effective. By February 11 the nurses had interviewed hundreds of people and initiated "triage nursing," a mechanism for channeling the exposed through the monitoring process.[5] Responsible for organizing all the medical files, the nurses compiled 335 health records and helped Binghamton General draw blood samples. On February 14 they received and began to catalogue test results from the biochemistry analyses. The next day the nurses oversaw the transfer of all records from City Hall to a trailer adjacent to the three-building complex, and, two days after that, to the Broome County Health Department.

An apparent consensus also existed as to which organizations should be responsible for what tasks. As the state's local representative, BCHD assumed administrative and medical responsibility, while the state accepted fiscal responsibility and offered expert advice to the county. Binghamton General's lab director explained:

At this time [about two weeks after the fire] the state was playing a kind of lord-overseer role. The only thing they were involved in, supposedly, was the money. They came [to visit the CEO at Binghamton General] and myself, and we gave them a price that was

5. Triage is a practice taken from military medicine; the injured are separated by treatment category (in the military, by immediate need), thus increasing the efficiency and effectiveness of health care delivery.

extremely reasonable [for the biochemical tests], plus the $30 apiece for the PCBs to be done at Chemlab. They agreed they were going to make us a one-payment type of thing—guaranteed payment. (Slaunwhite interview, December 24, 1981)

Medical surveillance seemed to be off to a productive beginning. Some details were neglected, but testing was instituted soon after the accident, and the samples were being analyzed. Also, there was no apparent disagreement that medical surveillance was an appropriate response to toxic-chemical exposure. A rationally ordered division of labor appeared to be developing among organizations, giving the project an efficiency predicted by theories of interorganizational relations. In these respects, medical surveillance was successfully under way.

Turmoil and Tumult

Under the best of circumstances—that is, circumstances that would yield reliable and valid data—a methodical plan would have been developed by officials, with the advice of experts, and implemented carefully from the beginning. Subjects would have fasted before blood samples were taken, and testing would have preceded chemical exposure. To ensure that no symptoms were missed, occupational histories, physical examinations, and tests for all conditions the chemicals might cause (e.g., accumulation of PCBs in body tissue) would have been taken. Given a sufficient sample size, these conditions would provide physicians and epidemiologists with a reliable baseline of data that could later be compared with data from the nonexposed, thus permitting an estimation of the effects of contamination. A clear design, or medical surveillance protocol (complete with standards to judge the meaning of test results), would also have been written. This detailed protocol would have provided a basis on which to estimate the amount of resources (fiscal, personnel, etc.) necessary to complete the task. Finally, an appreciation of those resource constraints would have led the Broome County Health Department and the New York Department of Health to distribute the tasks accordingly.

Of course, health officials did not enjoy the best of circumstances. Schecter, who had spent several years practicing medicine for the U.S. Army, likened his position to that of a wartime surgeon: "I was tied up, as a physician and scientist, in the middle of the biggest professional challenge of my life. . . . Like a surgeon in the middle of a battlefield where you don't stop to think of what's going on, you just do what you perceive as your job" (Schecter interview, August 10, 1981). Nurse Lee described the early state of the program:

> I was supposed to [be in charge of medical records]. Schecter said one morning, "You are now working on PCBs. Go upstairs and meet the nurse from the state." So I went up there. I happen to have a degree in medical records . . . so I knew what I was doing. Most people didn't know what they were doing at that time. . . . It was total disarray.

To make matters worse, it was not obvious what a scientifically sound protocol should entail, although the preliminary data revealed several troubling facts. Ninety-three persons reported symptoms often associated with toxic chemical poisoning (including tingling and numbness of upper extremities, and black particles in phlegm; a third reported abnormal skin conditions). Of 259 SMAC-20 blood analyses, 23 percent were abnormal in some way. Yet, the causes and consequences of PCB poisoning (and later dioxins, furans, and other chemicals) were not well defined. It was therefore very difficult to predict which tests would be most useful for monitoring health. Because assessing exposure was so ambiguous, BCHD's policy was to test anyone who suspected he or she had been contaminated. The director explained: "I wanted to test everyone who was exposed, and that was maybe one or two thousand people. See, the garage was contaminated heavily, . . . [which] meant that any county, state, or city employee or the general public [should be included]. So I wanted to get everyone that had been exposed" (Schecter interview, October 3, 1983).

Finally, the organization of resources at BCHD was less than efficient. According to Nurse Lee:

> With all these tests that were coming in, I asked Dr. Schecter what he wanted to do with them. He said, "Call [a doctor at Binghamton

General] and tell him I want the residents to do the physical exams." I told him [the doctor wouldn't] do that, because you can't do that without a protocol. . . . These are the details that were never worked out that would later come back to haunt him. Who is going to pay for it? What tests are you going to do? What body systems should they include? I knew no doctor would touch that with a ten-foot pole because there was no protocol. Very little planning was done for medical monitoring. For example, he just ordered the tests. Then we started getting back all the monitoring stuff, the tests. But there was no chart set up. There was no plan or strategy.

One flaw in BCHD's medical surveillance was that there was no method for transmitting patients' records to their physicians. Many of the results indicated abnormal health conditions, and if the program were to be useful, doctors would need their patients' data. But signed releases were not obtained from the patients, and the records could not leave the county health department without them. Worse, many patients did not have personal physicians, so the nurses had no one to whom they could send the records. Some of those who were exposed were transients who had been brought to Binghamton by OGS to clean up the building, and they were difficult to locate.

In late March 1981, nearly two months after the first blood samples were drawn, a letter was sent to the patients for whom BCHD had medical records. The letter asked that they sign medical release forms so copies of their records could be sent to their physicians. Three months after that, in June, test results were actually forwarded for those who could be located. Without a written protocol and without a way to interpret the test results for patients and their doctors, the value and use of the data could be questioned. Indeed, these problems created the possibility that the whole project might be dismissed.

Within a month after the accident, BCHD and DOH were at loggerheads over control of the medical monitoring process. Schecter was in daily contact with the media, and, as mentioned earlier, considered the media an efficient tool for public education. Meanwhile, officials in important organizations in Albany—DEC, DOH, and OGS—were now routing all requests for information from the press through the Albany public relations offices, preventing local officials from answering question in Binghamton. This restrictive policy was directly opposed to that of the county health department.

On February 25, 1981—the day before the OGS commissioner disclosed the presence of dioxin in the soot—Schecter reported to the county executive a conversation with DOH Commissioner Axelrod:

> The State Health Department position is that they are *advisors* to the State Office of General Services and the OGS cleanup team. The State Health Department is thus *not* acting in its usual regulatory role . . . [and] . . . the Broome County Health Department is responsible for the health of the residents of Broome County—its usual role. . . . Unlike the usual arrangement between State and County Health Department, the laboratory data which we need to answer *our* urgent county health concerns is not being sent to us. Under these conditions I cannot be confident of the well-being of our employees, or others in or around the affected building. (Schecter to Young, February 25, 1981)

The county health director then attempted, but failed, to enlist the executive's support in closing the State Office Building to any further activities, pending further testing.

While Schecter and BCHD worked on the problem of medical monitoring, DOH was increasingly defining *Schecter* as the problem, rather than the SOB: "I think if you were to talk to Axelrod, you would understand how he wished that [Schecter] had never been [designated as DOH representative].[6] There is a difference between what a public official in that rank has to say sometimes publicly and sometimes do publicly, as opposed to what they *think* might be the best thing" (Taylor interview, December 11, 1981). Although Axelrod had appointed Schecter as his on-site representative, DOH restricted Schecter's access to important information, in spite of the deputy commissioner of public health's claim that DOH "made continuous efforts to" keep him informed. One official recounted: "We tried to be pretty careful to make sure things were in fairly final form . . . long before [they] got to [Schecter] for any sort of

6. Axelrod declined to be interviewed.

review. We tried to give . . . information that went out at the public meetings and basically [tried] not to give him anything in writing ahead of time but [instead] to all who were involved. Basically, then, you assume [we were issuing] press-type information" (Taylor interview, December 11, 1981).

In addition, BCHD's requests for funding to finish the testing were rebuffed. In early March Schecter asked OGS for $22,000 to

> contract for one nurse practitioner and two clerical persons to handle medical records. . . . These people will, under my supervision, work on all medical records, notify the . . . exposed persons and their physicians of their exposure, of abnormal laboratory values, with possible interpretations and schedule and perform history and physical examinations and refer occasional patients to the appropriate specialist. (Schecter to Wahl, March 2, 1981)

The request was denied, as was a second appeal two days later for $2,000 to pay a local hospital "for purposes of immediate chart review to be performed by physicians in internal medicine and family practice" (Schecter to Mosher, March 4, 1981).

As the conflict and negotiations continued, key DOH officials came to believe that there was, in fact, no point in conducting any medical surveillance. But DOH was unable to halt the program because too many resources and too many organizations had begun working on the blood tests and their results. By early March, Chemlab had returned more than three hundred PCB test results to Binghamton General Hospital, none of which showed PCB quantities over twenty micrograms per liter, the lab's level of detection.

One alternative that *was* open to DOH was direct action against BCHD. Although DOH personnel approved the testing procedures, they later denied that they had prior knowledge of the PCB tests, that state officials had approved the testing by Chemlab, and even that there was any value in PCB blood tests. The incident was interpreted by DOH as evidence of Schecter's lack of foresight. One epidemiologist (and physician) at the state health department related the problem thus: "Schecter requested that bloods be sent off for PCB levels on people and [claimed] that you could define their exposure based on PCB levels. It was a very naïve thing to do" (Taylor interview, July 8, 1981). The same scientist pointed out, however, that because no standards or quality-control programs exist for labs that do PCB analyses, the only way to tell if a laboratory is adequate is if it actually detects PCBs in the samples. Chemlab, he said,

> used a gas chromatograph [for determining levels], which is pretty much state-of-the-art equipment, and the chemists may be very good, but, . . . well, virtually everybody in the U.S. has a blood level [of PCBs] if you use sensitive enough equipment. . . . The lab had insufficient experience in running PCBs. Basically they found no PCB in the bloods, which Arnie Schecter may choose to interpret as comforting; I choose to interpret it as [inadequate lab procedures]. (Taylor interview, August 4, 1981)

The problem may not have been bad science, but the ambiguity involved in interpreting the results:

> PCBs are a mixture of 210 different compounds. They come off this chromatograph, blip after blip, and you have to know which blips to count. It is not [as] if you measure blip 63 from the left-hand side of the page at a retention time of 29 minutes [and] that is the PCB of interest. There is an enormous amount of interpretation [involved]. It is not a black-and-white thing. It is not like going into the hospital to find out, say, yes, you had a heart attack or, no, you did not. And you can get people who can look at the same chromatograph, the same tracing, and argue about, "You know, it looks to me like there is a little shoulder on this blip and that means that there is something else hidden underneath there." (Taylor interview, August 4, 1981)

Bad methodology was probably not the most serious problem with Chemlab's tests. When pressed, the scientist quoted above responded, "I don't know enough about their methods, but I don't believe that I would disagree with them." Nor was the problem that PCB blood tests were worthless, for DOH scientists later ran their own. Rather, the medical situation was fraught with ambiguity about what constituted reasonable scientific behavior and appropriate medical judgment. Private physicians did not have the necessary data to judge the health of their patients; and even with those data, there would be no way to tell if their patients were going to get sick, or what could be done if they got sick. The New York Health Department at first acted as if exposure posed no health threats but then apparently reversed its position when the Broome County Health Department began the medical monitoring program. In addition, the county health department, although explicitly assigned the responsibility for surveillance, was not supported even by those state officials who had assigned responsibility. As state and county agencies labored under these uncertainties, the tests and test results became tools in a series of struggles for organizational legitimacy and power.

Malleable Science

The meaning of information depends on the larger context within which information exists. As contexts are constructed, meaning is bestowed on the information, thereby transforming it into knowledge. The way knowledge is produced and presented to experts and publics is a very important part of the decision-making process regarding risks. This process does not occur in a vacuum but is affected by the structures within which decision makers function.

In the two months between February 5 and early April 1981, some scientists suggested that the contaminated soot in the SOB might not constitute a significant health risk because of "carbon love." The carbon-love hypothesis posits that tight bonds between the carbon in the soot and the toxic chemicals would render the toxins incapable of being absorbed by the body. If true, this hypothesis would mean that exposure to the soot posed no important risk. Scientists also needed some way to measure the risk of the soot *in toto*. Two top DOH scientists described the problem in a preliminary report:[7]

7. The report, "Preliminary Report: Chick Embryos as a Probe of the Relative Toxicities of Soot Samples from a Polychlorinated Biphenyl-Containing Transformer" (Tumasonis and Kaminsky), is not dated. It contains a reference, however, to another report on Binghamton dated October 1, 1981. Because other reports were produced by DOH in early 1982 that might have been relevant to the problems addressed in this "Preliminary Report," but none are cited therein, I estimate the date of this paper to be November 1981. All quotations below, unless otherwise noted, are from this paper.

Predictions of the toxicity of the soot based on the known concentrations and toxicity of 2,3,7,8-TCDD and 2,3,7,8-TCDF are suspect for a number of reasons: Not all contaminating components of the soot can be determined, the toxicities of all polychlorinated dibenzodioxins and dibenzofurans is not known, the role of the soot matrix was not shown[8] . . . and the potential for synergistic or antagonistic effects of the pollutants on the toxicity of other pollutants is unknown. Thus there was a requirement for a toxicological assessment of the soot where it would be treated as a single compound.

To test the carbon-love hypothesis, a series of experiments was run wherein groups of chicken eggs were exposed to the polluted soot (by injection), as well as to control substances. The eggs were then incubated to the eighteenth day of gestation (the gestation period for chickens is twenty-one days), and then examined for defects or death.

I will not describe in great detail the conduct and findings of these studies, because it is not my intent to evaluate their scientific merit. Briefly, the researchers hoped to find a method for rapidly analyzing large numbers of soot samples without expending "enormous resources of personnel and equipment." Toxicologists dispute the appropriateness of chick-embryo tests for determining teratogenesis (birth defects—literally, "production of monsters"), partly because the tests are very sensitive. DOH scientists therefore limited their research question to the induction of lethality. They nevertheless thought it important enough to report that, for the chicks that survived to the eighteenth day, many displayed some form of birth defect (including curled toes, short beaks, edema, the brain formed outside the skull, lack of eyes). More than 50 percent of the embryos were dead by the eighteenth day at a level of 2 milligrams (1 mg = $\frac{1}{1000}$ gram) of soot for each egg (also called the LD50, or the lethal dose required to kill 50 percent of a sample). They estimated that "at a dose of 2 mg soot/egg there was . . . approximately 2 ng 2,3,7,8,-TCDD/egg and 100 ng 2,3,7,8-TCDF/egg" (1 nanogram = 1 billionth of a gram). Car-

8. That is, the soot itself might be toxic.

bon and fireplace soot were both used as separate controls, but "in no case did the control articles result in embryo lethality."

The chick-embryo experiments, carried out over a period of several months,[9] seemed to measure the toxicity of the contaminated soot. Unfortunately, the New York Department of Health did not apprise people in Binghamton of this new knowledge, nor did the department even let them know that the tests were being conducted. In fact, they deliberately concealed the experiments from Binghamton officials.[10]

On August 10, 1981, the Office of General Services and the state health department met publicly for the first time in Binghamton (six months after the fire). There the director of toxicology for DOH asserted that the soot was "in the category of a mildly toxic substance" and compared it to Malathion, the pesticide then being used against the medfly in California (Geimann 1981g). He reported that guinea pigs had been fed the soot and that it took 600 milligrams of soot per kilogram of animal weight to kill half the animals (i.e., the LD50 was 600 mg/kg). Similarly, DOH's deputy director of public health asserted that in free form the chemicals were extremely toxic but that the data from the guinea pig experiments supported the carbon-love hypothesis. Schecter, who had unofficially learned of the chick-embryo tests from an inside source at DOH, asked if there were any other tests then under way. DOH officials replied that there were none.

By not releasing incomplete information, state health de-

9. The tests were conducted at least until February 1982 (Eadon to Carpenter, February 2, 1982).

10. A DOH scientist, Richard Ilka, resigned his position as deputy director of the State Division of Laboratories and Research, partly as a result of the way these test results were handled. On October 8, 1981, a reporter for the *Binghamton Evening Press* quoted Ilka as saying: "I disagree personally and professionally with the way that group [the exposed people] is being handled. That's one of the reasons why I'm resigning" (Fecteau 1981m). The next day DOH hastily convened a press conference in Albany (the *Binghamton Evening Press* was not notified beforehand), where Ilka maintained: "I want to stress that the implication in which it is suggested that I had resigned in protest . . . is completely untrue" (*Binghamton Evening Press*, 1981b). In May 1982 a reporter for *Newsday* interviewed Ilka in Arizona, and he confirmed his original statement: "The real reason [I resigned] was the sheer incompetence I found" (Fischkin 1982).

partment officials were trying to avoid what they considered unnecessary alarm. One official stressed the importance of presenting information to the public in the proper manner, so that mass hysteria, such as that at Love Canal, could be avoided. He said in an interview: "You can speculate on a lot of things, take what bits and pieces of scientific data you have and speculate on what they mean, but I believe this does a great disservice to the public. These speculations have no meaning and aren't useful until the study is conclusive" (Haughie interview, October 8, 1981). Rather than releasing "bits and pieces" of information, officials argued, the responsible way to balance the dilemma of informing the public while preventing hysteria was to test, collect all the data, and then interpret them within a context that "people could understand." There is, however, more than one way to interpret this precept.

There was no public mention of the chick-embryo tests by DOH (until reporters later learned of them through a Freedom of Information request). Yet DOH did not hesitate to release the data on the guinea pigs, even though that information, too, was hardly "complete" in that it provided no valid assessment of levels of risk. Local officials bitterly complained of how they were deceived when their several direct queries about other tests were answered negatively.

There was some merit to their claim of a cover-up. As a DOH scientist admitted: "Each time there was such a [public] meeting, there was a [prior] meeting to discuss the meeting . . . to go over details . . . and what might have been ready at that point to be discussable . . . because there *were* things that. . . . The conclusion was that the tests are bothersome, but we don't really have any basis for comparing. We couldn't interpret them" (Taylor interview, December 11, 1981).

Why did the New York Health Department conceal test results that suggested the soot was highly toxic (even though the chick-embryo tests could not be used to reach conclusions about the soot's threat to human health) yet release information that suggested otherwise? Part of the answer is that DOH had a preconceived notion that the SOB did not pose a health hazard. Seven months after the accident, the deputy director of public health related DOH's position concerning long-term medical surveillance: "At this point in time, we cannot devote our resources to this question" (Haughie interview, October 8, 1981). The debacle at Love Canal also played a role. One official, who had spent the summer of 1981 working on epidemiological problems at Love Canal, explained:

> The precedents that were set [at Love Canal] people attempt to carry over, and I think that very many of the precedents involved overreaction and overdoing. . . . There is no demonstration of bona fide . . . health problems [at Love Canal]. As far as I am concerned, there is next to no good information [that has been gathered] in a bona fide fashion [that proves] people are adversely affected. . . . I have no question in my mind that there have been some pathologies at Love Canal, but I think it has all been psychological trauma. I think the same thing exists at Binghamton. . . . At this point, we have little information on the proven toxicology of anything that people would have been exposed to in Binghamton. (Taylor interview, July 8, 1981)

The chick-embryo tests, it bears repeating, were not intended to reveal the degree of threat posed to human health by toxic chemicals. As we have seen, though, the findings were nevertheless troubling enough for scientists to label them "bothersome"—suggesting that the results were not completely irrelevant to the question of health hazard. But two more important points can be drawn from this illustration of how organizations produce and use science. First, a finding that all the chick embryos died or were malformed as a consequence of exposure to the soot would still not reveal clearly the risk to humans. Extrapolations to human health from animal toxicity studies, whether they involve chick embryos or guinea pigs, are only suggestive, not conclusive. It is in the context of this ambiguity that the chick-embryo tests should be interpreted. Scientists and administrators could not know with much certainty the extent to which *any* animal test results were appropriate.

Second, building on this last conclusion, we might wonder (as did citizens of Binghamton) why alarming test results were hidden but reassuring ones readily released. The answer is found not in imputing devious motives to officials but in understanding the presumptions underlying their actions. Given the premise that the State Office Building did not represent a health threat, the only results that really made any sense were those that confirmed established beliefs. Psychologists Daniel Kahneman and Amos Tversky show that individuals use a heuristic system to make sense of perceived risks in a way that systematically biases the information considered relevant vis-à-vis making decisions (see the collection of articles in Kahneman et al. 1982). There was a similar use of heuristics in Binghamton, although they were based on organizational, rather than cognitive, factors. These heuristics led to biases in the sort of information that health officials defined as relevant and therefore appropriate for public release. Interestingly, it was not the results of the chick-embryo tests that alarmed the public most; rather, it was the discovery that DOH (whose job it is to protect public health) had intentionally concealed important information. There is a measure of irony here, because the decision to conceal the "bothersome" results was designed to mollify public concern.

*

The Emergent Division of Labor

All of this, of course, occurred within the general disorganization of organizations. One attempt to impose order on that chaos took place on March 11, 1981, about five weeks after the accident, at the Broome County Health Department. Attending the five-hour meeting were Director Arnold Schecter, two representatives of the state health department (John Eadie and Philip Taylor), and a nurse.[11] The administrative center for medical surveillance had by then been moved from the city office building to the state building annex, about half a mile from the contaminated SOB. The medical records, however, were still at BCHD.

11. I interviewed all the participants at this meeting except John Eadie, whose office would not return my calls. I wrote Eadie twice, requesting an interview, the second time using certified mail. The letter was signed for but, unfortunately, went unanswered. Although the meeting was less than cordial, the participants' reports did not differ concerning topics of discussion or what was said.

Until this meeting no systematic proposal for conducting medical surveillance or analyzing the data had been developed. One purpose of the meeting was to create such a protocol: "The discussion of the meeting was medical surveillance. . . . It was what to do about everything in general, physical exams, anticipating follow-up" (Taylor interview, December 11, 1981).

Another issue under negotiation was responsibility for the exposed people. According to a nurse who took notes at the meeting, the BCHD said: "'They are [our] people.' State was saying: 'No they are not. Most of the people who were contaminated are [our] people.' After [the meeting] we, I thought, had the protocol down and a way of doing things. . . . They were going to monitor their people, and the county was going to [monitor] theirs" (interview with nurse, anonymity requested). It was no accident that state health department officials met with Schecter soon after Chemlab began returning the PCB test results. According to Taylor, "When I learned that [Schecter] had sent those bloods to Chemlab, I was dumbfounded. John Eadie and I sat in Schecter's office [and] . . . I was trying to tell him what . . . idiocy [it was to] send those bloods off to Chemlab" (Taylor interview, December 11, 1981).[12] Another point of contention between state and county was BCHD's policy of defining the population at risk as anyone possibly exposed, including workers in the city and county buildings and those who had walked past the SOB during decontamination.

In this early stage, state officials frequently suggested that *any* medical surveillance was a waste of resources. During the summit meeting at the county health department, they questioned even the possibility of meaningful surveillance, arguing that it was impossible to believe that anyone had experienced significant exposure. Taylor, in particular, also doubted that it was possible to determine the relative contribution of exposure inside and outside the State Office Building. Moreover, DOH believed (erroneously) that Chemlab had allowed many of the samples to thaw, rendering them unusable, and that the data from the biochemical tests were only slightly more valuable be-

12. Recall that state officials, at least in the beginning, believed PCB blood tests were worthless.

cause not everyone had fasted prior to giving blood. BCHD's view was radically different. In the first place, there were indeed real, and extant, health problems. "There *are*," said Schecter, "skin rashes, and there are people with headaches, and there are people with abnormal liver function tests." Second, and most important, Schecter was arguing that "unless you have a good medical surveillance you don't know what is causing this. You just don't know" (Schecter interview, August 10, 1981).

The meeting was a struggle over access to and control of important resources. One of those resources was the collection of medical records at BCHD. Taylor, acting as a functionary of the state health department, argued: "It was a matter of where the records were primarily going to be housed. The thing is, that if he had control of the data then. . . . The information was being paid for by the state. So that establishes who owns the data" (Taylor interview, December 11, 1981). Although initially uninterested in the data, DOH was now eager to control them. According to Taylor, the records were to be taken to the SOB annex to be photocopied; the photocopies would then be given to BCHD. But Schecter had heard, reliably, that DOH personnel had asked a state nurse to fetch the records from the county health department and take them to the state's local headquarters, with or without his permission. DOH was trying to take possession of something BCHD then controlled. Taylor, in a fashion, agreed: "We probably anticipated Arnie being obstreperous about moving them, and we probably suggested . . . that [the nurse] and I just pull the car up and just take the files down and haul them off. It was simply a matter of—frankly— getting out of the hornets' nest" (Taylor interview, December 11, 1981).

For both BCHD and DOH, this meeting crystallized their disagreements. The day after the meeting, Schecter chained the file cabinets shut, moved the files from the third floor to his office, and had a new lock put on his office door. (He agreed to provide the state with copies of the data.) These desperate actions were symptomatic of the marginal position BCHD was being forced to assume. Nearly ten days later, the other DOH representative who had attended the March 11 meeting (John

Eadie) met with officials at Binghamton General to discuss the hospital's role in medical surveillance. On April 1, 1981, Eadie wrote to Binghamton General to "simplify and clarify" that role:

> Specifically, the State is designating seven persons who can order laboratory tests on behalf of the State. Five are physicians . . . from the Broome County Medical Society. The sixth person will be Dr. Philip Taylor who is coordinating the medical monitoring process. The seventh person will be Mr. Edward Mosher of the State's Office of General Services. Dr. Taylor will be physician of record for tests ordered by Mr. Mosher. No one else is authorized to order laboratory tests at State expense. (Eadie to Slaunwhite, April 1, 1981)

As Schecter had done previously, DOH directed the hospital to collect three tubes of blood in this new effort. The intent of the directive was clear: There would be no more PCB tests. Eadie wrote: "The frozen bloods are to be sent by the hospital . . . to Dr. Philip Taylor in the State Health Department. . . . Nothing *else* is to be done with the frozen samples" (Eadie to Slaunwhite, April 1, 1981). If DOH could not directly quash the source of its troubles, the other way to wrest power from BCHD was to manipulate BCHD's environment. Thus, DOH representatives demanded that Binghamton General hand all test results and medical records over to the state. Further, they demanded that these records *not* be given to the county:

> During our discussion of March 23, you advised me that Binghamton General Hospital has retained the PCB blood level reports which were ordered by Dr. Schecter at State expense. . . . Please be advised that for the time being, reports you now hold or subsequently receive, are to be released to *no one*. . . . If the reports are transmitted to anyone before you receive authorization from the State Health Department, the State cannot be expected to pay for the laboratory testing. (Eadie to Slaunwhite, April 1, 1981; emphasis in original)

DOH also prescribed that people who had been in contaminated areas be referred to one of five doctors designated by the county medical society to serve as a referral panel.[13] For reasons not specified, however, DOH directed that those who had never been in contaminated areas should be referred to the county health department.

The New York Department of Health was not simply making clear the assumptions under which these organizations would interact in the future; it was also demanding that Binghamton General withhold *previous test results* from the county health department, even though the department's director was legally the physician of record. These demands presented Binghamton General with a difficult problem. Although payment for any further tests was not at issue, the bill from Chemlab, coupled with administrative costs, was nearly $25,000, and the hospital had not yet received any payment. Slaunwhite asserted that DOH

> reneged on every one of their goddamn promises. They didn't pay us. Then they made us turn around and refile [the claims through workers' compensation], which meant that we had to go through and recalculate everything and [send] them into comp. Comp refused to accept them and sent them back to us again, so we had to turn around again. [DOH had agreed to pay us before we sent off the tests.] Mr. Eadie was sitting right there, and so was [the DOH] local comptroller. They said, "Just submit the bill for the patients to us—everybody is getting the same thing. We like your prices, and we will give you the check." (Slaunwhite interview, December 24, 1981)

Nevertheless, because Schecter was the physician of record, New York law, as well as medical ethics, prescribed that he alone should have access to the files. Without medical releases from

13. In early April, DOH asked the county medical society to nominate five physicians (four specialists in internal medicine and one in dermatology) to serve on this panel. People who had symptoms believed consistent "with exposure to the contaminants" were to be referred to the panel. In the letter to the five doctors, DOH repeated the requirement that "any individuals who call in who were never in the contaminated area will be referred to the County Health Department" (Taylor to five physicians, April 1, 1981). Interviews with several of these doctors indicate few, if any, people made use of the panel. The panel, it seems, was not intended to examine all the contaminated people; rather, the doctors were to be available for people who did not already have their own physicians.

the patients, hospital administrators maintained, it would have been illegal to allow anyone *but* BCHD access to the documents. Furthermore, some of the test results indicated adverse effects, and the county health department and Binghamton General were not convinced that DOH would take any results seriously, given its informal but oft-repeated policy that medical surveillance was without medical or scientific value. The hospital's administration feared that political considerations would interfere with medical judgment and that public health might be compromised for the sake of organizational interests.

Binghamton General was eventually paid by the state, and the records were transmitted to BCHD as they arrived, although DOH was not notified. It might be argued that attempting to monopolize the data was another instance of DOH trying to prevent public hysteria and panic. In fact, there was another reason for the policy. As a DOH official put it:

> I think we were really trying to close the gate on having Schecter send anybody and everybody who had ever walked by the building but never been in it over for free testing. . . . For example, everybody that worked in the county office building or city building who wanted [to be tested] got sent over. As far as I am concerned, they weren't really exposed. The little bit of exposure that might have been traipsed into those buildings hardly constitutes a significant exposure. (Taylor interview, December 11, 1981)

If BCHD had lost control of the records, its ability to affect health policy would have been greatly diminished. If the county were relegated to a secondary position, DOH could more easily give it only "press-type information." Without inside information, the county department's ability to influence projects in early stages would have been considerably lessened.

DOH eventually did succeed in denying BCHD the requisite resources for influencing the course of the medical surveillance program. The process through which this was accomplished served to reduce some of the most bedeviling ambiguities in this interorganizational garbage can. Finally, a definite structure of relations began to emerge among the organizations, with the state health department in clear control of medical monitoring.

Postscript to Medical Surveillance

The events described in this chapter illustrate some of the mechanisms that organizations use to define policies and programs designed to ameliorate risk. Obvious explanations for these events—such as callous bureaucracies or unfeeling politicians—do not account for significant features of the data. The role that interorganizational conflict plays in determining which actors will be able to construct policy and science, especially, can be understood only at a structural level of analysis. Some theories of interorganizational relationships, such as exchange theory (Levine and White 1961) and resource dependence theory (Aldrich and Pfeffer 1976), might predict that because the Broome County Health Department and the New York Department of Health both had formal mandates to ensure public health, they would be likely to agree on policies designed to fulfill that goal, implementing the most appropriate technology to meet it. Such a prediction obviously would have missed the mark in the case of the Binghamton SOB.

After DOH assigned BCHD the responsibility for medical surveillance, BCHD began a comprehensive health-monitoring program. Because the county health department could not internally generate the resources necessary to carry out the project, the Office of General Services and the state health department became involved. But radically opposed ideas of what was chemically dangerous, politically responsible, and organizationally possible led to important disagreements between state and county agencies. As the negotiating process proceeded, DOH came to regard BCHD (and especially its director), not toxic chemicals, as the most immediate risk. One consequence was that a final plan for medical monitoring was not developed until nearly a year after the initial exposures.

The surveillance program is not complete (as of June 1988), but the state health department has released several papers that report initial findings (Fitzgerald et al. 1984, August 1985,

November/December 1986; Youngblood and Weinstein 1986). The program has two objectives: (1) to provide medical information to individuals and their physicians (termed "public service" by DOH); and (2) to investigate a possible association between exposure and selected adverse health outcomes.[14] The research is based on a model (fig. 1) that hypothesizes a relationship between exposure to toxic chemicals and short-term adverse effects on health, as measured by standard biochemical tests and tests for PCB levels in the blood. The authors of this early research are explicit that it is not designed to measure or assess long-term health problems. All those in the medical surveillance program, 482 people, are defined as "the population at risk," but only those who were actually in the building (327) are defined as exposed. (The range of hours of exposure was from about one hour to more than a thousand.) The rest of the subjects "were permitted to participate because of the program's public service nature." The study attempts to relate data from biochemical and PCB tests to the length of contamination.

The nature and extent of exposure, however, is not easily determined, given that several factors need to be taken into account: location within the SOB (some areas were more heavily contaminated than others); activity (e.g., firefighting, cleaning, repairing); whether or not protective gear was worn; duration of exposure; and intensity of exposure (i.e., concentrations of chemicals during exposure). These factors are combined to form an "index of exposure" (table 3). Subjects were assigned to one of three groups, apparently using multiples of one thousand on the index to determine how they would be grouped.

The first exposure group was assigned an index score of zero. DOH does not consider the 155 participants in this group exposed, because their route of exposure was outside the building (even though in table 4 this same group is designated "low exposure"). This first group serves as the control group for those who were exposed within the SOB. The second group,

14. Data for this discussion come from interviews with the epidemiologist primarily responsible for the medical surveillance program and DOH papers (Fitzgerald et al. 1984, August 1985, November/December 1986; Youngblood and Weinstein 1986).

Figure 1. New York Health Department's Model
Connecting Exposure with Outcomes

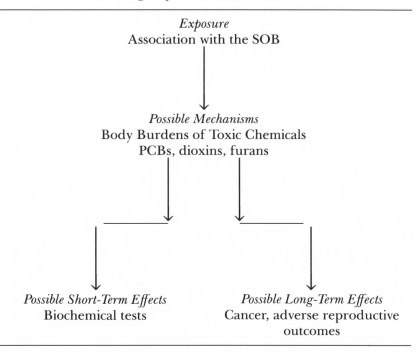

SOURCE: Fitzgerald et al. 1984.

NOTE: Words in italic type are concepts; words set in roman type are operationalizations.

termed moderately exposed, is defined as those with scores between 1 and 1,000; it, too, was made up of 155 persons. The remaining 163 people, the highly exposed group, are those with scores of more than 1,000. (Data were missing for 9 people.)

Recall the PCB blood tests that BCHD ordered soon after the fire. The state health department also uses PCB blood levels as an indicator of ill effects. The mean PCB levels for the three groups are shown in table 4. This study finds that, over time, the PCB levels in blood declined (thus suggesting exposure to the SOB had measurable effects) and that the decreases for all three groups were roughly the same. The study also compares blood samples for 301 people for whom there were paired data

Table 3. New York Health Department's Exposure Index

Factor	Weight
1. Place of contamination	
a. primarily from basement	2.5
b. secondarily from basement	1.5
c. never in basement	1.0
2. Activity in building	
a. primarily firefighting	20.0
b. primarily cleaning or repairing	10.0
c. secondarily cleaning or repairing	2.5
d. none of the above	1.0
3. Protective gear worn in building	
a. rarely or never	20.0
b. sometimes	10.0
c. usually	1.5
d. always	1.0
4. Hours in building	.5 through 998.0
5. PCB air level in building	
a. February 5, 1981	6.90
b. February 6, 1981	6.17
c. February 7, 1981	5.43
d. February 8, 1981	4.69
e. February 9, 1981	3.96
f. February 10, 1981	3.22
g. February 11, 1981	2.47
h. February 12, 1981	1.73
i. February 13, 1981 and beyond	1.00

SOURCE: Fitzgerald et al. 1984.

on PCB levels (i.e., it was possible to match 301 samples from the initial and follow-up tests). The mean PCB level for these people at the initial test was 7.08 parts per billion (ppb), and 6.15 ppb at the follow-up. (Using mean levels, incidentally, obscures individual pathologies and changes.)

The papers DOH has released support the conclusions that no significant exposure occurred as a result of contact with the contaminants and that there are no significant outcomes from exposure. But several assumptions and conclusions in the study

Table 4. Mean Blood PCB Levels

	Initial Test	*Follow-Up Test*
Low exposure	5.40 ppb	4.73 ppb
Medium exposure	6.39 ppb	5.73 ppb
High exposure	7.26 ppb	6.23 ppb

SOURCE: Fitzgerald et al. 1984.
NOTE: Measured in parts per billion.

are open to question. By focusing exclusively on PCBs, the study ignores possible effects of furans or dioxins, even though each of those chemicals is considered far more toxic than PCBs. (Schecter reports results from studies on sixty of the exposed, including subjective data and liver and fat biopsies specifically designed to measure furans and dioxins. The subjective data show fatigue and loss of energy; the biopsies show liver damage, skin rashes, skin cancer, and elevated cholesterol and triglyceride levels. He notes, however, that it is not certain that the toxic soot is the cause of these maladies [see Boffey 1983; Schecter et al. 1984; Schecter and Tiernan 1985; Schecter and Ryan 1985; Schecter et al. 1985; Tiernan et al. 1985].) This problem is exacerbated because any potential additive or synergistic effects of PCBs in tandem with the other, more dangerous, toxins are ignored. DOH argued that "exposure to [furans] and [dioxins] can be assumed to parallel the exposures to PCB," but there is no evidence that parallel exposure is the same as parallel effect.

Moreover, although the first group is defined as not exposed (or as only trivially exposed), there is in fact no real control group against which to compare the study's results. DOH concludes there is no significant difference between those who were exposed within the building and those exposed outside it (Fitzgerald et al. 1984).[15] Yet, without comparing these two groups against a sample of truly nonexposed, the similarities

15. Nevertheless, a 1985 paper observes that "one hundred ninety-eight participants [52.2 percent] stated that they had at least one problem in *any* of the four major systems [skin, eyes, gastrointestinal, and neurological]" (Fitzgerald et al., August 1985).

between them could just as well indicate abnormal levels of PCB as provide solace that the little difference between them indicates no adverse effects.

Further, the weighting factors for the exposure index were arbitrarily determined. The only variable in the index that is a true ratio is the number of hours spent in the SOB, and that variable was determined through the subjective indicator of asking people—some six to twelve months after the fire—how much time they had spent in the building. (Even the status of this variable as ratio is open to question, because we do not know if four hours of exposure is twice as much as two hours of exposure in terms of health effects.) Although the DOH questionnaire provides space for reporting abnormal conditions, much more weight is given to the biochemical tests such as liver enzymes and serum lipids. The reasons for this, according to DOH, are that the latter are more objective indicators of exposure than "self-reports," that these kinds of data are more easily adaptable to "standard and well-known statistical techniques," and that DOH failed to collect the more "subjective" data in the follow-up. The criticism of subjective data notwithstanding, the state health department's study is itself dependent on subjective reports of duration of exposure.

Even though the evidence on adverse health effects appears more equivocal than what is presented in state reports, it is not my intention to make the case that the State Office Building actually was (or is) a threat to health and that the New York Health Department failed to follow the proper prescriptions for ensuring public health. Yet it is true that the assumptions embedded in the procedures of this public health program may not be the most conservative available. Some possibilities, in fact, are precluded from discovery because of DOH's choice of methods. For example, psychological and mental troubles have been associated with exposure, but very little attention is given to these possible effects. Associations between exposure and adverse effects might have been higher had subjects been asked about such symptoms.

At this writing, plans for long-term follow-up are unclear. A 1984 paper (Fitzgerald et al.) concluded that long-term surveillance was not necessary. But a more recent paper (Fitzgerald et al., August 1985) mentions only that present results cannot rule out such a program. The focus of this study is on easily measurable medical outcomes, the use of which supports DOH's position from the outset—that the State Office Building poses no risk to human health.

A larger range of possible solutions and technologies for measuring exposure could have been defined as acceptable. Psychological reactions to the accident could have been measured, although those measurements would have been less precise than measures of, say, liver enzymes. A true control group could have been used for comparative purposes, and the values on DOH's "index of exposure" could have been differently weighted.

Each of these alternatives, in one form or another, was initially intended to be part of the medical surveillance protocol. But as the pertinent organizations moved from a pluralistic situation—one where a multiparty construction of solutions was a primary feature—to a situation characterized by a clear division of labor, those solutions increasingly became defined as outside the realm of reasonable science and policy. An important factor in this progression from interorganizational anarchy to a well-structured configuration of organizations with an ordered division of labor was DOH's use of power to determine which elements of medical surveillance would be considered legitimate.

We have now examined the processes through which the solution to the problem of the exposed people was constructed. I have argued that the keys to understanding these processes are bounded rationality, organizational power, and control of strategic resources. In the next chapter, which addresses solving the problem of decontaminating the State Office Building, we see similar processes at work.

SIX

Organizing Decontamination

We're getting the attention of the world.
—Commissioner,
Office of General Services

When organizations attempt to define and mitigate risks, they face several types of difficult problems, the most obvious of which involve technical issues. When the Chernobyl plant nearly destroyed itself, for example, the world's attention was riveted on Soviet efforts to contain radioactive fallout and extinguish the burning reactor core. After the catastrophic chemical leak in Bhopal, enormous effort was expended to understand the plant's technological failures and recovery devices. In the Binghamton case, the accident also created a set of important technical problems, chiefly that of ridding the State Office Building of toxic chemicals.

As important as technical problems are, however, they are not as difficult as some less obvious social problems. For instance, who should define safety levels, who will create policy, and who will be legally accountable for exposure? Although these issues may appear fairly unproblematic, a closer look reveals some interesting ambiguities in defining exactly how they are resolved. That is our task in this chapter.

Binghamton's banks and government are located downtown, so many people go there frequently. But it is odd for the accustomed focus of human activity—downtown—to suddenly be a place that people cannot enter because of a cancer risk. The SOB is ten stories higher than any other building in the area, standing as both a question mark and a potential health hazard. As was true for medical surveillance, the task of rehabilitating the SOB has proved formidable. By July 1988, about $30 million had been spent on several cleanups of the building. In contrast to the difficulties involved in the medical surveillance, however, it has been easier to measure the effects of those ameliorative efforts. Interestingly, the techniques that organizations used to make sense of the ambiguities involved in decontaminating the building were similar to the techniques used in medical surveillance.

Chemical Problems

Levels of chemical concentrations were an important part of defining the severity of the problem within the SOB, and thus of measuring the effectiveness of attempts to certify its safety. Acceptable risk, political choices, and solutions to technical and social problems have all been couched in terms of these chemical levels.

Two technical points need some explanation. First, the chemicals of concern to those deciding the fate of the SOB, and to the people who will most likely work there, were PCBs, furans, and dioxins; excluded from testing and measurements of cleanup progress were other chemicals such as 2,3,6,7 tetrachlorobiphenylene, although there is evidence that these toxins are as dangerous as dioxins (Stalling, March 31, 1981). Second, chemical concentrations were measured both in the building's air and on its surfaces. Toxic air levels are expressed as the ratio of mass per cubic meter (usually in micro, nano, or picograms/ m^3). Some surface samples from the building were gathered with swabs, usually expressed as the ratio of grams per square meter ($\mu g/m^2$; μg = micrograms); some were collected in bulk and expressed as a proportion of the sample from which they were taken, usually in parts per million or billion (ppm or ppb) or sometimes as the proportion of chemical to soot weight (i.e., as percentages).

The New York Department of Health reported some precleanup PCB levels, but we need not dwell on these numbers, for there is no way of knowing how accurately they reflected the distribution of contamination within the building.[1] An ex-

1. Various sources reported that air samples averaged 1.48 $\mu g/m^3$; that the highest surface concentration was 1995 $\mu g/m^2$; and that the average on horizontal surfaces was 162 $\mu g/m^2$, and 6.76 $\mu g/m^2$ on vertical ones (PCB

tremely wide variation in the amount of toxins was found among different samples, as low as nondetectable levels of PCBs in the air two weeks after the accident, and less than .1 μg/m² on surfaces (averages and some of the highest levels are given in note 1). One test for furan was as low as 5.4 μg/g (Stalling, March 31, 1981), and dioxins were measured at levels as low as 1.2 ppm. Even though officials often used averages in public meetings, press conferences, and risk assessments, the meaning of those averages is especially ambiguous. For example, it is difficult to interpret the 1.48 μg/m³ PCB air-sample average because we do not know if the samples were taken when the air was circulating.

The difference air circulation makes is illustrated by comparing two samples taken from the Binghamton City Hall. Before the air conditioning was turned on, PCB was detected at 6.8 μg/m³; after the air was circulated, PCB was detected at 12 μg/m³ (Hawley to Kim, May 1, 1981). Similar increases in surface-level PCBs were reported by DOH in the State Office Building. Moreover, there is little reason to believe that the pattern of chemical distribution within the SOB was random. Thus, without comprehensive sampling it is difficult to interpret the meaning of any of the average toxic levels, or even the maximum levels. Nevertheless, I report the figures because they were the ones most often referred to by the New York Health Department and the Office of General Services in documents and public statements issued to experts and the public. More important, these measurements were *the only way* to gauge the progress of decontamination.

A point of comparison will be useful for conveying the meaning of the chemical levels. At Seveso, Italy, a cloud of vaporized toxins—including dioxins—from an explosion at a chemical

---

contamination in closed file cabinets averaged 74 μg/m² [New York Department of Health, February 24, 1981]). As a proportion of chemical to soot, PCB was found at 100,000 ppm (OGS, August 4, 1981); PCB was also found to be 10 percent to 20 percent of some samples. Furans were found at 2610 ppm (Rappe to Haughie, June 1, 1981), and 756 μg/g in soot samples (Stalling, March 31, 1981). Apparently, there were no early attempts to measure airborne dioxins, but they were found to be 24 ppm in samples of soot (Smith et al., February 20, 1981).

plant was dispersed over several thousand people. Thomas Whiteside recorded some of the effects:

> Many of those who had been outside quickly developed burnlike sores on their faces, arms, and legs. Adults and children alike developed other symptoms, among them headaches, dizziness, and diarrhea. Within two days, small animals in the area . . . began to sicken, and many died. Birds that had flown through the cloud or had been enveloped in it while they were perched in trees died quickly—many before they could even fly out of the area. (1979, 33)

Dioxin was detected in the soil around Seveso at .03 ppm. One DOH scientist compared the levels of dioxin in the SOB to those discovered at Seveso: "We're talking the same ball park of contamination as Seveso. . . . We don't know the exact calculation of how much material was released into the building yet, but we think it's similar" (Fecteau 1981f). The director of public health for DOH also compared the chemical levels at the State Office Building with those at Seveso (Fecteau 1981f).

The levels of PCB, furan, and dioxin were too high to be background contaminants. But the problem was not so much that chemical levels were too high, but that there was no way to know what levels would be low enough to allow reoccupation of the building. An engineer for OGS said soon after the accident, "We are writing the book here. This is unknown." We will now turn to the question of how, and why, that "book" was written.

An Attempted Solution

The technical problems posed by the toxic chemicals were indeed difficult. The State of New York (and its consultant, VERSAR, Inc.—discussed below) developed cleanup technologies for which there were few precedents. Yet the technical problems were not insurmountable, for their solutions could at least be based on techniques developed for other situations of chemical contamination. The *social* problems, however, were another matter. The most important barrier to cleaning up the building was dissension between those who claimed authority to decide what constituted reasonable danger. The Office of General Services could have removed the last traces of toxic chemicals (at least to levels of nondetection), scraping the walls, floors, and ceilings and burying the building's contents, but the task of creating a structure of responsibility and norms of acceptable risk would still remain. From the view of the state, competing claims to participate in key decisions precluded such consensus. The deputy commissioner of OGS conceded: "If we clean and then say, 'Okay, it's clean,' and the public has no confidence in us, then the building isn't clean" (Hudacs interview, October 8, 1981).

Joseph Gusfield (1981) persuasively argues that the relative abilities of social actors to establish themselves as the "owners" of risk are important parts of the process of constructing solutions to public problems. In the Binghamton case, this means tracing the process of distributing responsibility among organizations, making some solutions more likely to be pursued than others. Thus, to anticipate my conclusion, once the Office of General Services "owned" the problem of the SOB's risk, it was not likely that the alternative of destroying the building would be publicly considered.[2] Earlier, ownership of risk was not as clear. For example, after the first (janitorial) cleanup there were extensive charges from various groups that OGS (and New York State more generally) faced a conflict of interest. How, some wondered, could an agency be trusted to define adequate cleanup procedures while being held legally liable for the failure of those procedures? Others complained that OGS lacked the expertise to tackle the problems. A clear structure of authority was needed, one that established rights to make decisions and access to organizational resources.

One social fix for this problem, the use of scientific legitimation, was tested by OGS (and DOH) two months after the accident. On March 25, 1981, state officials announced that a 13-member panel of experts on environmental health and toxic substances would meet in New York City. According to Gover-

---

2. It is clear from internal documents and interviews that destruction was considered by state organizations.

nor Carey, the sole reason for creating the blue-ribbon panel, which first met on April 3, was to "satisfy the unions." He explained that unions could prevent their members from working in the SOB if their consent was not secured. DOH Commissioner David Axelrod was more circumspect. He said the panel's major purpose was "to attempt to define the conditions under which reoccupation of the building can be considered" (Panel Packet, April 3, 1981).[3]

These efforts to establish legitimacy were contested, however. Officials in Binghamton complained that the expert panel was not being convened in their area. The county executive and the Binghamton mayor, for example, argued that because the SOB was in their community, local officials ought to have access to those who might define acceptable risk for their constituents. Some of these officials, in addition to the local press, asked that the meeting be held in Binghamton. But Axelrod argued that the panel's discussions would be too technical for the general public. Once a decision had been reached on the goals and methods of the cleanup, he said, state officials would express them in terms laypersons could understand (Fecteau 1981i).

Several important questions were asked of the experts:

- What level of exposure to the various chemicals . . . is permissible?

3. The original members of the panel included Richard Dewling, acting regional administrator, EPA; Donald Grant, acting chief, Toxicology Research Division of the Health Protection Branch of Canada's Health and Welfare Department; Douglas Harding, senior medical consultant, Ontario Ministry of Labor in Canada's Special Studies and Research Branch; Clark Heath, director, Bureau of Chronic Diseases at the CDC; Renate Kimbrough, research medical officer, CDC; Philip Landrigan, director, Division of Surveillance, Hazard Evaluations, and Field Studies, NIOSH; John Moore, deputy director, National Toxicology Program, and associate director, National Institute of Environmental Health Science; David Stalling, chief chemist, U.S. Fish and Wildlife Service; Robert Tardiff, executive director, National Academy of Science's Board on Toxicology and Environmental Health Hazards; Arthur Upton, head of environmental medicine at New York University Medical Center; David Wade, Division of Epidemiology, Michigan Department of Public Health; and Alvin Young, Major, U.S. Air Force. A large packet of materials was given to the experts at the meeting. For convenience I cite materials from these documents as Panel Packet, April 3, 1981.

- What kind of testing should be done to monitor . . . any decontamination effort?
- Should all areas of the building be subject to the same guidelines regardless of differences in potential human exposure? (Panel Packet, April 3, 1981)

As Axelrod claimed, these questions involved highly technical issues. For example, toxicology, animal testing, limits of detection, and threshold values for the induction of cancer were all discussed in detail.

But the panel of experts did not produce the solution that state officials had hoped for. Most of the renowned scientists called for more tests, observed that the unprecedented nature of the task precluded easy answers, and claimed that more data were needed before risk could be accurately assessed. Although the panel did not succeed in defining acceptable risk, two of their suggestions deserve mention. Renate Kimbrough, an expert on toxic chemicals at the Centers for Disease Control, argued both at the meeting and in an interview with the author that the toxic levels were not high enough to occasion inordinate concern and suggested a method that would help diminish them: If people are exposed, she said, "they would in many instances be exposed only intermittently, and every time somebody was exposed, some of the material would be removed [from the SOB], so the amount that would remain in the building gradually decreases" (Kimbrough interview, July 15, 1981). Kimbrough was undoubtedly correct, but the Office of General Services did not pursue the notion that people's bodies were an effective decontamination tool. More to the point of dealing with the social problems in Binghamton, Air Force Major Alvin Young counseled:

> The public needs to . . . hear "positive" information. . . . The "Doom and Gloom" team constantly maximizes any threat at the expense of perspectives and probabilities. In truth, we have no information that the low levels of PCBs, [dioxins], and [furans] encountered in the environmental monitoring programs or in the decontaminated areas pose a threat to man or his environment. We must not let emotion dictate that the State Office Building and all its contents be destroyed. (A. Young to Haughie, May 7, 1981)

Major Young prescribed other public relations devices that would help create a less gloomy impression of toxic contamination. He suggested that establishing a more or less permanent "Binghamton Authority" in Binghamton would send a clear message to the press and the public that the SOB was being taken seriously by state decision makers, and he also suggested that strict control be instituted over the dissemination of technical and political information. The major knew what he was talking about. He had been heavily involved in Agent Orange studies that many took to refute the hypothesis that exposure to the defoliant placed soldiers at inordinate risk (cf. Smith 1985). State officials followed the spirit, if not the letter, of Young's advice.

Although the experts did not answer the questions put to them, convening the panel nevertheless had potential as a solution to the state's problem. One interpretation of the panel's purpose, the one espoused by state officials, was that the gathering of experts was an attempt to amass a wide array of information and to generate alternative answers to problems of cleanup and medical surveillance. As most theories of decision making would have it, the best way to arrive at an optimal solution is to create conditions that foster serious consideration of a wide range of alternatives, each of which has some credibility and some potential for implementation. But was this a valid description of the panel's operation?

Two observations suggest that the official version of the panel's purpose and operation was not altogether useful. First, those chosen to serve on the committee did not represent a wide variation in opinion. DOH and OGS solicited opinions only from experts they considered legitimate. Had the panel included exposed workers, citizens of Binghamton, and County Health Director Schecter, more serious criticisms would have been likely. The state's refusal to hold the meeting in Binghamton also served to stifle potential dissent, and therefore alternatives. There can be little doubt that the conviction to reopen the building, rather than destroy it (as some officials and Binghamtonians were suggesting), would have been criticized more if the panel had met in Binghamton rather than two hundred miles away in New York City. Second, and more important, is that the panel's agenda was structured to preclude certain options.

The Context for Decision Making

Officials making decisions regarding risk frequently complain about the hazards of information that is misinterpreted because it is released to the press and the public outside its proper context. For example, fifty thousand people die on U.S. highways every year (almost as many as were killed in the Vietnam War). This grim statistic tells the risk of motoring only in absolute terms. To understand how grim the number is, it must be made relative to some comparison point, for example, to the number of miles driven every year or, better yet, to the number of miles traveled per hour of exposure. These ratios are an important aspect of the context of the risk of driving because they allow comparisons with the risks of other activities. We can understand still more about the risks posed by the highway system if the death rate on highways is compared to the death rates of alternative ways of moving large numbers of people.

Similarly, OGS and DOH officials frequently complained that the media (and those considered alarmists) too often drew attention to PCB levels within the SOB without also noting that PCBs are ubiquitous in the environment, that fluorescent light fixtures and refrigerators (whose capacitors often contain the chemical) contaminate us daily, and that benefits accompany the risks of using PCBs. Although it was not his intent, the governor reminded everyone that absolute safety was an unreasonable goal when he announced at a press conference that "there's no such thing as a risk-free existence, as long as we have a free press" (Geimann 1981b).

If risk is always relative, then it is essential to ask: "Relative to what?" Risks are important only because they jeopardize the values of some group in some way. The governor implicitly referred to the social nature of risk when he tried to explain his remark that, with a few good workers and some vacuum cleaners, he could render the SOB safe:

> I want to warn everybody in this state that we can sacrifice jobs in this state, we can interrupt the public process by not having people

working if no one is willing to take a risk. But life is a risk. We'll use all the reasonable and available means that we can to clean that building. I believe that a tolerable level of dioxin should be reached, then we should move back into the building. (Geimann 1981c)

The governor's remarks angered nearly everyone. Negative public opinion was expressed in letters to newspapers and in my interviews in Binghamton. The media added the governor's comments to a long list of what they deemed his frivolous behaviors (such as dyeing his hair orange). Local officials, and labor unions, interpreted them as evidence that he did not take their problems seriously. The governor's own commissioners of health, general services, and environmental conservation were suddenly in situations similar to ones at Love Canal. Carey's threat may have been idle, and his contention that decontamination would be easy unreflective, but his implication was certainly correct: Decisions regarding hazards reflect distributions of power, as some groups allocate hazard and others bear those allocations. Moreover, the governor was explicitly stating some assumptions that are often hidden in the arcane discussions of experts: Threats to public health are also threats to other social resources. The nearly $30 million spent cleaning the SOB suggests that the building was a risk not only to the health of those who entered it (and those who will, most likely, enter it again) but also to the organizations that constitute the State of New York. If risk is a relative concept, then it is also appropriate to ask *whose* risks were being ameliorated with the OGS's cleanup, and what, exactly, were the risks being mitigated?

Underlying the complaint about risk assessments being interpreted out of context is the presumption that people make decisions and evaluate threats to values on the basis of information. If the databases of decision makers are systematically biased, however, then it stands to reason that their judgments will also be biased. It is important, then, to consider some of the information that helped form the context for the expert panel.

The panel was given a packet of materials that established the premises of the alternatives it considered. Among the materials were, as I indicated, several questions that, it was hoped, the experts would answer. Also enclosed was a short description of the fire, an account of the first cleanup (the janitors were not mentioned), and an explanation about how the discovery of dioxins and furans led officials to close the building. Also included was a "sampling plan" that described how samples of soot were taken from the building and claimed that the geometric mean on surface levels decreased nearly 700 percent after "an initial surface cleaning on the seventeenth floor." Next in the packet were four tables showing PCB measurements. The first table showed PCB levels inside the building, and the others documented levels taken from control locations, including the SOB's basement, the County Office Building, and the garage of a local bank. All of the control levels were much lower than those in the first table. Also included in the packet was a report from the New York Health Department, dated February 20, 1981, entitled "Analysis of 2,3,7,8 Tetrachlorodibenzofuran and 2,3,7,8 Tetrachlorodibenzo-p-dioxin in a Soot Sample from a Transformer Explosion in Binghamton, New York" (Smith et al., February 20, 1981). This paper was also put in several Binghamton libraries. A breathless, highly technical analysis, the paper reports the 2.9 ppm of dioxin and 273 ppm of furan that state officials most often quoted. It closes with a discussion of DOH's method of detecting dioxins in the soot, a description that, as Axelrod claimed, would indeed have been opaque to a layperson.

There are several things to note about this packet. First, the meaning of the average chemical levels the panel was to consider was more ambiguous than their contexts suggested. Second, the highest level reported for samples taken from the garage was 51 $\mu g/m^2$, although another DOH analysis, dated March 12, 1981—three weeks before the panel first met—reported the concentration to be 240 $\mu g/m^2$ (Hawley to Kim, May 1, 1981). Third, all the surface samples were collected using "dry wipes." Hexane wipes, however, almost always yield higher levels than dry wipes. It is difficult to be confident that the panel based its discussions on the best information available at the time.

Finally, there were two versions of the paper, "Analysis of 2,3,7,8 Tetrachlorodibenzofuran and 2,3,7,8 Tetrachlorodibenzo-p-dioxin in a Soot Sample from a Transformer Explosion in Binghamton, New York." The one given to the panel, the media, and the public was nearly five pages of dry chemistry. The unreleased version had another page and a half and three extra citations, which were intended to place the SOB's contamination levels (low estimates though they were) in perspective. "A brief comparison with other episodes [of accidental chemical poisonings] may serve to emphasize the magnitude of the soot contamination," explained the report.[4]

In the extra material, chemical levels in the SOB are first compared to "Yusho," an incident in which a thousand Japanese ingested rice oil contaminated with PCBs, as well as with the more toxic furans. "The most common manifestation of disease was a swelling of the eyelids followed by acneform eruptions [i.e., resembling acne] and skin pigmentation." Other symptoms included "nausea, headaches, jaundice, and neurological disorders." The paper then estimates that someone need ingest only 12 milligrams of the contaminated soot particles "to reach 1 percent of the [furan] dose that proved toxic to the Yusho victims."

The unedited paper also describes three other incidents of dioxin exposure. It tells how in 1971 three horse arenas in Missouri were sprayed with a dust-control oil that had been accidentally contaminated with dioxin: "Over a period of 3 years approximately 70 horses who were exercised in the arenas died. Two adults and four children developed chloracne of varying severity after exposure to the soil. One of the children, a 6 year old girl, who played regularly in the most heavily contaminated area, developed more serious medical problems including hemorrhagic cystitis and focal polynephritis."[5] The little girl's playground was contaminated with about 33 ppm TCDD (dioxin). Dioxins in the State Office Building were detected at levels as least as high as 24 ppm (Smith et al., February 20, 1981).

The dioxin contamination of the SOB soot was also com-

4. All quotes in the remainder of this section are taken from the report in Smith et al. (February 20, 1981) unless otherwise noted.
5. Cystitis is inflammation of the urinary bladder; hemorrhagic means bleeding; nephritis means kidney inflammation.

Table 5. Comparison of TCDD Levels on Particulate Matter
          After Environmental Accidents

Sample Area	TCDD ppm	Sample
New York	24.00	soot
Missouri	33.00	soil
Seveso Zone A	.03	soil
Seveso Zone A	.002	dust
Love Canal	.005	soil
Love Canal	.203	organic leachate

SOURCE: Smith et al. 1981.

pared to dioxin levels discovered at Love Canal, where "certain medical problems including reproductive failures have been reported for people who lived near the dumpsite." The final comparison is to the Seveso incident, where "the only established medical problem in the human population has been the occurrence of chloracne among approximately 180 people, mainly children."[6] This last section of the report is careful to point out that the situations are not "directly analogous," although it concludes with the information presented here in table 5.

The Binghamton case is indeed not "directly analogous" to other instances of dioxin contamination, mainly because of the difference between the types of samples and because most of the Binghamton toxins were kept inside the SOB. The data also suggest that the State Office Building was *more* dangerous, at least in terms of acute exposure, than either Love Canal or Seveso (see table 5).

It is true, as experts and officials say, that contexts are important for making sense of pieces of information. Contexts are particularly important for decision makers because they place an alternative within a range of choices and thus permit them to choose a solution they deem most reasonable. At least two possible contexts were suggested in the DOH report, each created by a different "vocabulary" of risk. One uses the vocabulary of acceptable daily intakes, geometric means of micro-

6. See Whiteside (1979) for evidence of more damage.

grams per square meters, bioassays, chromatography, and reproductive failures. When OGS placed several reams of documents on file in Binghamton's libraries for public inspection, most of them bore titles (which accurately reflected their contents) such as "Engineering Report on Air Filtration and Pollution Control System for the State Office Building in Binghamton, New York." Missing from those documents, however, were the terms of another, complementary, vocabulary of dead horses, swollen eyelids, and children with dread diseases.

The consequences of creating a context for making decisions about acceptable risk are clearly important. Some contexts draw attention away from certain potential effects of toxic chemical exposure and turn the spotlight toward others. Risk can be characterized in a way that is directly accessible to the public and the media, as well as to experts. Such characterization leaves little doubt about the effects that dioxins, PCBs, and furans can have on human health. Another kind of characterization is remote from human experience and is therefore less easily understood and criticized by groups lacking technical training.

The Solution

In June 1981, about four months after the accident, the Office of General Services contracted with VERSAR, Inc., an engineering firm specializing in the study and control of hazardous materials, to assume broad control of cleanup. One of VERSAR's first tasks was to find a way to vent the State Office Building. In the process of decontaminating the building, dust and soot would be stirred around and some of the chemicals would vaporize. Also, because the toxins were distributed throughout the building via the ventilation system, the air ducts and plena contained the largest amounts of contaminants. A cleanup that did not include circulating the air in the building would therefore be incomplete. Besides, the decontamination effort would be difficult work, so the air had to be circulated for the comfort of the cleanup workers. The SOB's ventilation system could operate without releasing the air to the outside, but VERSAR's cleanup plan required ventilation to the environment because the stale, toxic air could not be recirculated indefinitely. On August 11, 1981, at a public meeting where officials announced that the tainted soot was about as dangerous as a common, garden-variety pesticide, a VERSAR engineer promised that the vented SOB air would be cleaner than Binghamton's general environment (Fecteau 1981k).

"Toward the end of the month of August [1981]," an official history of the SOB saga declares, "the Office of General Services completed an Environmental Impact Assessment in accordance with the State Environmental Quality Review Act. The assessment concluded that the preliminary cleanup of the Binghamton State Office Building would not have any significant adverse effect upon the environment" (OGS 1982, 15). This assessment was necessary before OGS and VERSAR could begin the second cleanup.

As noted earlier, there are two ways to conform to New York's Environmental Quality Review Act. The first (which OGS claims to have used) would have required the drafting of an Environmental Impact Statement (EIS). An EIS is not complete, however, without a detailed cleanup plan, replete with risk assessments supporting assertions that the cleanup posed no additional risk to the surrounding community or to the cleanup workers. An EIS also requires that public hearings be held so that interested parties can express their views and directly question authorities about their decisions. OGS did not, contrary to the official history, choose this option.

The legal equivalent of an EIS is a "Negative Declaration," which is presumed to have the same consequences as an Environmental Impact Statement. Using the declaration rather than the EIS implies that the procedures described and justified in an EIS would not change under any conditions. An official in New York's Department of Environmental Conservation explained that VERSAR and OGS were "following the intent, if not the letter" of an Environmental Impact Statement. The experts, he said, were reviewing VERSAR's plans, and the periodic public meetings put together by OGS served the same function as the formal hearings that would have been held with an EIS. The DEC official compared the State Office Building decontamination to similar situations in which private companies were involved. In the latter cases, he explained, companies must clean up the property and equipment and prove they are safe for human exposure. An EIS is always required in those cases. In part, an EIS serves to protect workers and the public, but it also serves another purpose. As a DEC official put it, Environmental Impact Statements are "great because they take the heat off us. Any time we have a politically hot topic, we just go through the hearing route, and that takes the heat off" (Lanahan interview, October 7, 1981).

But the State Office Building accident was different from typical environmental contaminations in two important ways. In the first place, the official explained, OGS was exempt from obtaining the kind of permit required of a private corporation because the SOB was considered an ongoing emergency, and permits are not required for emergency cleanups. Second, and more important, the SOB was not, for DEC at least, a "politically hot topic." In chapter 3 I chronicled the mechanisms DEC used to buffer itself from the controversy surrounding the accident at the office building. The most important mechanism was defining the enclosed structure as separate from "the environment." Thus, DEC required no public hearings to deflect the political heat.

The Negative Declaration asserted that the proposed cleanup would "not have a significant adverse effect upon the environment" (OGS, August 28, 1981, 1). Before an extensive decontamination could be undertaken, as much soot as possible would have to be removed from the SOB. The declaration did not contain formal risk assessments, but it did have a detailed "work plan" outlining the measures to protect the cleanup workers. It also described an air-filtration system utilizing "negative pressure" during the cleanup. Negative air pressure meant that by using fans on the roof air would be drawn through the building from the ground floors up. The fans would pull the air in through doors and vents and then push it through filters on the roof, recirculating the air into the building and sifting toxic chemicals from the good air. In this way, control would be established over the direction of the airflow and, presumably, over the release of contaminants into Binghamton's environment.

An important difference between a Negative Declaration and an Environmental Impact Statement is that, for the former, public hearings are not required and explicit risk assessments do not have to be performed and made available for public perusal. We cannot know if OGS and VERSAR would have behaved differently if an EIS had been drafted rather than the Negative Declaration. It is nevertheless reasonable to assume that public hearings would have slowed the cleanup effort and generated more public criticism of the OGS's tacit assumption that the cleanup would have no effects beyond the boundaries of the SOB.[7]

A Negative Declaration and the more elaborate Environmental Impact Statement both claim to other parties that an organization is making responsible decisions. Both announce that a thorough and rational decision-making process generated their conclusions of safety. They are both formal accounts of an organization's decision that the benefits of some activity outweigh its costs and a signal to other groups that problems are not insurmountable. A Negative Declaration, however, is directed to groups not at risk: organizations. An Environmental Impact Statement is directed toward publics, or to those who presumably will *bear* the risk of the activity being negatively declared.

VERSAR was the state's solution to the social problems created by the contaminated State Office Building. Its officers constructed plans, protocols, risk assessments, and procedures for safety and cleanup. But, as a high-level official who requested anonymity told me: "The major problem is not cleaning the building, but convincing people that it is safe to reenter. This thing is more of a public-relations problem than a technical one. The science isn't hard—the political process, the public relations, the sociology, the psychology of the whole thing is the problem." New technologies were developed to decontaminate the building, but the really difficult tasks were creating a consensus among actors and mollifying public concern over risks posed by the cleanup and over the state's assumption that the

7. For an argument that Environmental Impact Statements are a mechanism of political accountability, see Taylor (1984).

building *could* be reopened. A knowledgeable official explained how the consensus among the experts would be constructed:

> We will have to get a working consensus of everybody in the world who is an expert as to what is a safe level. We need the weight of the scientific establishment behind it; there also cannot be any loud dissenters. We will prepare risk assessments, and those will be distributed to everybody in the scientific community and they [will] all say, "Gee, we have all these problems." Then we will revise it *X* times. We will keep revising it and sending it out until they get tired of commenting on it. There is no other way of doing it. (interview with official, anonymity requested)

It would be a similar process for the public, he said: "There is more stuff in the library and papers than they want to read. The key is, first, to get them satisfied that we are doing a good job, and then get them bored, and then go in and clean up the building."

The important organizational problem regarding decontamination was creating a structure of authority that would forestall the potential for other bases of conflict—no "loud dissenters"—to arise and challenge official definitions of acceptable risk. The social technology employed for achieving this end was effective. Before OGS contracted with VERSAR, state officials often reacted to criticism in a blunt, unforgiving, and sometimes condescending manner. OGS officials sometimes directed scathing criticisms toward those who challenged cleanup methods. For example, at a public forum, the guard who was on duty in the SOB when the accident occurred asked officials to explain why samples of fat (where toxic chemicals tend to accumulate) were not taken from the exposed people as part of the medical surveillance program. Her question went unanswered. Instead, she was subjected to a tongue-lashing on the dangers of smoking. Creating consensus and inducing public boredom were not likely in such a highly charged atmosphere. After VERSAR began working for the state, official response to dissent took a marked turn. About nine months after the accident, I was told: "VERSAR has done this before and found that people lose interest fairly quickly. Nobody will care at some point if the press work is done right. A few people are still interested in the details of the medical stuff, interested in residual levels around the building, a little interested in the safety precautions in the cleanup, but that is a minor part of it" (anonymity requested).

The advent of VERSAR brought a change in the interaction between OGS and its critics. Minor details, rather than the fundamental assumptions of the Office of General Services' decisions, became the focus for discussion. Further, as New York State began to create a structure of responsibility and authority for decontamination, the roles of other, more critical organizations and the public began to be less significant. As with medical surveillance, the reduction of the number and type of actors involved helped to prepare the way for defining acceptable risk.

Symbolic Risk: Decontamination or Destruction?

There were essentially two alternative solutions to the problem presented by the SOB: clean it up or tear it down. Ridding the structure of the chemicals was a Herculean task, given the vast range of pathways to the goal of decontamination, from removing every bit of soot by scraping, washing, and wiping to gutting the entire structure. Still, officials seemed convinced from the beginning that the building would not be destroyed and that hygienic conditions could be restored. "Once it is decided how clean the building has to be to be safe," said the president of VERSAR, "we will prepare complete engineering specifications for the cleanup" (Fecteau 1981j). Several months after the accident, VERSAR's president estimated that it would cost between $45 and $55 million to tear the building down and replace it, and added, "I don't think that will be necessary. I think we can come up with a plan to clean it. But the first thing to do is to establish how clean it has to be" (Fecteau 1981j). Similarly, the cleanup engineer declared three days after the fire that the building would probably be closed only another ten days (Fecteau 1981b). The commissioner of OGS reflected his organization's commitment to decontamination on September 10, 1981: "I wouldn't retreat on any of the things we did, but our public relations did slip. . . . I'm thoroughly convinced we're going to

clean it and get it opened, and that's not Pollyanna talking. . . .
I can't be a doom and gloom guy. I've got that much confidence
in this country" (Fecteau 1981l). Implicit in all these pronouncements was the unfailing faith that the SOB could be
cleaned, that it *must* be cleaned and reopened, and that the notion of taking the building apart and carting it away was ludi-
crous. Yet there was little objective evidence on which to base
this conviction. Because the accident at the SOB was unprecedented, there was no way to be sure the building could be
cleaned. Because there were no legally established safe levels
for dioxins (for example, by EPA or OSHA), there was no way
to be sure acceptable levels could be reached. Even if safe levels
could be defined, there would still be no predictable end to the
amount of resources the project would require before the
building would be usable. These organizations implied that
they would "stop cleaning the building when it is clean." But
this, surely, is a platitude.

Our theories lead us to believe that organizational behavior
is goal-directed and that behavior not so oriented is nonrational. One of the panel experts warned state officials that a
decontamination attempt without a clearly defined end would
lead them into an abyss of ambiguity: "You are faced with a
monumental decontamination task," he cautioned, "which, unfortunately, has the potential for becoming an albatross around
the neck of the New York Department of Health for many years
to come. . . . However, decontamination efforts are pointless
unless you have a goal-oriented program. Thus, interim standards must be established concurrent with decontamination actions, lest you be faced with the dilemma of when to stop cleaning" (A. Young to Haughie, May 7, 1981). If we think of the
decontamination process in operational terms, the cleanup
seems like a twist on Karl Weick's argument that organizations
often do not know what their goals are until they have acted
(1979). That is, when explanations were demanded from state
officials for their actions, the goal of "cleaning until it is clean"
was easily produced. But with no available levels of acceptable
risk, or levels of contamination, toward which the cleanup
could be directed, the Office of General Services was not pursuing "a goal-oriented program," as the expert put it.

To better understand these behaviors, consider the disadvantages posed by the destruction of the SOB, as opposed to its decontamination, from New York State's point of view. In interviews, I often asked officials why they did not simply tear the building down and bury it in some landfill. Unlike decontamination, this solution would indeed be final. (Moreover, there was a precedent. In the early 1970s dioxin-contaminated portions of a chemical plant in the Netherlands were encased in concrete and dumped in the sea near the Azores.) Policymakers replied that they had no choice in the matter. The building, they explained, could not be dismantled because doing so would expose the contaminated interior to Binghamton's environment, thus releasing the toxins. Therefore, toxic levels within the building would have to be at least as low as ambient levels before the State Office Building could be destroyed. And if the levels could be lowered to those outside the SOB, the building would, for all practical purposes, be decontaminated, and might as well be reopened.

There are several flaws in this reasoning: First, the building was never airtight. Locking most of the SOB's doors, restricting access, and preventing the roof hatches from opening undoubtedly prevented some toxic chemicals from escaping. But a VERSAR engineer told me that outside air was exchanging with the air inside the SOB every twenty-four to thirty-six hours; i.e., Binghamton's environment was already contaminated. Second, the building could have been gutted, leaving only the structural steel and outer walls, neither of which was contaminated by the toxic soot. Although gutting would have disturbed the soot more than cleaning would have, the contents of the building could have been sealed before being taken out. Finally, OGS and DOH had long ago abandoned ambient air levels as an acceptable goal of the cleanup (such a level for dioxin would probably be zero). Thus, there were few practical reasons *not* to destroy the building and replace it.

Indeed, the logic of balancing costs against benefits suggests that the most sensible course of action would have been to dismantle and replace, rather than decontaminate, the building. Assume, for the sake of argument, that the SOB could have been decontaminated to the point where there were no differences between it and any other comparable office building. Average levels of PCBs, furans, and dioxins would be computed from a representative sample of buildings, compared with similar measurements from the SOB, and found to be the same or higher. OGS could then have declared the building safe and moved the seven hundred employees back into it. According to national statistics, about 20 percent of the people who work in and visit the SOB can be expected to develop some form of cancer in their lifetimes; similarly, about 3 percent of the babies born to women who would work in the building can be expected to have some form of birth defect. (Using cancer death rates in New York State [2.1/1,000, using data from 1976 to 1980] would yield a more conservative estimate [*New York Times* 1983].)

At the same time, given the uncertainties and difficulties of determining the long-term effects of exposure to toxic chemicals, few independent experts would be willing to testify in a courtroom that a case of cancer or a malformed child could not possibly have been caused by a residual molecule of dioxin or PCB left in the building. As one DOH official said, "It's impossible to remove every molecule of PCB. [After decontamination] there will be PCBs at levels above those at the time of the explosion" (Fecteau 1981e). It is not hard to imagine a jury—faced with persuasive arguments from medical and legal experts and with a deformed child or a cancer-ridden mother of three—finding in favor of a complainant. (Chemical companies frequently settle out of court, even though statistics support their cases, because of the plausibility of this scenario.) Given the plethora of excellent reasons to destroy the building, how is it possible to explain the state's determination not to do so?

The way to understand the behavior of state organizations is not to focus exclusively on defining safe chemical levels. Instead, the decision to decontaminate rather than destroy the SOB may best be understood by looking at the *environment* of OGS. Government officials for Binghamton and Broome County, for example, shared the state's commitment that the building could and should be cleaned; the expert panel seems not to have considered destruction a viable alternative; and NIOSH, the state health department, even the media, almost always couched their recommendations, criticisms, and comments in terms of the difficulties, or inadequacies, of cleanup attempts. But no group in the environment of OGS ever forcefully pressed the possibility, or the desirability, of destruction.

In addition to the lack of external pressure, internal forces at OGS served to defeat the alternative of destruction. From the first few days after the accident, various government officials, from the governor and the commissioner of OGS down to lower OGS functionaries, declared their intention that the building would someday be reopened. It would be imprudent to estimate the moment, but at some point it became impossible for leaders to retract their convictions of certainty, claim that enough had been learned, and begin a project of destruction. I am not speculating about the motives of New York's policymakers; nor am I making any assertions about elite personalities. Rather, I am suggesting that a process of commitment to a course of action occurred, wherein promises were made or implied without knowing how those promises would be fulfilled. If organizations say loudly enough and long enough that they are going to do something, they can create a situation in which that action *must* follow their proclamations (Salancik 1977; Staw and Ross 1978).

Another part of the reason the building was cleaned was the potential political costs of destruction. As one OGS official explained: "The building is not a free-standing building. It's part of a complex. [The city, county, and state] share the plaza. But to have launched the demolition of the largest building in the place would have caused additional damage to the surrounding areas. And I don't know what the political implications would have been in terms of making that judgment" (Rings interview, December 4, 1984).

Finally, New York State has had its fair share of well-publicized "toxic time bombs." These include Love Canal, PCBs in the Hudson River (DOH advises pregnant women not to eat fish from the river), Hyde Park, and the widespread contamination of Long Island's potable water. Science and effective organizations are expected to be able to handle problems without resorting to radical solutions. Destroying the office building in Binghamton would have effectively announced that problems of toxic chemical contamination can be beyond expert abilities. Eliminating, rather than rehabilitating, the SOB would have supported a risk assessment that, in effect, presented the incremental risks to human health posed by PCBs, dioxins, and kindred chemicals as unacceptable.

.   .   .

The process of defining acceptable risk requires that some agent, or set of agents, establish a "domain consensus," or a general agreement, concerning a distribution of authority. Without a domain consensus, the definition of acceptability cannot be resolved, because too many discrepant interests, goals, and values are competing for attention. In the context of the State Office Building case, this meant that as long as meaningful dissension persisted among the many actors involved just after the accident, it was impossible to resolve the dilemma of what to do about the building. Before that dissension could dissipate, a stable structure of authority for decisions and allocation of resources had to be organized. The primary mechanism through which that structure was created was the establishment of VERSAR as the official cleanup agency whose word would be more or less final regarding the technical issues. The secondary mechanisms through which dissent was defeated were the state's use of a Negative Declaration rather than an Environmental Impact Statement, and its structuring of debate agendas by assembling scientific materials so that safety rather than jeopardy was emphasized. The Negative Declaration ensured that open and public debate over the dangers of decontamination would not arise. Presenting incomplete evidence to the expert panel and the public without meaningful comparisons to similar situations narrowed the agenda of reasonable alternatives.

This process was not fully rational. For the decision-making process to have been completely rational, state officials and organizations would have had to array a fairly complete set of options (from doing nothing to complete destruction), evaluate each one of them on a number of dimensions (cost-benefit analyses that dealt with a wide range of values), and choose the one that maximized as many values as possible. Clearly, no alternative other than decontamination was seriously considered by the state, even though there were very good reasons to demolish the building.

Thus, the process of organizing the decontamination of the State Office Building was decisively shaped by organizational interests, the bounded rationality of decision makers, and the social environment of their organizations. The main conclusion of this chapter is that uncertain and unstable social conditions prevent organizations from defining acceptable levels of risk. Before I pursue the implications of this conclusion more fully, another set of actors in Binghamton needs to be heard: those who considered themselves victims of exposure.

SEVEN

The Exposed

> Do I worry? I don't worry about it twenty-
> four hours a day. You'd be neurotic. But the
> concern is there. Always.
>
> —Cleanup worker

As organizations fashioned solutions to the State Office Building's problems and set the terms for what would be considered acceptable risk, they evaluated the hazards not only to themselves but also to workers and Binghamton's public. Organizational sociology does not have much to say about exposed individuals, of course, but there were interesting similarities between individual and organizational reaction to the SOB's risks—the topic of the first part of this chapter. The second part is concerned with the Citizens' Committee on the Binghamton State Office Building, an association whose members considered themselves victims of the SOB. In examining the Citizens' Committee, I seek to answer the question of why this group was unable to have its interests reflected in policy. Unfortunately, there is no way to know the extent to which these groups represented Binghamton's general population.[1] However, after interviews with members of the Citizens' Committee and exposed workers, it is clear they were not simply a cadre of

1. Attempts to secure funding for a survey of Binghamton's population were unsuccessful. I obtained a list of most of the workers included in the state's medical surveillance program, but ethical considerations prevented me from contacting them (see Appendix B). Nevertheless, I was able to gather data on two sets of exposed workers. The first was the wave of people in the building during the first couple of months after the accident. The second was part of a more organized cleanup effort that began in October 1981, eight months after the fire. These workers are not part of the state's surveillance program, and because they are employed by a private company, I was unable to obtain an accurate estimate of their number. The perceptions and positions of the second group were similar to those of the first, and so I interweave their testimonies.

malcontents or a group whose worldviews were radically different from the rest of their community.

Exposed Workers

Grievances

The janitorial brigade was the first major group to be exposed to toxins in the SOB. That cleanup lasted about three weeks, until the building was "closed" on February 26, 1981. State officials, predictably, blamed the workers for the ineffective program. The deputy commissioner of OGS reflected the official view when he proclaimed: "The process of cleaning that we used is still a good process, but not with that group" (Hudacs interview, October 8, 1981). Similarly, the official directly responsible for the brigade said: "There was just no way we could keep watch on all the janitors" (Beaudoin interview, October 6, 1981). In these declarations, officials mimicked the "operator-error" excuse so common when untoward events attract publicity. I do not intend to evaluate the degree to which the opposing views were or are correct, but rather to trace out the areas of disagreement and the basic, underlying issues.[2]

If the supervisors held the workers responsible for their own exposure and for spreading the toxins, workers responded that it was their bosses, not they, who left fire-escape routes unlocked and gave permission to flush the building's toilets. "When you talk about negligence [by the state] beyond your wildest dreams, you don't know the half of it," said one worker (Fecteau 1981p). Although some of the members of the initial cleanup crew apparently failed to appreciate the imprudence of tracking contaminants outside of the building, they maintained that officials were not following the rules they themselves had promulgated. About two weeks after the accident, some county employees distributed a petition in which they complained of their exposure: "This has occurred either by use of

2. Some workers disregarded obvious safety precautions. In March 1981, 131 lottery tickets were stolen from a newsstand inside the SOB. A year later, $3,000 in presumably contaminated cash was stolen from a safe in the office building.

county vehicles which were deemed safe after the mishap or by going to the basement to obtain vehicles" (Broome County Employees, February 18, 1981). These petitioners were worried about birth defects and cancer.

Cleanup workers claimed they were not told that dioxins were in the SOB or how to use their protective equipment. In a typical account, one worker said that, on one job, he worked without

> a suit because the store's clerk . . . said the area was not contaminated. [On another job] I worked with a protective suit and respirator, gloves, and boots. Nobody instructed me how to put the suit on or how to use the respirator. There were no safety checks made. My job was to tear down drapes, [and] I got a face full of soot. There were no goggles. The boots . . . kept coming off and ripping [and] . . . the sleeves of the suit would ride down when I reached over my head. My arms were covered with soot. The inside of my respirator filled with soot, so I took it off. I then took off my suit improperly since there was no instructions on how to do it, in the same place that I put it on. . . . My eyes started to burn at this time and I asked [the] director of clean-up what to do about my eyes. [He] wasn't sure, but he said to wash my eyes out with cold water. . . . I then went to the men's room in the City Hall to wash up. I had a scabby rash around the eyes and was sent to the hospital. . . . They did not know what to do.[3]

The first cleanup squad also reported nausea, headaches, trouble with swallowing, lack of coordination, disorientation, extreme irritability, faintness, fatigue, insomnia, and cold sweats following their work in the building—all symptoms associated with dioxin exposure. The decontamination worker quoted above later hanged himself, apparently because of the depression and anxiety he experienced as a result of his work in the SOB. (Following his attempted suicide, he went into a coma for several years and then died.) It is impossible to be certain that toxic exposure caused his troubles, but anxiety and mental disturbances are among the symptoms associated with exposure to PCBs, furans, and dioxins.

3. Some of the testimony from the janitors comes from affidavits they completed in February 1981 for the Civil Service Employees Association, whose cooperation I gratefully acknowledge.

Nearly a year after the janitorial cleanup, better-trained and more informed workers (employed by Allwash, Inc., the state's cleanup contractor) voiced many of the same concerns.[4] Indeed, judging from the interviews, I found it difficult to distinguish the later cleanup workers from the earlier ones. Allwash workers alleged that officials were taking shortcuts that threatened their health, as well as the health of future inhabitants of the building. "The word 'clean' is a joke," said one. "The state is really concerned with money. You'll say to someone, 'We can't clean this. It'll have to be thrown out.' 'No, no, no,' they say. 'We'll clean it up.'"

These workers were very concerned that their protective equipment failed to shield them from exposure and argued that self-contained respirators (i.e., those that continually supply fresh air) would have been more appropriate for such hazardous work than the simple air filters they were given. One worker explained that because "you have three layers of clothing on and you're doing strenuous work, you begin to sweat. The outside of the respirator mask is rubber, and therefore it gets lubricated by the sweat on your face, and your mask starts to slip back and forth if you have a lot of head movement. On one occasion I . . . got some of the dust into my mask and started choking." Another worker described what it was like when the mask was contaminated: "Once you get something inside your mask . . . it won't go out. It just stays there, and you breathe it, breathe it, breathe it." These workers reported headaches, chest pains, and regurgitation of blood (Seely 1983).

Besides distrusting the measures taken to protect them, the initial cleanup crew, as well as employees in the neighboring city and county buildings, were troubled that the state senate ma-

4. On October 8, 1981, OGS announced that Allwash had been awarded the contract to decontaminate the SOB (VERSAR remained the directing organization of this effort). Interviews with the Allwash workers are taken from verbatim transcriptions kindly provided by a reporter then with the *Syracuse Herald American,* Hart Seely, who interviewed a score of workers involved in the project. At Seely's request, I do not use the workers' names. As a point of interest, no women were allowed to work on the cleanup because of the potential threat to their reproductive systems. It should be pointed out that there is evidence that dioxins can adversely affect male reproductive systems as well (see Smith 1985).

jority leader salvaged personal effects from his office and that contaminated files had been removed from the SOB. They were also disturbed that a judge was trying to retrieve cassette tapes from his office. A labor representative wrote to the OGS engineer in charge of cleanup to protest the judge's request:

> Such a request is of grave concern to all employees. . . . There are several young women of childbearing age presently working in this building who may needlessly be exposed to toxic PCB material. Indeed, the person whose normal function it is to handle these tapes is pregnant. . . . I have personally spoken to at least a dozen state employees now working [where the tapes would be taken] who have expressed an objection to [the judge's] proposal. (Weigert to Seiffert, February 26, 1981)

Upon closing the building, state officials announced that it would thereafter be restricted to all but authorized personnel and that nothing should be taken from the State Office Building. One week *after* the official closing, however, the deputy county health commissioner wrote to an on-site OGS representative: "Tuesday evening I received a call from [a worker at a local] car wash who was concerned because he discovered that a New York State car that he had cleaned inside and out had been parked in the garage at the time of the explosion" (Gaffney to Mosher, March 5, 1981).[5]

Firefighters also questioned official policy. They had not been given answers to some important questions. "I think most of the guys have gotten over the uneasiness," one remarked, "but no one really knows what will happen. . . . I think we're going to be a batch of guinea pigs." These workers feared not only for their own health, but for that of their families as well. "I claim my men are strong," said the assistant fire chief, "but there is only so much that anybody can take. If he has got a constant worry on his mind that he's got a carcinogenic problem, it affects not only him, it affects his family" (Faughnan interview, August 13, 1981).

Most research on risk perception is conducted on survey re-

5. This memorandum, according to Gaffney's notes at the bottom of it, was never sent, but its contents were discussed over the telephone.

spondents and experiment subjects (e.g., Hohenemser, Kasperson, and Kates 1977; Fischhoff, Slovic, and Lichtenstein 1978; Cole and Withey 1981; Slovic, Fischhoff, and Lichtenstein 1982). But the reactions of those exposed to the SOB's toxins suggest it is also useful to elicit the views of those who actually bear risks. One of the lessons from the evidence reported here—along with evidence from the exposed at Love Canal, Michigan, and Three Mile Island—is that what we usually think of as "at risk" should extend well beyond physical health. Psychological well-being, family health, friendships, and communities are all exposed, in a sense, when groups of workers confront an increased probability of contracting cancer, liver disease, and other ailments that attend occupational hazard.

Reactions

In addition to examining workers' perceptions, it is necessary to explore reactions based on these perceptions. Some workers reacted with resignation to a fate beyond their control. One engineer, whose superiors pressured him to enter the State Office Building several times without a protective suit, conceded: "At that time I guess our attitude was kind of, well, you know, if it's going to get us, it's going to get us. We are going to die of something anyway, so we just kind of had an attitude of, well, if it does it does, and if it doesn't it won't" (interview with engineer, anonymity requested, February 22, 1982). Similarly, the guard who was contaminated at the time of the fire, although disconcerted that no one had told her how deadly the chemicals were, scorned others' protests: "I, for one, hope . . . that I will be called [to testify] for the state. There is nothing I would like better than to cut these money-hungry people down and let them end up paying court costs as well as their attorneys" (Foldes 1981).

But with time, resignation turned to distrust and anger. The engineer quoted above eventually refused to enter the SOB:

One [reason] for my decision was . . . that I would pick up a paper one day and they would say, 'Oh, yes, this stuff is very deadly. Just a little bit will kill you,' and the next day you see that some scientist says, 'Well, they are making more of this than it really is.' So, I got to thinking, well, if they say one whiff of this thing will kill you, at least you know what you are up against, or if they say no, definitely it's okay . . . I started to wonder that maybe we really don't know what we are up against.

Even the frustrated guard, after several months, decided she would go back in the building only "if the Pope said it was okay." Obviously, something had changed, as these workers came to believe that those who professed they were protecting public health were not. The guard said, in marked contrast to her earlier statements: "I think we're facing another Love Canal. Look how much those people had to fight to get what they wanted. I'm getting the feeling New York has more environmental disasters than any other state and apparently, they don't know how to handle them. You'd think by now they'd be experts" (Fecteau 1981n).

From nearly everyone subjected to the toxic chemicals came a common refrain: "We are guinea pigs." One of the workers was rueful: "Let's face it," he said, "even with guinea pigs they write everything down and make sure it's a controlled experiment. I don't think they do that with us."

Another response of these "workers at risk" was organized, albeit modest, protest. In addition to the petition mentioned above, another petition was circulated in early March of 1981 among city and county employees, many of whom feared they had been exposed to the tainted soot. These petitioners were moved by "considerations of personal health as well as for the future safety of our immediate families," asking:

- What is the nature and extent of scrubdown of the city building's restrooms and water fountains, which were heavily utilized by the cleanup personnel during the first stages of PCB cleanup?
- What is the condition of the elevator and stairwell areas that link the affected sub-basement and basement levels by persons carrying contaminated materials from the state building? What current safeguards are being utilized to control this unauthorized traffic?

There were other questions in their petition. The signers explained they were not convinced the state was protecting their interests, and therefore they requested "an immediate and thoroughly detailed explanation of the above mentioned items. Moreover, we want to know the specific plans of the State regarding the present and future safety protection of our health and welfare" (City and County Workers to Schecter, March 3, 1981). The petitioners received no response to their requests.

Certainly, officials did not perniciously plot to contaminate employees, and the "guinea pig" metaphor is somewhat overdrawn. Some would argue that the workers' fears reflected an unreasonable expectation that experts and organizations always have satisfying answers. If so, then authors such as Raiffa (1980), a pioneer in the field of risk analysis, are correct when they assert that the key problem in situations of risk is an ill-informed and unpredictable public (also see Schwing and Albers 1980). In this view, the remedy for maladies of hazard is to educate the public about the realities of making difficult trade-offs in a context of scarce information and resources.

From this perspective, workers become overly alarmed, even panicked, when experts disagree. But a closer examination of the evidence suggests we should exercise more caution before hastily dismissing the worries of these workers as another instance of an overreacting, ill-informed public. When pressed, workers do not really expect experts and officials to be omnipotent: "I had one of the experts tell me what I consider to be the truth, and he said, 'We don't know what the far-reaching effects are'. . . . He said, 'We just don't know.'" What *does* concern workers is that officials refuse to acknowledge their uncertainty. "We've heard nothing," the assistant fire chief said, "[not] even . . . the results of those other blood tests and now they're talking about more blood tests. The more I hear the less satisfied I am" (Fecteau 1981n). Dorothy Nelkin and Michael Brown interviewed some of Binghamton's firefighters for their book *Workers at Risk* and report similar evidence: "We were getting everything from you're going to die to it's good for you. . . . These were supposedly medical experts. So we're still in the dark as to what's what" (1984, 157).

Overall, the types of responses and perceptions among the

exposed workers varied widely. This variation was remarkably similar to much of the organizational behavior chronicled in the previous chapters. Ambiguous contexts elicit contradictory behaviors from individuals *and* organizations, suggesting that it is not irrationality, but the difficulty of making sense of unfamiliar environments that allows or facilitates unusually flexible reactions. However, an important difference between officials and exposed workers is that there were no risks of cancer, birth defects, or chloracne for the former. Workers will develop a certain measure of cynicism toward policies and programs when they are asked to bear the costs of possible failures.

The literature on risk assessment is of little help in understanding workers' reactions, mainly because there are few studies of subjects facing actual risks. But Levine's (1982) research on Love Canal residents, Walsh's (1981, 1985) studies of people living near Three Mile Island, and Nelkin and Brown's (1984) study of chemical workers in a variety of occupations, in addition to the evidence from Binghamton, suggest that an important element in the development of distrust of officials and organizations is the extent to which the aggrieved themselves are defined as part of the hazard by organizational decision makers. As an alternative, these decision makers could concede the possibility that these complaints come not from an abstract and uninformed "public," but from people who have borne, and will be asked to bear, the negative consequences of public policy.

Risk Assessments

In addition to the grievances of exposed workers and their reactions to official policy, there is one more component of their risk assessments: An interesting question to ask is why the cleanup crews—both the untrained janitors and the Allwash employees—would volunteer to work in a dangerous environment like that of the SOB. Some versions of economic theory would argue (e.g., Viscusi 1979) that they do so because of the extraordinary compensation for extraordinary risk. But the janitors received only their regular hourly wage, plus overtime and expenses. And most of the Allwash employees received about $5 per hour, usually with a $97.50 per diem, which turned out to be insufficient to retain some workers:

> Say I had a really menial job. . . . You'd expect to be paid $3.35 an hour. Okay? But in a job where you're cleaning up hazardous wastes, and the state is paying a two-digit number for the company that hired you to do the work, [they're] only paying you $5 an hour. On top of that you get a per diem. . . . And [the company] takes a percentage of that, also, which I don't think is fair. Because it's our health that's on the line, it isn't [theirs].

"Revealed preference" theory proposes another explanation for why these workers would accept the SOB's risks. This theory posits that an individual's notion of acceptable risk can be inferred from her or his behavior. But because revealed preference theory assumes that people have complete freedom of choice, it fails to take into account social structures that limit the discretion to choose and therefore affect the formation of motive. The OGS janitors felt constrained by the informal structure of their organization: "There were rumors going around," said one, "that if employees did not work, they would get in trouble, and it would reflect on employees' evaluations and job security." Later, the Allwash employees faced a similar dilemma that pitted safety against livelihood:

> I'd say almost every day you could tell some material had gotten into your mask. At first, I'd report it and go out [of the building]. But very quickly you'd find that's frowned upon. After a couple of times they'll say you'd better get the problem fixed or you won't go back in the building [which meant being fired]. There is a limit to how many times you can do it. It's an unspoken limit, but you catch on pretty quick. (Seely 1983)

Another said: "When I started, if you had to shower out for any reason—even going to the bathroom—they were pretty lenient; they'd let you shower out. But as time goes on, more and more people are finding they have to go to the bathroom, and . . . they decided that if a person had to go to the bathroom, they were kept out of the building for the remainder of that shift, and they were docked for their hours."

It seems too obvious to observe here, but it bears emphasizing that workers tolerate job-related risks because they need to make a living. "These happen to be trying times," one worker explained. "There are a lot of people out of work. We all need a job." One of Nelkin and Brown's respondents summarized the predicament succinctly: "You can never balance the wage against the risk; you balance the wage against the alternative. The alternative is starving" (1984, 180).

Organizing Dissent

The Citizens' Committee on the Binghamton State Office Building first took form in mid-October 1981, about nine months after the accident. Although aggrieved, the committee initially adopted a conciliatory stance toward the state and county. One of the committee's founders explained that they wanted "to work with the State and be its partners in the protection of our lives and those of our children" (Citizens' Committee meeting transcript, October 26, 1981). The Citizens' Committee was an association of homemakers, lawyers, firefighters, exposed workers, and others who will someday have to decide whether or not they will again work in the State Office Building. In this way, the association resembles many other citizen action groups.[6] As is true of other such groups, few committee members had heard of toxicology, chemistry, and epidemiology—subjects remote from their everyday lives. With time, though, its members developed the skills to converse in these strange languages, asking reasonable questions of those making the decisions that would affect them, and understanding the answers they received. The Citizens' Committee became adept at recognizing official assertions of safety that hid the more important issues of relative risk.

Committee members believed the Binghamton case to be in the same genre of other, more famous, incidents. "Binghamton

6. In a study of 242 community organizations involved in environmental health issues, Freudenberg (1984, 445) found that the occupation most commonly listed by members was "homemaker."

now has the dubious distinction," one member noted, "of rank-
ing with Three Mile Island, Love Canal, Seveso, Italy, and other
localities where environmental pollution has become a health
threat to its citizens" (Fecteau 1981p). But the Citizens' Committee was not demanding the shutdown of multimillion-dollar
power plants or the purchase of a neighborhood. It sought
something much more modest—answers to some simple questions: Who will decide what is safe? On what authority? What
will be done to protect the health of workers and Binghamton's
environment? These questions, members thought, were not especially alarmist. Rather, they were the basic questions of individuals who would someday have to shoulder the consequences
of official definitions of acceptable risk.

One of the committee's specific concerns was that the medical
surveillance program did not include all those who were indirectly exposed. They protested, in particular, that it did not
include the family members of exposed workers, even though
toxicological evidence suggests that such indirect exposure can
be dangerous. The Citizens' Committee also tried to find out
why no attempt had been made to discover whether their
neighborhoods and the downtown area were contaminated. An
oft-repeated sentiment was that if the decision makers had
dioxins in their own neighborhoods, more would have been
done to ensure public health.

The members of the Citizens' Committee thought their goals
were reasonable. They were not asking for absolute definitions
of safety; nor were they demanding that a large fraction of New
York State's budget be diverted to their problems. They *did*
complain of what appeared to be senseless organizational behavior; echoing rationalist theory, they objected to actions that
were not directed toward well-defined ends. They had witnessed more than eight months of official dismissals of the
problem of the SOB and its victims, as well as promises that no
expense would be spared to protect their health. They had
heard certain declarations of safety and were subjected to plat-
itudes, such as the governor's assertion that "life is a risk." Committee members pointed out that state experts had been quick
to judge the soot nontoxic when the "carbon-love" hypothesis
was suggested, and equally quick to conceal the results of the

chick-embryo tests that suggested otherwise.[7] They argued that because they, and others like them, were the ones who inhabited cost-benefit ratios, they should have some voice in deciding what level of risk was acceptable. One member observed that "many actions have already been taken by the State, and others are being planned, without anyone knowing whether those actions were or are desirable and necessary, meaningful, effective or safe. Because the planning and execution of the plans [were] undertaken without input from the citizens, we were and may still be seriously shortchanged and unnecessarily endangered" (Citizens' Committee meeting transcript, October 26, 1981). The committee, in short, was demanding political accountability from policymakers.

On November 4, 1981, the committee staged a public meeting and invited the media, local health officers and politicians, and officials from the New York State Department of Health and the Office of General Services. The state officials were cordial during the meeting and explained that they wished for an environment of cooperation. They volunteered the truism that risk is defined by society and asserted that safety would not be determined on the basis of technical criteria or fiscal costs. The committee's leaders again stressed their own desire for a "cooperative partnership" and pointed out that "everyone knows by now that we have no saints and no magicians on our public payrolls."[8] The committee asked state officials the hard questions:

- Why, nine months after the accident, has a clear medical surveillance plan not been instituted?
- Why have data been withheld?
- How, exactly, will a safe level of toxins be established?

In other words, the Citizens' Committee was asking these representatives what their goals were, how they planned to reach

7. The "carbon-love" hypothesis (see chapter 5) proposed that bonds between chemicals and the carbon in the soot would render the chemicals harmless.

8. These quotations were taken from a verbatim transcription of the meeting.

them, and the role they intended the public to play in the process of defining acceptable risk. State Health Commissioner Axelrod denied that any data had been withheld and that positive but inconclusive data were readily released. He also told the gathering: "We have always proceeded from the fact that the citizens of this state represent a very well informed and intelligent community, and I would not presume at any point to underestimate the intelligence of any body of people who ultimately pay my salary."

Axelrod also told the citizens that "'safe' is a political term" and that the risk of reentering the State Office Building "will not be any greater than the risk of entering any other state office building within the state of New York." He clarified the official view of the proposal that the Citizens' Committee could be a partner in determining policy when he told them they would "have the opportunity to comment on whatever levels are going to be recommended. . . . That is [why we are here]," he said, "to offer you the opportunity to comment." Simply commenting, however, was not what the committee had in mind.

Not much came of the committee's meetings with state officials, except to gain a small measure of publicity for the committee in the local press. Its leaders and members both were disappointed with the officials' lack of candor and thought they had been subjected to more instances of "informing the public." State health officials, for the most part, imparted "press-type information," and representatives from OGS read long, self-evident statements that had been delivered at previous public meetings.

After the November meeting the committee became somewhat more adversarial. "We are getting into that stance, whether we like it or not," one of its members explained, "because the state wants to sit on some very unfortunate information, and [we are being] *forced* to assume this stance" (Stuckart interview, April 29, 1982).

Nevertheless, the Citizens' Committee on the Binghamton State Office Building was unable to garner enough power to become an effective constraint on the decision makers who would define acceptable risk for the public. One of the reasons for the committee's failure, several members confided, was that many of them worked for the county and state, and they feared reprisals for "going public." One of the committee's leaders told me: "I have had people tell me that all kinds of terrible things could happen to them if they join" (Stuckart interview, April 29, 1982).

. . .

A common theme pervades scholarly work on risk. Of all the research topics that might fall under the general study of risk, the most common address arguments and assumptions regarding the role of unorganized, and unofficially organized, publics. A frequent and consequential assumption in many studies is that the public is irrational and overly alarmed about hazards. From that assumption it is no great leap to the conclusion that publics should play a *reactive,* rather than a *proactive,* role in determining policies regarding risk. When Raiffa (1980, 340) notes that "public perceptions and reality dramatically differ," he is echoing a common view of those who make important decisions and policies regarding risk. But such views ignore the *structural contexts* within which publics assess risk.

Fortunately, some recent progress has been made on the study of publics, as more attention has been accorded to structural issues rather than to the psychology of risk. Adeline Levine's study (1982) of Love Canal activists and Walsh's studies of Three Mile Island (1981, 1985) provide rich evidence of the strategies and tactics used by protest associations to achieve goals in a context of threats to public health. Nelkin and Brown's (1984) research chronicles structural factors such as the range of occupational alternatives open to workers and the opportunities workers have to engage in meaningful protest that shape their perceptions of risk.

It is true that the notions of acceptable risk held by exposed workers in Binghamton were not based on probability distributions of the likelihood of contracting cancer, and it is true that their risk perceptions differed from those of experts. But it does not follow that the solution to problems of risk is therefore public "education," if "education" means convincing publics to accept official definitions of safety. For Binghamtonians who perceived the building as a threat, the crucial element in the debate over the acceptability of the SOB's risks was that the officials are not the ones who will live and work there. As a committee member pointed out, "There is a big difference between going in for an hour or so for an opening celebration and spending forty hours a week in there."

Despite the efforts of the Citizens' Committee, it was clearly unable to achieve its goals. In 1984 it succeeded in having Ellen Silbergeld, a respected toxicologist, appointed to the state's expert panel. Nevertheless, the committee and the state organizations never became "partners" in any meaningful sense, and there is no evidence that official policy was in any way shaped by the demands or existence of the association. Why the failure?

Most of the risk analysis literature is rooted in the psychology of individual fear, so little research has been conducted on how public values are reflected in policy choices. One explanation, however, is suggested by the revealed preference theory mentioned earlier (see Starr 1969; Cole and Withey 1981; MacLean 1982). According to this view, individual behavior mirrors individual definitions of acceptable risk. If millions of people smoke cigarettes or live near a nuclear power plant, they must consider the risks of smoking and atomic power acceptable; otherwise, they would quit smoking or move away. One reason the Citizens' Committee failed, according to its leaders, was the committee's inability to convince people to protest openly. Perhaps we may assume, from the behavior of the citizens, that they thought the hazards posed by the SOB were not severe enough to serve as a rallying point for their grievances and that they approved of official policy. After all, massive protests were not staged in the streets, the workers' unions were fairly inactive, and officials were not kidnapped in protest, as EPA officials were at Love Canal (Brown 1979).

Nevertheless, even if we ignore the inherent tautology in revealed preference theory, it still cannot explain the failure of the Citizens' Committee. First, some segments of the public were indeed quite concerned about the building's risks. Second, the revealed preference hypothesis assumes, as Nelkin and Brown (1984) point out, a wide array of choices unconstrained by social structures. Yet it is clear that the Citizens' Committee enjoyed little or no effective connection to policymakers. For preferences to be revealed in behavior, there must be some way both to transmit goals to decision makers and to ensure their enforcement. But the Citizens' Committee, and the public more generally, was excluded from the political arena. Any possible contributions they might have made were therefore thwarted and became expressions of anger, frustration, or resignation instead. If we are to understand how "society" evaluates, distributes, and accepts risk, we must therefore address the issue of the structural connections between those with power and those without it.

Comparing the Binghamton case, on the one hand, with Love Canal and Three Mile Island, on the other, shows two differences that help explain why the Citizens' Committee was unable to establish connections with policymakers. First, aggrieved citizens and workers in Binghamton were unable to attract outside support—in particular, the attention of the national media. Although the event received a modicum of national and international attention—several newspapers covered it, it was reported in *Science* magazine, National Public Radio did a small piece on it, EPA changed some regulations concerning electrical transformers, many papers on the incident have been presented in environmental and trade journals—it never received the extensive publicity that Love Canal and TMI did. We have no studies of the processes through which the national media come to regard some public health threats as serious enough to warrant major coverage (cf. Schoenfeld, Meier, and Griffin 1979). But the Binghamton case, in conjunction with others, suggests that national media coverage is necessary, if not sufficient, before grass-roots associations can gain enough power to become real forces.

The second difference between Binghamton and other cases is that the Citizens' Committee did not form until *after* most of the major issues were resolved. By the time members of the committee began to voice their objections—nearly nine months after the accident—decision-making structures were already in place, lessening the impact of the committee's challenges. The major sociopolitical battles among the various organizations were also settled, so that state agencies were firmly ensconced as the "owners" of the building's risks. State organizations were the only ones left to propose solutions to the problems created by the contaminated building. In late October 1981, the same month the Citizens' Committee started to organize, OGS began a publicity campaign designed to remedy popular distrust of state policies. A series of open meetings (discussed earlier) were held in which the public was given symbolic.opportunities to influence decisions. State officials also met with editors of the local papers and convinced them to soften their previously critical stance. Thus, the timing of intervention and association is an important, albeit neglected, variable in research on citizen protest (Walsh 1985). Associations of dissent, it seems, are more likely to achieve their goals the earlier they claim a legitimate role in the process of defining what constitutes acceptable risk.

EIGHT

Organizing Risk

Conclusions about the Binghamton case must begin on a positive note that nevertheless has grim implications. Although the
accident was not as bad as it could have been, similar accidents
are likely to occur again and to have even more dire consequences. In a sense, the PCB solution used in the coolant mixture for the building's transformers was a blessing. Had the
transformers used a nontoxic coolant mixture based on min-
eral oil (the common coolant before PCBs, and still used in
many buildings), the State Office Building would probably have
burned to the ground. Binghamton's fire chief testified that
such a traditional coolant would have created "a towering in-
ferno." In that event, the problems of toxic chemicals would not
have plagued the building, the exposed people, or decision
makers. But we must remember that the complete contamination of the SOB was an accident, and as such is a relatively rare
occurrence. Towering infernos would occur more frequently if
there were no PCB-containing transformers. Important advantages obviously attend the use of risky technologies (Wildavsky
1979).

The fortuitous timing of the accident—early in the morning
(5:30 A.M.)—also moderated its potential for disaster. Had the
accident occurred a mere four hours later, more than seven
hundred people working and conducting business in the building would have suffered acute exposure to toxic chemicals far
surpassing the levels at Seveso, Love Canal, and Michigan.[1] We
cannot know if deaths would have resulted from exposure of
that intensity, but it is possible that many would have died in
the panic to get out of the darkened building. It is certain that
an accident during working hours would have increased the
probabilities of chronic ailments. "If this building had gone up

1. See, respectively, Whiteside (1979), Levine (1982), and Egginton
(1980).

at three o'clock in the afternoon," one DOH official remarked, "this would have been a horse of a different color. . . . Be grateful" (Fecteau 1981f). Thus, we survive to discover that the accidents our organizations create can always be worse.

Another paradox in the story of the State Office Building is that, in some sense, the accident could not have happened in a better place. The scientific and engineering apparatus used by the Office of General Services and the New York Department of Health are regarded, even by their counterparts in the private sector, as among the most advanced in the world. Instruments to measure traces of dioxin, for example, are very sophisticated, and the scientists who use them are highly trained. If the accident had occurred in Montana, the very low measurements taken and used by OGS and DOH (however haphazardly collected) might not have been available for us to examine critically.

Similar accidents have been reported in Chicago, San Francisco, Tulsa, Toronto, Clearwater, Florida, and Syracuse and Albany, New York, but none was as extensive. We can only hope that the timing of future accidents will be as forgiving as this one was.

Throughout this book I have sought answers to two main questions: How do organizations behave under conditions of ambiguity? What can organizational sociology teach us about risk management and risk assessment? In this chapter, I first trace the process through which solutions to the SOB's problems were constructed. Along the way, I evaluate the ability of extant theories to explain that process. Next, I more explicitly mine organization theory for clues to interpret the Binghamton case, arguing for a modification of currently favored models of decision making. In concluding, I return to the twin themes of this book—ambiguity and the organizational context of risk assessment—and propose some directions in which I think the sociology of risk should move.

All important accidents, by definition, produce social disruptions (Erikson 1976; Kreps 1984). Accidents with the potential to affect innocent bystanders (those who cannot be aware of the risks) and future generations pose dilemmas that are peculiar to modern technologies (Perrow 1984). One of the most important dilemmas decision makers must resolve is the proper bal-

ance between organizational and public health. Before turning
to this topic in the final section on risk assessment, let us examine the SOB accident to see how organizations make sense
of the inherent ambiguities that beset such situations.

Disruption of Routine

Imagine the day before the accident at the SOB, February 4,
1981. Federal agencies such as the Environmental Protection
Agency are adjusting to the Reagan administration's budget
cuts and policy changes. The National Institute of Occupational Safety and Health, which advises the Occupational Safety
and Health Administration, is running experiments and conducting epidemiological research. At the state level, the New
York Department of Health is engaged in its multifarious programs to oversee the medical profession in New York, certify
hospitals, inspect restaurants, issue directives to branch offices,
and conduct biological, epidemiological, and chemical research. The two major divisions of the state's Office of General
Services—the design and the construction and maintenance divisions—are busy doing the work of engineers and keeping
New York's buildings operating. The New York Department of
Environmental Conservation is monitoring private corporations for violations of pollution and toxic-substance laws, certi-
fying landfills, and otherwise trying to keep a step ahead of
New York's myriad threats to environmental integrity.

At the local level, both city and county governments are pre-
occupied with the prosaic but important functions of bud-
geting, legislating, and public relations. Most of the Broome
County Health Department's resources are engaged in administering its Women, Infants, and Children program; inspecting
hotels; and maintaining its schedule of home health care visits
for the indigent, old, and disabled.

On February 5, the accident disrupted these routines, creating, from all accounts, social chaos (at least in terms of the
proper response to the SOB and its victims).[2] As we have seen,

2. There are two main differences between disasters such as the SOB,
Love Canal, Michigan, Bhopal, and TMI, on the one hand, and natural disasters, on the other. First, for natural disasters experienced agencies exist to

the event created two general classes of problems. First were the technical uncertainties of how to run medical surveillance and decontamination: Who should be covered? What ailments should be anticipated? Would a medical monitoring program help the exposed? Should a surveillance study even be run? Could the building be rid of the toxins, and, if so, how? When should cleaning stop? How safe is safe? The second class of ambiguities—which might be termed sociopolitical—involved the lack of any semblance of social structure for the distribution of legitimacy, authority, responsibility, and power among organizations.

It will help to organize the narrative by separating it into two phases. Figure 2 (opposite) graphically represents the progression of events in Binghamton. It also illustrates the relationship between the sociopolitical and the technical ambiguities. As time passed, a division of labor gradually emerged from organizations negotiating over definitions of authority and responsibility. I argued in previous chapters that the organizations needed to settle these negotiations before the more technical solutions to the problems of the contaminated people and the contaminated building could be constructed. As the Binghamton story unfolded, the technologies of medical surveillance and decontamination became increasingly sophisticated, arcane, and elaborate. A series of interorganizational conflicts had to be resolved, however, before these technologies were defined, accepted, and implemented.

Phase One: An Interorganizational Garbage Can

The early phase of the crisis set into motion organizational behavior as abstruse to outside observers as the accident was to

---

mitigate the harshest effects of dam breaks, earthquakes, fires, and floods (treating the sick and injured and burying the dead). Second, the rescue effort for toxic disasters is necessarily more limited than it is for victims of natural disasters. If a flood demolishes a town, the sooner the rescuers and the victims meet, the sooner will follow public (and individual) health. Once a dioxin exposure has occurred, the best rescuers can do is monitor victims for early signs of disease. For these reasons, studies of natural disasters would be of little help here.

Figure 2. Organizing Risk: The Binghamton State Office Building

---

Phase One: An Interorganizational Garbage Can
February–September 1981

1981
Intense interagency conflict under ambiguous conditions
  • mandates and jurisdictions ill-defined

February

Enter Broome County Health Department
  • assigned responsibility by state, works with media, gains legitimacy as public health protector

Janitorial cleanup (Office of General Services)
  • city building contaminated
  • toxins vented to environment
  • official total of exposed individuals: 482

Media have easy access to organizational personnel

April

Most organizations exit

Three organizations left in garbage can: Broome County Health Department, New York State Health Department, New York State Office of General Services

Three organizations negotiate over medical surveillance and decontamination control
  • people and building relegated to secondary status
Mid-September
  • county health director fired

Phase Two: State's Assumption of Risk
October 1981–present

October
State "owns" SOB's risks

Public relations campaign initiated by state

Media co-opted; access to information restricted

End of October
Citizens' Committee on the Binghamton State Office Building forms; unable to garner power

1982

Protocol for medical surveillance and plan for cleanup written

Formal risk assessments generated

the organizations that had to contend with it. Within two days after the fire in the SOB, the Office of General Services sent a team of untrained janitors into an extremely toxic environment, risking lawsuits as well as workers' health. OGS, as if to mock organization theorists (Goodman and Pennings 1977), acted as the model of bureaucratic efficiency, applying a very effective solution, but to the wrong problem (i.e., the building was contaminated, not just dirty). In the subsequent three weeks, this first cleanup effort served mainly to spread, not contain, the toxins because of doors left unlocked, petty theft, and documents and cars that left the building. The New York Department of Health responded much as it had to Love Canal, trying to minimize the importance of the accident, and therefore aggravating the negative consequences over the long term (Levine 1982). The Broome County Health Department began a program of medical monitoring whose lack of order reflected the department's lack of requisite personnel, expertise, and funding and its relative isolation from agencies such as EPA and NIOSH. Physicians, unable to tell their patients if they were sick or would become sick, or indeed what could be done if they became sick, were concerned about possible lawsuits, or, as they saw it, being put in a position of responsibility for the blunders of others. The local media also reflected the general chaos, reporting contradictory facts from officials who contradicted one another.

The first phase of the story, which lasted about nine months, is best described as an "interorganizational garbage can" (Cohen, March, and Olsen 1972; March and Olsen 1979). This multiorganizational garbage can possessed several characteristics. First, there was *no clear definition of the problem.* In the chapters on medical surveillance and decontamination I criticized the assumptions that underlay the technologies of the medical surveillance study and that defined acceptable levels of contamination. During the first phase, even the *possibility* of medical surveillance and cleanup was being negotiated by several organizations, mainly the Broome County Health Department, the New York State Health Department, and the Office of General Services. The first surveillance efforts by the county health department created a normative constraint on DOH to follow through with the study. BCHD framed the question of the value of medical monitoring early on and in such a way that if DOH terminated the program, it would be taken as an admission that public health was not being taken seriously.

Looking back, there seem to be functional reasons why the county health department could not have directed long-term medical surveillance. Pfeffer and Salancik (1978), who represent an important perspective on relations between organizations (known as resource dependence theory), argue that in our world of scarcity, organizations cannot internally generate all the resources necessary for attaining their goals and must therefore exchange resources with others in their environments (see also Aldrich and Pfeffer 1976). Another reason organizations enter into formal and informal arrangements is that problems sometimes arise that are beyond the capabilities of any single organization to solve (Gottfredson and White 1981; Metcalfe 1981). Normally, resource dependence theory maintains, exchanges between organizations lead to interdependencies, from which shared expectations can develop (Levine and White 1961; Aldrich and Whetten 1981). In the Binghamton case, the cost of the PCB blood tests alone was more than $40,000, not including the opportunity costs of labor, machinery, and public relations. Resource dependence theory and common sense suggest that medical surveillance would require a great many resources if it were to have any longevity and validity. Thus, an efficient and effective study would *have* to be run by the New York State Health Department. Upon closer inspection, however, it is clear that functional necessity was not the reason for these events. Contrary to resource dependence theory, the emergent division of labor in Binghamton did not reflect either the demands of efficiency or an agreement on which values should be pursued. For example, it was not until the PCB test results began to be returned from Chemlab that the state health department took an active interest in medical monitoring.

Neither the demands of the tasks themselves nor the imperatives of trading scarce resources led to the eventual distribution of tasks. Instead, organizations negotiating a definition of acceptable levels of risk played a major role in determining responsibility. These conflicts and disagreements were not simple disputes between technicians over trivial details, but political battles over basic questions of legitimacy and accountability. During phase one, "the problem" came to mean other organizations, not the SOB itself. Until interagency competition abated, the demands of the exposed individuals and the building cleanup were relegated to a secondary status.

In one sense there was a chorus of agreement: The players in the State Office Building drama all professed—sincerely, I believe—a strong commitment to public health. Yet, as I have argued, meta-goals such as "public health" and "acceptable risk" are of little help in understanding how organizations make tragic choices. Given the uncertainties engendered by the SOB fire, these goals could hardly be more than wishes for a remote and vague future. Goals such as these are master metaphors for the processes through which social goods are organized and allocated. Behind the metaphors are organizations with choices to make, struggling among themselves over ways to control one another and their environments.

A second mark of this interorganizational garbage can was that *no organization, or set of organizations, possessed an obvious right, obligation, or mandate to deal with the tragedy.* OGS owned the building, but the effects of the accident transcended its walls. Ownership was therefore not a necessary and sufficient condition to establish authority over its disposition. In the language of garbage can theory, the situation lacked an "access structure" (March and Olsen 1979, 28–31).

Access structures are patterns of interaction that direct solutions to problems. The term "solution" does not necessarily imply meeting the requirements of a task so that a problem no longer exists. It simply denotes a range of alternatives, each of which might reasonably qualify as organizational policy. I have argued, as have March and Olsen, that organizations can be conceived of as repositories of solutions. Mechanisms (or the lack thereof) that direct organizations toward or away from problems are therefore social technologies used in making choices. Because the organizations in the garbage can phase lacked mandates and norms that clearly demarcated responsibilities, the flow of solutions to problems was not well regulated. As a result, the potential to influence decisions was fluid. We might hypothesize that access to decision making is pluralistic when access structures are not well defined.[3] This is one of the most important reasons why the county health department was able to shape policies in Binghamton, at least during phase one, even though it did not command superior tangible resources.

Another important consequence proceeded from the lack of an access structure among organizations. In chapter 3, I described the ease with which local, state, and federal government organizations were able to buffer themselves from the demands of the SOB. Indeed, of the potential pool of participants, most organizations were able to avoid becoming central players. In almost all those cases, administrators cited their lack of expertise. Closer inspection reveals, however, that lack of expertise explained these demurrals in only a few cases. Instead, a constellation of political demands both constrained and gave discretion to organizations seeking to distance themselves from the accident. When most organizations left the garbage can, what remained were the New York State Health Department and the Office of General Services, on the one hand, and the Broome County Health Department, on the other, to form an uncooperative set of organizations to whom the media, public, and other organizations turned for answers.

Political positions polarized early in phase one, as BCHD, OGS, and DOH tried to define what problems should receive attention and who should be the arbiter of reasonable policy. The organizations disputed control over resources and control over symbols. Throughout phase one, medical surveillance languished as organizations constrained one another into inaction. BCHD controlled the data from the blood tests and was committed to an extended study because, as its director put it, "like

---

3. Following a similar logic, Laumann, Knoke, and Kim (1985) argue that in turbulent environments the degree of interest in a policy domain is a crucial determinant of policy outcomes.

asbestos, these chemicals remain in the body and are carcino-
gens, so chronic surveillance seemed the best first reaction; the
study can always be limited later." But DOH sought to wrest
the data and unanalyzed samples from BCHD, doubted that
the SOB posed any important risk, and thus doubted the very
merit of medical surveillance. DOH finally agreed that some
type of surveillance was appropriate, but state and county officials could not agree on who should qualify for inclusion in the
program. BCHD proposed testing everyone who might have
been exposed, "maybe one or two thousand people." State officials, however, wished to confine the definition of exposure to
those who could prove they were actually in the building (thus
excluding those whose route of exposure was the contaminated
garage or the surrounding environment). The two health departments disagreed on how surveillance would be conducted,
what body functions should be monitored, who should talk to
the media (and what should or should not be said), who should
be included in the study, and how the public should be informed.

BCHD maintained that DOH control of medical surveillance
entailed a conflict of interest, that more body functions should
be watched, that warnings should be given to pregnant women,
and that a disinterested expert in environmental medicine
should run medical monitoring. While under Schecter's direction, the county health department exhibited a policy of openness with the media, proposed the inclusion of four times more
subjects in the study than the state health department, and pro-
moted a relatively open decision-making process. After several
futile attempts to iron out these differences, and some critical
exchanges in the media, DOH threatened not to pay a local
hospital for services it authorized and withdrew BCHD's warrant to state funds, seven weeks after the accident. Not until
after Schecter was fired, at the end of what I have labeled phase
one, was a research protocol developed for medical monitoring. (Indeed, an organized medical monitoring program did
not begin until a year after the fire.) The state's study includes
only those who can prove they were exposed within the State
Office Building.

But BCHD was able to wield another type of influence even after losing control of important tangible resources. Under ambiguous conditions, as March and Olsen (1979) suggest, symbols play a heightened role in social interaction. By maintaining close contact with the local media, acting as one might expect a cautious health department to act, BCHD gained access to an important social stepping-stone between state decision makers and their environments. As long as that relationship continued, BCHD was able to force OGS and DOH (as well as county officials) to respond to criticism and thus to modify important policies. It was not until the end of the first phase that state organizations gained symbolic control of the SOB.

A final characteristic of this interorganizational garbage can was that *mechanisms for information exchange were unrestricted.* In phase one, the media had direct access to administrators and workers, even though state organizations issued an order, on March 1, 1981, that only official representatives were authorized to speak to the media. Until September 1981 (nine months after the accident), interchanges among officials, scientists, and the media were frequent and published. As one might expect, this relationship was not always cooperative. Officials were not always candid, and there was the occasional inflammatory headline ("State May Leave Some PCBs," "The Tower of Death"). But media access to policymakers and experts facilitated relatively open, if somewhat crude, public debate over important issues. Scientists, bureaucrats, and policymakers could barely mention plans about public health and cleanup without reporters questioning reasons and intentions (and sometimes suggesting alternatives of their own).

At first, reporters were as unfamiliar with the strange, deadly substances as everyone else, so they developed their own networks of experts to explain the complexities and dangers of what they were trying to report. This mining of technical expertise allowed reporters to ask informed questions about public health and policy. In arming themselves with technical minutiae, reporters often served as links between opposing views. Although not frictionless conduits, these links were often more effective than official dialogues. Fortified with the testimony of a chemist, for example, who had discussed the minuscule amounts of dioxin necessary to induce birth defects, reporters would then ask those in policy-making positions what they intended to do to avoid the dread effects. It would stretch the point to argue that the media served as watchdogs, but they did serve as an important mechanism through which the question of acceptable risk could be posed to those with the political responsibility to decide such issues.

These observations about the media are important. Risk assessment literature tends to view the media as conveyors of misleading or inaccurate information regarding risks (Combs and Slovic 1979; Slovic, Fischhoff, and Lichtenstein 1979; Wildavsky 1979; Douglas and Wildavsky 1982), thus causing the public, and others, to hold unreasoned and unreasonable positions concerning hazards. The progression of events in Binghamton suggests that this perspective is not very useful. During phase one, the media did not display the sensationalism one might expect from ill-informed reporters, but, rather, struggled in earnest, and usually with success, to understand what they were trying to report. When given access, reporters interviewed decision makers and experts as frequently as possible. Of course, this meant contradictions were bound to appear, because officials and experts were contradicting one another and themselves. But there is no evidence, from Binghamton at least, that accurate portrayals of these contradictions and the internal conflict in organizations (whose task it is to solve problems) necessarily lead to irrational publics or demands for excessive caution. Indeed, because definitions of acceptable risk, like most important public issues, are fundamentally about political value and moral choice, there is every reason to *encourage* the media to report conflicting and contradictory positions.

These contours—competing definitions of the problem, lack of centralized authority, and political accountability (through the media) of decision makers—were the major characteristics of the interorganizational garbage can in phase one.

Phase Two: The Action Set

By the beginning of phase two, all the organizations except for BCHD, DOH, and OGS had extracted themselves (or been pushed away) from the problems in Binghamton. As phase two progressed, BCHD's role was lessened, and authority, information, and power became centralized in state organizations. An amorphous collection of more or less independent organizations emerged, with a structured division of labor—or what Aldrich (1979) calls an "action set." An action set is "a group of organizations that have formed a temporary alliance for a limited purpose" (see also Aldrich and Whetten 1981). Like organization sets (Evan 1966) and, sometimes, networks (Milner 1980; Mintz and Schwartz 1985), action sets tend to develop a normative order for effective decision making and efficient allocation of resources. Implicit in this idea is that the members of an action set hold a domain consensus (Levine and White 1961), or mutual agreement on a division of responsibilities, and that the allocation of tasks among the organizations is based on comparative advantage. Although by the beginning of phase two there was indeed a structure to the organizational field (Warren 1967), the ability to structure the participation of other groups in key decisions was more important to the process of constructing solutions than either expertise or efficiency.

In phase two, state organizations established themselves as the legitimate "owners" of the SOB's risks, thus resolving the issue of symbolic or ideological control. Gusfield (1981) argues that the ability of actors to establish "ownership" of risk centrally shapes the construction of solutions to public problems. In the context of this study, this means that once issues of responsibility and legitimate authority were settled, some solutions to the problem of the toxic SOB had a higher probability of being pursued than others. After state organizations successfully came to own the building's risks, there was little likelihood that the destruction of the building would be publicly considered. Similarly, the scope of medical surveillance became very narrowly defined, excluding potentially important symptoms (reproductive failures, mental health) of concern to the exposed individuals.

After open challenges to the state's authority began to wane, the Office of General Services began a publicity campaign to dispel the widespread distrust of its policies expressed by the media, the public, the Citizens' Committee, and others. In a series of open meetings, the public was granted symbolic opportunities to influence decisions. At these meetings, DOH and OGS officials explained, "in laymen's terms," what they intended to do and how. But it would be a mistake to describe these gatherings as an attempt to involve the public in defining acceptable risk. The agendas of the meetings were arranged so that substantial criticisms did not arise, data were not released until the meeting, and the presentations were arcane and did not answer the questions to which outsiders sought answers. Sometimes the meetings were held during working hours, which prevented most citizens from attending.

By the end of phase two, the only legitimate interpretations of scientific data and solutions were those proposed by the state's department of health and the Office of General Services. Questions of acceptable risk and adequate medical surveillance no longer received the public attention they once had (although Citizens' Committee meetings, letters to the editors of the local papers, and Schecter's speaking engagements tried to rekindle debate). Once state organizations owned the State Office Building's risks, plans for decontamination and medical surveillance began to take shape. In phase two, the state hired a professional toxic-cleanup firm to develop plans for decontamination. That firm, as I argued in chapter 6, was an important part of the solution to the toxic problem.

As the structure of relationships among organizations developed, the production and dissemination of information became centralized. Questions from public representatives were increasingly referred to public relations personnel, who distributed "press-type information." One consequence of this tight coupling of organizations with information was that issues once debated openly (e.g., Acceptable to whom? Healthy according to what standards?) became inaccessible to all but those most closely allied with state organizations. In addition, state officials met with editors of the local papers and convinced them to relax their criticism of state actions. During phase one, reporters spent a large part of their time researching the intricacies of toxic chemicals and interviewing the many people who might influence policy. They interviewed dissidents and tracked down unofficial leads. During phase two, reporters relied far more heavily on quotes from officials. Thus, accompanying the state's assumption of the SOB's risks was the elimination of an important mechanism of political debate—the crucial element, of course, in all questions of acceptable risk.

Interestingly, formal risk assessments (which, according to rationalist-decision theory ought to be mechanisms that structure social action) were not generated until *after* the key decisions had been reached (see fig. 2, last line).

The Structural Basis of Individual Dissent

The role of Dr. Arnold Schecter in the Binghamton case warrants comment. It is true that some of Schecter's personal characteristics were important in the Binghamton case. His training in preventive medicine and occupational health, his extraordinary energy and ability to articulate reasonable criticism in a short reaction time, and his willingness to openly question the authority of New York State both endeared him and made him a valuable asset to members of the media. During the State Office Building crisis, Schecter and the media developed a mutually beneficial relationship. He provided good copy by criticizing the state; the media, in turn, served as a mechanism through which he could voice his concerns. There are, nevertheless, at least two larger lessons.

First, it should be noted that Schecter did not overstep his mandate as the local health officer. Although state officials were quick to denounce Schecter and his actions as alarmist or self-serving, his actions and decisions were in fact those we might expect of any public health officer. At the same time, it is also true that by openly criticizing state, and sometimes county, policy Schecter was putting his job as county health director in jeopardy, and in this sense his actions were *not* what we might expect from any public health officer. The solution to this apparent puzzle is not found in Schecter's personal qualities but in his structural position. Although Schecter was director of the

Broome County Health Department, he was also a tenured professor at SUNY Binghamton's medical school. He thus had a secure position enjoyed by few county health commissioners. To the extent that Schecter was responsible for generating public debate regarding important policies and decisions, he was able to do so because he was occupationally secure. This observation is disturbing, for it suggests that in instances like Binghamton's, the public may not be able to count on local health officers to protect their interests.

Second, although during phase one the media and the county health director frequently traded information, after Schecter's ouster, he no longer enjoyed the status of quoted critic. Why? The local papers were not co-opted until *after* Schecter was ousted, so that does not account for his subsequent neglect by the media. And Schecter's expertise as a physician and public health official did not disappear simply because he no longer worked for the county. One lesson to learn from Schecter's role is that access to an organizational base of power is an important intervening variable in disputes over legitimacy. Even given Schecter's personal qualities, it is the office that is important, not the person, whatever the person's qualifications. Losing his institutional legitimacy meant losing his status as expert, and being known as an expert increases the probability of attention from the media (Gans 1979; Pearson 1984).

Theories of Choice

Theories about how problems are solved highlight certain aspects of organizational behavior and, by necessity, neglect others. In the simplest model, complete and valid information is passed through the organization to those at the top, who then choose one solution from several or many. In this model (the theory of rational choice), selection of alternatives is governed by demands of efficiency and the criteria of organizational effectiveness. The theory requires these criteria, as well as decision makers' preferences, to be well defined. Otherwise, enough uncertainty is introduced into the model that its predictive powers are considerably lessened. Obvious uses of this overly rational model of decision making are elusive. The model is slippery because it is more often assumed than argued explicitly. No theorist of decision making (save perhaps the neo-classical economist) openly argues completely rational choice. Yet any given issue of *Administrative Science Quarterly*, a major scholarly journal on organizations, will contain an article that covertly adopts the tenets of rational choice theory. Most often, these tenets are found in works that do not directly address decision making, thus obscuring the authors' rationalist assumptions. But this should not lead us to think the theory of rational choice is chimerical.[4]

Garbage can theory was developed to counter theories in which power and rationality drive decision making (Lutz 1982; Tasca 1983). In this view, the components of an organizational system—people, problems, solutions, choices—are only loosely coupled and often vary independently of one another (Weick 1976). In theories of rational choice, the power to command, hierarchically structured offices (each with a regulated amount of authority), and the demands of completing tasks are the keys to understanding how choices are made. March and Olsen (1979) argue, instead, that a choice results from the fortuitous coincidence of the components of an organizational system. James March (1978, 592) explains that the garbage can model emphasizes "the extent to which choice behavior is embedded in a complex of other claims on the attention of actors and other structures of social and cognitive relations." What is important in choice situations is not the interests of elites, but rather the constellation of competing demands on potential participants' time: the opportunity costs of making decisions. People cannot attend to many problems at once, do not have stable and ordered preferences, and often are unable to understand what their organizations are or should be doing. In this model, ends and means bear no obvious connection to each other, nor are action and intention always related. Instead, organizations act and produce goals only when they are chal-

4. Even if it were impossible to find a theory of rational choice, there would still be value in creating one, if only to serve as a background against which alternative views could be compared.

lenged to render sensible accounts of their actions (Scott and Lyman 1968; March and Olsen 1979, 71–75).

The garbage can metaphor is useful because it provides a way of thinking about organizational processes that differs from deterministic models (Mohr 1982). It is especially useful for drawing attention to organizational behavior under ambiguous conditions, i.e., situations in which goals are unclear, technologies are ill defined, and rights to participate in major decisions are in flux. Rather than coordinating their behaviors so that organizations move toward well-understood ends, participants often behave in ways that reflect no plan. Situational rationality reigns in ambiguous contexts. Garbage can theory has caused us to research *the conditions under which* rationalist theories can explain organizational behavior and the conditions under which they cannot.

The model underestimates the importance of power in organizational life, however, and I doubt that the elements of an organizational system are as "randomly organized" as garbage can theory would have us believe. In universities (supposedly the ideal-typical organized anarchies), for example, power may be more widely dispersed than it is in an oil company, and departments may be more loosely linked than they are in an army, but it is still not usually the case that lower participants enjoy the same probability of influencing important decisions as do those at the top of the hierarchy. Although this is admittedly an oversimplification, *single* organizations are more accurately described as a division of labor based on legitimated authority, with the subunits designed to transform some raw material, than as a conglomeration of disjointed elements, randomly colliding in a system in which meaning is forever equivocal.

A *group* of organizations, however, *is* more like a garbage can (or a crowd), having neither an institutionalized structure to coordinate its members nor a centralized office that issues orders. Moreover, with an *inter*organizational garbage can, as in the first phase in Binghamton, entry and exit into decision opportunities are relatively easy, and there is no hierarchy that clearly delimits authority and power among organizations. The principles of garbage can theory are thus most applicable at the level of *interorganizational* analysis.

A variant of this nonrational model of decision making, specifically cast at the level of interagency relationships, has been suggested by Norton Long (1958), who analyzed organizations within communities and asserted that a local community should be conceived as "an ecology of games." Games are activities in which social players such as organizations, interest groups, and publics vie for participation. The rules of any single game are fixed and known, but the "social game," or the general creation of social order, is neither well structured nor understood by the players. A community is not a single structure of services and power; rather, organizations in a community pursue their own interests and in the process mesh their behaviors with that of others to produce social equilibrium. Because all these games (read "organizations") are relatively isolated from one another, there is scant formal coordination. Long's metaphor is problematic because it assumes, much as March and Olsen's does within organizations, that the lack of formal interagency coordination means that the distribution of power among a group of gamesters is inconsequential. Although the insights of March and Olsen and Long are most useful at the level of interorganizational analysis, their theories must be modified to accommodate the role of power in models of decision making.

The nature of power changed during the two phases in Binghamton. In the first phase, nodes of power often shifted from organization to organization in a relatively unpatterned, if not completely random, manner. Later, after most organizations had "exited" the garbage can, power became stabilized in state organizations. The kind of power in Binghamton was not the overwhelming, direct control of one actor by another (although there were significant examples of this). Instead, power was important in Binghamton because it helped to determine what would be considered the legitimate content of policies.

Gusfield (1981) studied how the popular image of the "killer drunk" was created. He found little objective evidence that drunken drivers are a major social problem. Among the most important factors that contributed to the "killer drunk" myth were the institutional interests that defined the terms of the drinking and driving debate. One consequence of the influence of various organizations on defining drinking and driving as a social problem was that individuals are viewed as a major threat on our highways. Yet there is nothing inherent in traffic accidents that requires a focus on individual action (Gusfield 1981, 174). Other ways to name the problem might be "an unforgiving automotive design" or "a highway system that induces tragedy." Attributions of responsibility change when tragic choices (or any choices) are placed in a larger context that includes other factors.

Similarly, if control of the State Office Building's risks had been more broadly distributed, rather than the state assuming all decision opportunities, different solutions to cleanup and medical surveillance might have been applied.

Symbols and Organizational Deceit

At several points I have examined how symbols—expert knowledge, scientific studies, risk assessments—are used in situations that entail important choices. Sometimes these symbols were used as devices to conceal certain facts or interests. Yet, in only a few of those instances was there a deliberate organizational plan to defraud an environment. Instead, each instance of deception made sense within the immediate context of making trade-offs between organizational and public health. It is true that officials setting policy for DOH, for example, often constructed an organizational face that was opaque to the public. Facts, studies, findings, and problems were sometimes presented in ways that did not accurately reflect how they were being used and studied within the organization. There were also several instances in which DOH suppressed "alarming" evidence of the SOB's hazards, but readily released "calming" evidence.

In each of these instances there were important differences between what organizational representatives said and what they did. One explanation for this discrepancy, popular in Binghamton, is the "steamroller theory," which holds that officials were lying, incompetent, and callously conspiring to deceive a public unable to resist manipulation. This theory conjures up an image of a New York State juggernaut, its organizations unified in purpose, agreed on means, and politically homogeneous. The steamroller explanation fails, however, because it implies omniscient rationality and extraordinary cunning among elites, and complete integration within and among organizations. Even during the second phase, when conspiracies and cover-ups would have been easiest to carry out, less than perfect coordination and homogeneity prevailed. Instead of full rationality, we witnessed tightly bounded rationality, as elites muddled through ambiguous situations, constructing solutions before goals were known, and without any assurances they would solve problems (Lindblom 1959, 1979). Far from incompetent, policymakers and scientists in the bureaucracies of New York State are widely regarded by their peers as among the best in the world.

A more plausible explanation for the difference between what elites do and what they say is that institutional environments demand rational accounts from organizations (DiMaggio and Powell 1983). One task of organizational leaders is to advance interpretations of their agents' behavior that will make sense outside the organization. For example, when the janitorial cleanup turned into a scandal, OGS officials nevertheless maintained that the effort was successful, although by any objective measure the cleanup succeeded only in increasing the likelihood that New York would incur lawsuits (and increase the risk to workers). The use of symbols in events and policies involving organizational deceit—particularly where ambiguous risks are involved—is therefore best understood as an attempt to conform with environmental demands for rationality. Unfortunately, we can take little comfort from the implication that deliberate lying and treachery are probably not very central problems in situations involving hazards to public health. In instances of significant risk, organizations most often take into account the expectations and demands of other organizations when constructing policy and devising action. In these cases, publics, as unorganized masses without access to concentrated resources, must find some mechanism that will synchronize their interests with those of organizations if they are to have their interests represented in official policy. In a world where important risks are defined and accepted mainly by organizations, the term "public interest" is a fiction.

The Sociology of Risk

One of the major themes of this book has been the organizational context of risk assessment. Most of the risk analysis literature has a decidedly psychological cast (for reviews, see Fischhoff 1977; Kates 1977; Cole and Withey 1981; Einhorn and Hogarth 1981; Covello, Menkes, and Nehnevajsa 1982). The major concerns of this research are the cognitive processes involved in individual assessment of hazard; experiments and attitude surveys are the major tools of data collection.

Two criticisms of the risk assessment literature are relevant here. First, psychological studies of risk lack a conception of social structure that connects perceptions of risk with the formation of policy. Instead, the literature assumes that individuals are the crucial assessors and acceptors of risk in our society. It therefore rests on the premise that policymakers are determined by, and will reflect the views of, society as a whole. But the evidence from Binghamton, Love Canal, Three Mile Island, Michigan, Times Beach, and Bhopal suggests—contrary to the psychology of risk—that organizations, not disparate members of the general population, are the final arbiters of hazard. Such studies have neglected the processes by which important decision makers evaluate and accept risks, and so have missed the crucial processes through which risk assessment proceeds.

Second, the field of risk analysis seems to presume that choice among hazards should follow a rational model of decision making. As I indicated, much of this research focuses on individuals' risk perceptions (Cole and Withey 1981; Slovic, Fischhoff, and Lichtenstein 1982). Many argue that individuals' sources of information (mainly television and newspapers) systematically distort the data on which individuals base their assessments (Lichtenstein et al. 1978; Combs and Slovic 1979). Moreover, because people cannot digest the large amounts of information available for popular consumption, they devise ways to order those data—they make sense of hazards in ways that confirm stereotypes about the way the world works. The stereotypes often fit the data well (Slovic, Fischhoff, and Lichtenstein 1980).

To determine when subjects' guesses are accurate, their risk assessments must be compared to some standard. One standard for comparison is a model of rational decision making, where "rational" means logical and systematic information search. With this method, subjects' guesses are compared with statistical compilations of probability distributions of risks to human health. For example, Slovic, Fischhoff, and Lichtenstein (1979) found that students and members of the League of Women Voters estimated the risk of accidental death as more likely than death caused by disease, even though disease claims fifteen times as many lives per year as accidents. Another standard for comparison is expert knowledge, where the public's risk assessments are matched with those of experts. Slovic, Fischhoff, and Lichtenstein (1979) report that when experts confine their guesses to their specialty areas, they offer better estimates of risks than do nonexperts. One explanation for the differences between these groups is that nonexperts are unaware of actual data on the risks of certain technologies and activities. Nonexperts, for example, consistently underestimate the aggregate hazards of lawn mowers and overestimate the likelihood of a major accident at a nuclear power plant.

Using either of these two standards (probability distributions or experts) yields comparisons that can be interpreted to mean that feared risks receive disproportionate attention, or, to put it simply, that people worry too much. Lester Lave (1984) and Aaron Wildavsky (1979), for example, two well-known authors in the field, respectively argue that low-level risks should be dismissed, and that conflicts between groups over questions of hazard may cripple our economic system.

These findings imply that risk analysis could be used to inform decision makers, providing them a way to rank their preferences, thus facilitating a more rational process of choice. Meyer and Solomon (1984, 246), for example, argue that formal risk assessments "may yield better policy judgments" than other ways of decision making (such as reacting to the demands of interest groups or complying with federal regulations). Risk assessment, in this view, is a method of purging values and political judgments from choice opportunities. Meyer and Solomon argue, in effect, that policymakers could be more effective if their decisions more closely conformed to the dictates of instrumental or formal rationality (Weber 1978, 24–26). It is possible that under certain relatively clear conditions, risk analysis can indeed serve as a tool to gather and systematize information for rational choice.[5] But under ambiguous conditions, decision makers are confronted with too much information whose meaning is equivocal (Sabatier 1978; Feldman and March 1981), and meaning must be clear for ordered preferences to be of value.

If risk analysis were indeed a tool of rational choice, we would expect a clear, agreed-upon definition of the hazard and an extensive data-collection effort on a wide variety of options. This information would then be used to construct alternative goals. Because, strictly speaking, the acceptability of risk is a political, rather than a scientific, issue (Kantrowitz 1975; Fischhoff 1977; Kates 1977; Calabresi and Bobbitt 1978; Mac-Lean 1982; Otway and Thomas 1982), we would expect to find the values of many groups reflected in the evaluation process.

But sociological research suggests that risks are rarely, if ever, assessed in a rational manner. Allan Mazur (1973), in a careful analysis of debates over water fluoridation in the 1950s and nuclear power in the 1960s, shows that institutional location is strongly associated with how experts (the quintessential risk assessors) pose questions and choose methods to answer them. Mazur's research shows that scientific data are more ambiguous than we usually presume. Consider, for example, a controversy over whether or not to build a nuclear power plant on an earthquake fault that has been inactive for forty thousand years. Proponents of the plant will argue in favor of construction because the fault is obviously stable; opponents will argue that building the plant is foolhardy because the lengthy interval since the last

5. The following are conditions under which a rational model of risk assessment might apply: (a) where structures of authority and power are unambiguous and stable, (b) where goals are familiar and easily defined, and (c) where technology is readily available (Clarke 1988).

earthquake means another is imminent. Mazur also found evidence that risk assessors tend to choose methods and data that support the position to which they are already committed. "We generally assume," he writes, "that informed scientific advice is valuable to political policy makers. However, in the context of a controversial political case, and when the relevant technical analysis is ambiguous, then the value of scientific advice becomes questionable" (Mazur 1973, 261; see also Mazur 1975). Rather than determining policy, risk assessments in controversial situations are more likely to *reflect* alternatives already chosen.

Had the process of determining acceptable risk followed a rational model in Binghamton, formal assessments would have driven decisions regarding what to do with the building and those exposed. Yet, formal risk analyses proliferated only *after* competing definitions of acceptable risk were winnowed out; instead of preceding actions, risk assessment followed them. In addition, policies to decontaminate the State Office Building and to conduct a medical surveillance program were instituted far earlier than calculations of the costs and benefits of those programs.[6]

The use of formal risk analyses in Binghamton suggests a process of choice that is not captured by decision-making theories that stress goal definition, consideration of alternative solutions, and implementation of an optimal choice. In addition to being tools for rational decision making, risk assessments are also tools that help an organization construct a reality whereby the actions it has already taken will seem reasonable to elements in its environment (Meyer and Rowan 1977; Meyer and Scott 1983). As I argued above, risk assessments are claims to legitimacy that are directed at other organizations.

---

6. Formal assessments were constructed by VERSAR, Inc., as well as by the New York State Department of Health. After a Freedom of Information request yielded a copy of the contract between VERSAR and OGS, I discovered that VERSAR was required to file weekly progress reports with OGS. There are extensive references in those reports to cost-benefit analyses and risk assessments, although no conclusions are reported therein. OGS refused to release any of those assessments, claiming they were "under litigation."

Organizations, not individual members of society, are the most important risk assessors in our society. To understand how choices about risk are made, we need to accord more attention to the structural forces that impinge on decision makers. Some of these forces originate in the organizations in which policymakers are embedded, and some originate in the environments of those organizations. These structures and processes coalesce to constrain decision makers to make trade-offs between organizational resources and public health, and vice versa. The Binghamton case has allowed us to examine some of the processes whereby alternatives are chosen and some of the mechanisms that organizations use to guide their behavior in circumstances that provide few clues about the proper responses.

Appendix A:
The Players

Below is a listing of most of the participants in the Binghamton story, arranged by organizational affiliation. The first section lists public organizations (which are then organized by level of government) and public figures, and the second lists private organizations and individuals.

Public Organizations and Figures

City of Binghamton
  Executive Office

Alfred Libous	Mayor
Owen Byrne	Personnel and Safety Director

  City Council

Judith Eggleston	President
James Testani	Chairperson, Municipal and Public Affairs Committee

  Fire Department

Edward Faughnan	Fire Chief
Donald Faughnan	Assistant Fire Chief

Broome County
  Executive Office

Carl Young	Executive
James Lee	Deputy Executive
John Murray	County Attorney

  Legislature

Cleon Barber	Majority leader; Republican
John Hanrihan	Public Health Committee member; Democrat
Jeffrey Kraham	Chairperson, Legislature; Republican
Deborah Quackenbush	Chairperson, Public Health Committee; Republican

Joseph Svoboda   Representative; Democrat
Health Department
Arnold Schecter   Director
Kathleen Gaffney   Deputy Commissioner, later
                                Health Commissioner
Roland Austin   Director, Environmental
                                Health Services
John Buckley   Consultant, State Office
                                Building

New York State
Executive Office
Hugh Carey   Governor
John Burns   Governor's Appointment
                                Secretary

Office of General Services
Arthur Beaudoin   Senior Public Building
                                Manager
Tom Cooper   Public Relations Officer
John Egan   Commissioner
John Hudacs   Deputy Commissioner
Edward Mosher   Engineer; advisor to Seiffert,
                                February 1981
David Seiffert   Engineer; director of first
                                cleanup, February 1981
James Wahl   Superintendent, Binghamton
                                State Office Building
Lois Whittemore   Guard in State Office
                                Building at time of fire

New York Health Department
David Axelrod   Commissioner
George Eadon   Director of Toxicology
John Eadie   Assistant Director of the local
                                Health Management
                                Department
Edward Fitzgerald   Epidemiologist
Glenn Haughie   Director, Office of Public
                                Health

Robert Huffaker	Associate Director, Office of Public Health
Patrick O'Keefe	Scientist, Division of Laboratories and Research
Susan Standfast	Physician
Philip Taylor	Epidemiologist

Department of Transportation

Gary Peterson	Regional oil-spill engineer

Federal

Environmental Protection Agency

Walter Barber	Acting administrator
Donald Barnes	Cochairperson, Dioxins Work Group
Paul Brown	Cochairperson, Dioxins Work Group
Joseph Lafornara	Scientist, Environmental Response Team
Peter Niemick	Attorney, Enforcement Division
Joseph Spitola	Scientist
Kenneth Stoller	Superfund Program Manager

National Institute of Occupational Safety and Health

Philip Landrigan	Director, Division of Surveillance, Hazard Evaluations, and Field Studies
James Melius	Physician
Philip Taylor	Epidemiologist

Centers for Disease Control

Renate Kimbrough	Director
Clark Heath	Director, Chronic Diseases Division

U.S. Congress

Alfonse D'Amato	Senator, New York; Republican

Daniel P. Moynihan — Senator, New York; Democrat

Small Business Administration
Michael Cardenas — Administrator
John Jennings — Office of Disaster Policy
Miscellaneous
Richard Schweiker — Secretary, Health and Human Services

Alvin Young — Environmental scientist; Major, U.S. Air Force, involved with Agent Orange studies

Miscellaneous
Norbert Adler — Founder, Citizens' Committee

Bruce Drazen — Binghamton businessperson; helped form an association of local business owners to ask for low-interest loans from Small Business Administration

Louis Giordano — President, Broome County Medical Society

John Moore — Deputy director, National Toxicology Program, U.S. Department of Health and Human Services

Christoffer Rappe — Chemist, University of Umea, Sweden

David Stalling — Chief chemist, Fish and Wildlife Service, U.S. Department of the Interior

Robert Tardiff — Executive Director, Board of Toxicology and Environmental Health Hazards, National Research Council

Thomas Tiernan — Chemist, Wright State University

| Arthur Upton | Chairperson, Institute of Environmental Medicine, New York University Medical Center |

Private Organizations

The Binghamton Press (Binghamton Press, Inc. owns the two local newspapers in Binghamton: the *Sun Bulletin* and the *Evening Press*. Reporters are identified by "SB" or "EP.")

Andy Cohen	Reporter (SB)
Mike Doll	Managing editor
Jim East	Reporter (EP)
Phil Fairbanks	Reporter (SB)
Lois Fecteau	Reporter (EP)
Steve Geimann	Reporter (SB)
Steve Jones	Reporter (EP)
Gail Roberts	Reporter (SB)
Steve Spero	Reporter (EP)

Schenectady Gazette

| Doug Miller | Reporter |

New England Pollution Control (NEPCO)

| Vincent Brigante | President |

Binghamton General Hospital

| Jason Moyer | Chief Executive Officer |
| David Slaunwhite | Administrative Coordinator, Laboratory |

Appendix B:

A Methodological Accounting

In this appendix I discuss the virtues and faults of my data sources, some justifications for a case study, and a few ethical dilemmas.

Interviews

The method I used to find people to interview was akin to snowball sampling. As my first contact in Binghamton, Arnold Schecter suggested the first "key players" to talk to. Because key players are always embedded in networks of other key players, I was led to about two hundred telephone interviews and sixty-five face-to-face interviews, approximately twenty of which were return visits.[1] Although I interviewed people across a broad spectrum of status and organizational location, I deliberately skewed my sample to represent those who were in positions to make important decisions. For the most part, organizations were the crucial players in the Binghamton case, and it has been their decisions and accounts on which I have spent the most time.

I conducted three weeks of interviews in Binghamton and one week in Albany.[2] I also conducted interviews in New York City and Washington, D.C. I tried to arrange interviews with everyone who played a role in developing policies concerning the State Office Building and the exposed people, as well as with workers, bureaucrats, scientists, engineers, and technicians. In general, I met little resistance in Binghamton. Respondents in Albany, however, were considerably more hesitant and were more suspicious of my motives. One DOH official accused me of being a journalist. State officials' reluctance can be explained by potential legal liability and the specter of Love Canal fresh in their memories. Despite this overall reluctance,

1. The list of interviews that follows the references reflects the interviews cited in the book. It is not a full accounting of all the interviews I conducted.

2. An excellent source on the methodology of interviewing—ways to build rapport, gather sensitive information, talk to people while guarding against being misinformed, and protect informants—is Woodward and Bernstein's *All the President's Men* (1976).

many state policymakers, and those close to them, granted me useful interviews.

One risk of interview data is the possibility that informants may not tell the truth, may distort facts, may be evasive, and in general may issue only "press-type information," to use the words of one of my respondents. This hazard confronts every field researcher (as it does every survey researcher). We invade people's personal and professional lives, ask them to divulge information they may not admit even to themselves, let alone to some stranger whose purpose is to analyze and publish what they say. The problem is pervasive in research such as that reported here, where lawsuits are on everyone's mind and people (especially elites) are regularly subjected to considerable embarrassment for saying things they must later retract ("The building will be open in two weeks"; "We will not do medical surveillance"). Indeed, this research challenge is endemic to all studies on organizations, because one of the things that bureaucracies do, after all, is keep outsiders from knowing where the skeletons are, by acting as if everything is rational and under control.

This last problem is particularly troublesome when one ventures beyond the boundaries of rational decision making. How is it possible to study anarchy and nonrationality when the basic research tool, the interview, demands that informants have good organizational sense and give rational accounts? Put another way, it is hard to imagine any of the Binghamton respondents saying something such as, "Well, no, we really didn't know what was going on, and, frankly, did not give enough thought to what exposed people might think, so we did the first thing that occurred to us." It is even harder to imagine that any respondent *could* say, in more academic prose:

> Our preferences were not well ordered, and a wide range of alternatives were not embedded in our standard operating procedures and, so, did not receive much attention. In fact, often we did not seem to have any preferences at all, contrary to what rational theory predicts, because they frequently changed in response to environmental demands. At times, we failed to properly scan our environments and so did not anticipate the reactions of other organizations. Our problem-solving processes were further distorted when we began to make trade-offs between organizational interests and public health.

The only effective way to study loosely coupled behavior is to compare actual behavior with what people say about their behavior, and then to compare both to predictions from available social theory. This strategy requires the frank admission that respondents can misinterpret important parts of their organizations and environments, thus raising the problem of deception.

Fortunately, deliberate deceptions are usually about facts ("I did not say that" or "We did not commit that act"), and if I was unable to verify a "fact" with another source, I did not use it. Fading memories and the reconstruction of events that differ from what actually happened are two other serious problems. As often as possible I double-checked facts and interpretations. For example, if someone relayed something that was not verified by other witnesses, I usually went back to that respondent for further clarification. Although there is no way to be absolutely sure that bad memories and selective reinterpretations did not contaminate my data, I believe that the data I gathered were of the highest quality possible.

A Possible Bias

The study began through my connection with Arnold Schecter. Because I had unrestricted access to him, some of my questions in early interviews were colored in ways that probably revealed our association to some of my respondents. For example, when I asked the county executive about points of contention between Schecter's lawyers and the county over the proposed consultant's contract, he could surmise only that, for me to have commanded so much detail, Schecter had to have been my source. I cannot estimate the extent to which people who knew of this association responded differently because of it. The most effective check on this bias is the skill of conveying impartiality that one develops in the field (see Douglas 1976).[3]

Interview Technology

The tape recorder as a data-gathering instrument is regarded with suspicion, the most common criticisms being that people are less likely to be open and that it dampens spontaneity, making responses less reliable. For reasons of efficiency, I nevertheless decided to try

3. However, there were also times when this association worked in my favor. Some informants were more open than they otherwise would have been, precisely *because* they thought I was Schecter's agent; i.e., they saw the chance to set me straight on questions about which I might have (in their view) been misled.

the recorder in face-to-face interviews, and I learned that tape does not seem to compromise the quality of responses. Generally, I found that politicians and those used to speaking in public did not mind the tape machine. Laypersons and scientists, however, were more reluctant to be recorded.

I developed another method that increased interviewing efficiency. After returning from my trips, I immediately transcribed the tapes and typed up notes from those I did not record. I then made a cleaner version of the nonrecorded interview notes, editing them for readability, and sent them to respondents for further comments or additions. My cover letter said I was sending my notes in order to verify their accuracy, explaining that there were some things I had missed in the interview or did not understand from my notes, and asked for clarification. If the interview had been recorded, I added a section at the end of the transcript that was more or less my interpretation of what the respondent had said. This addendum served several functions. First, for the unrecorded interviews, it allowed the respondent to correct any factual errors. Second, by including some interpretation in the interview notes, I engaged in some unobtrusive inquiry. There were always some questions I was not able to ask during the interview; also, sometimes, a question was so politically sensitive that to have asked it face-to-face would have jeopardized the interview. Thus, in the interview notes I sent to respondents for their perusal and correction, I included interpretations of what had been said that my informants had not offered themselves. Most of the time, I nevertheless received answers and clarifications that were clear and thorough. If the informant did not react to the nonanswers, I did not use them. Judging from the answers to my notes and questions, most respondents carefully read the interview notes. I always received a reply, usually with copious notes and useful additions. They *always* responded to the interpretive sections of the interview notes, sometimes simply with a shorthand indicating agreement (e.g., an "ok" in the margin), and sometimes going on to give their own perception of the problem—which, of course, was part of what I was trying to elicit in the face-to-face interview.

Newspapers

I relied on newspaper articles to reconstruct events and for quotations from officials. Using the mass media as a source is tantamount to using accounts of accounts and raises serious problems of validity.[4] I do not believe my use of this data source has biased this study. I used newspaper articles to reconstruct events mainly for the first few months after the accident. Even then, my reliance on the articles was for gaining leads into the kinds of issues that needed exploring and the kinds of questions I needed to ask.

Politicians often complain about the media. The lament they most often voice is that their words are taken out of context and used in ways they did not intend. But this complaint is not really about accuracy, but about the meaning a journalist conveys by reporting facts and statements from different sources in the same article, thereby creating a context of meaning with which officials may disagree. Because the media, especially newspapers, were key actors in the Binghamton story, I usually asked my respondents their views of the mass media. Although officials often disagreed with the reporter's "slant" in an article, they usually testified that they had been quoted accurately. That is, they objected to the way their words had been used, but not to the reporting of what they had actually said. Moreover, after several interviews with each of the main reporters assigned to the SOB story (there were three or four from both of Binghamton's papers), I developed strong confidence in their professional ethics and journalistic skills.

I subscribed to both of Binghamton's newspapers for about two years, which eventually provided a comprehensive collection of articles that I used to construct chronologies and assemble quotations. In addition, because of the scholarly nature of my research, the two newspapers granted me unrestricted access to their morgues.

Freedom of Information Requests

One of my most fruitful sources was state and federal freedom of information (FOI) requests.[5] One of the things bureaucracies do is

4. See Mintz and Schwartz (1985) for more detailed discussion of the value of using the mass media as a data source.
5. The Freedom of Information Service Center is a nonprofit organization that publishes guidelines for researchers, journalists, and scholars on how to use state and federal Freedom of Information acts; the center also provides sample letters and instructions on how to appeal denials and how to work the bureaucracy designed to handle freedom of information requests. (Write to FOI Service Center, 800 18th Street, N.W., Washington, D.C. 20006 for copies.)

produce files, and freedom of information requests give one (limited) access to those files. After the project had been under way for several months, one of my respondents referred to what he claimed was a fact. He also said his superiors would not be particularly happy if they knew it had been revealed. He told me that if I asked his superiors about the information, his identity would be apparent and would probably cost him his job. He suggested, however, that a freedom of information request—crafted vaguely enough so that the particular topic would not be revealed, yet targeted directly toward the area of interest—might yield confirmation of his story without implicating him. I thus submitted an FOI request to the public access officer at OGS for a copy of the contract between OGS and VERSAR, Inc., OGS's consultant. I learned from the contract that VERSAR was required to submit "weekly progress reports" to OGS. I also learned that VERSAR would be responsible for performing a series of formal risk assessments for OGS. I then submitted further requests for the weekly reports and risk assessments, which themselves suggested other documents of potential use. Another example of how FOI requests were helpful, this time with the state health department, was my use of bibliographies from DOH papers to find the titles of papers that had *not* been made public. I would then ask for these through an FOI request. In this way my collection of documents snowballed until, finally, the cost (usually 25 cents per page) prohibited further expansion of my file.

The Utility of Case Studies

Case studies, some hold, are the bane of organizational research (Campbell and Stanley 1966; Miles 1979; cf. Campbell 1975; Yin 1981). Case studies are cursed with a familiar list of faults: They cannot be used to generalize to a larger class of events (cf. Kruskal 1978; Kennedy 1979); they fail to provide enough controls, and therefore the most important factors cannot be isolated; and, worst of all, they lend an unchecked freedom of interpretation to the author. There are important qualifications, however, to this list of evils.

Any attempt to generalize to a class of events from a single case is doomed to fail, it is said, because the laws of probability do not permit extrapolation from an N of 1 (cf. Dukes 1965). This criticism of case studies is basically sound, but it should be qualified in two ways. First, case study researchers do indeed generalize to a larger class of events, but they do so with considerably less confidence than they would if their generalizations were supported by probability theory (Kruskal

1978). In the present case, I believe the processes reported here would probably be found in other cases in which several, or many, organizations interact in unexpected ways within an ambiguous environment. Of course, my confidence in this generalization is primarily based on sociological judgment and comparison with similar cases.

Second, case studies provide an opportunity to study social processes in depth. This advantage is not inherent in case study research, but concentrating one's research efforts on one case does allow maximum investment of data-gathering resources (e.g., time). As Diesing (1971) and Mohr (1982) point out, two basic sets of epistemological assumptions underlie most social science research. The first and most explicit set of assumptions is found in variance research. In such research, variables are chosen in advance, and the investigator's interest is to specify determinant relationships among them. Both the specific value and limitation of variance research is that the researcher focuses on a handful of the aspects of some situation, ignoring the rest (Diesing 1971, 269). In those cases, the scientists' concepts and procedures are, more often than in case study research, clearly defined, usually before the research begins. Case studies usually sacrifice opportunities to examine specific relationships, mainly because they typically lack the kinds of controls one finds in variance research. All research lacks something, and the trade-off is usually between comprehensiveness and detail (see Weick 1979, chap. 2, for a dissection of this dilemma). Basically, there are two ways to handle this problem: (1) study a carefully delimited set of variables, or (2) study a little of everything with the hope of rendering a holistic account (Diesing 1971, 279). One of the greatest benefits offered by case studies is the opportunity to investigate the full context of a social situation rather than being confined to the variables to which one has access.[6]

A potentially more serious charge against case studies is that the absence of statistical or comparative controls bars one from saying anything conclusive about the topic under study. For example, I can quite logically claim that the process of accepting risk is more a process of defeating dissent than creating consensus. But one could legitimately question how I know for sure that I have isolated the most important parts of the process of creating acceptable risk. Not by way of defense, but by way of putting this criticism into perspective, we should note that the only method that really solves this problem is

---

6. These are central tendencies, of course, and not inherent in the methods themselves. The factors that most constrain researchers from combining these methods are probably time and money.

the controlled, randomized experiment. Even observational studies based on large databases must confine their controls to the variables at hand rather than concluding that all possible influences have been canvassed. That is why there is always a substantial portion of unaccounted-for variance in statistical studies. Statistical studies resemble qualitative case studies in that both use an interpretive framework or theory to provide the mechanism for controlling for significant influences on observed outcomes. But statistical studies suggest which variables to measure for later use as controls, whereas, for qualitative studies, theory building is an inductive exercise, so that variables are not conceptualized before data gathering begins. I would add that, for most case studies, there *are* controls for the myriad factors that could produce an outcome, but the tools of control are alternative ways of *explaining* observations, instead of other *observations* (Allison 1971; Davis 1974).

The final indictment against case studies—that they grant the researcher too much interpretive freedom—is a criticism against which I have few defenses. The temptation to make the data fit the favored interpretation always exists, and case studies lack the kinds of controls that confer great confidence that an accidental confluence of events has not produced the outcome one is trying to explain. This does not mean, I think, that the researcher is free to impose *any* interpretation on the data, because standards of logic will render some interpretations more plausible than others. Nevertheless, case studies are still plagued by the problem of too much interpretive freedom, at least until enough cases have been accumulated to provide analytic constraints on that freedom.

Case studies, with their nagging problems, annoying limitations, and egregious but necessary sins against standards of rigor that most researchers endeavor to reach, are counterbalanced by the saving graces of holistic research and by opportunities to suggest hypotheses and new directions for research. Ideally, if not always practically, case studies are useful stepping-stones to questions that can be answered with more explicitly operationalized concepts and specification of relationships among clearly delimited variables.

Ethics

It is hard to imagine a project that requires field research methods that would not present the researcher with ethical dilemmas. Ethical conflicts seem to me inherent in research where one intrudes into people's lives to ask that they reveal things that may embarrass either themselves or someone else (often their boss). If conflict is endemic in society and the researcher's aim is to investigate the various meanings of conflict among people who occupy different social locations, then differences of opinion are bound to test the integrity of the researcher. Lofty values of respect, fairness, and rights to privacy run headlong into the pragmatic demands of probing, teasing, and cajoling the truth out of people. Indeed, these values are immediately and inevitably compromised as soon as researchers assume they have the right to investigate how other people live their lives. And the profession of sociology does not give much guidance on how to resolve problems of professional ethics. A search of how other authors solved ethical dilemmas provides little help, because there is a great deal of variation in what is considered ethical. Another potential source of wisdom for resolving ethical dilemmas is the network of sociologists in which the researcher is located. Consulting colleagues about problems of ethics, although useful in many ways, is inevitably frustrating because even experienced field workers expound the same admonitions found in chapters on ethics and values in "Introduction to Methods" textbooks. In the end, one is left with what one began: one's own judgments about reconciling the demands of thorough research with the rights of those being researched. I made three judgment calls in the course of this study that might have had important effects on either the State Office Building story or the way I told it.

First, although in most interview research the promise of confidentiality is sacrosanct, many of my informants' names can be discerned from the text. My selective use of confidentiality is tied to the notion of informed consent, so I begin with how I handled that issue. Because no deception was involved in the study, and because the formality of signing a document would have been a bad way to begin interviews, I petitioned my university's committee on human subjects to modify the usual procedure. I took two documents to interviews, one the formal consent form, the other a simple letter introducing myself and my purpose. I gave all respondents the letter, explained what it was, and then told them I had the formal consent form if they wished to use it. In this way a potential boundary to developing good rapport (signing ceremonies) was turned into a mechanism of creating trust. No one asked for the formal consent form, but most smiled in appreciation when I handed them the letter of introduction.

I included the following sentence in both the letter and the consent form: "Any information you may provide will be respected as confidential, according to your wishes, since information and candid responses are more important to the researcher than individuals' names." The phrase "according to your wishes" was constructed so that my informants knew confidentiality would surely follow a direct request for it. The SOB story would have been much duller to tell and read if I could not directly represent the people who were living with those fascinating problems. Moreover, disguising many of the respondents would have been impossible and absurd. The most important function of confidentiality is to prevent those who know the subject from finding out what the subject says, thinks, or does. But even if I had disguised the players, the people in Binghamton and Albany would still know who I was writing about. Thus, unless I was asked for confidentiality, or unless a quotation might conceivably place the respondent in jeopardy, I usually tied my quotes to the people who uttered them.

The second and third judgment calls resulted from the same source. Soon after Kathleen Gaffney replaced Arnold Schecter as commissioner of the Broome County Health Department, I traveled to Binghamton for some interviews. Gaffney and I were talking about the number of experts to whom Schecter had written about the contaminated parking garage, and she asked, "Would you like to photocopy the health department's 'Binghamton file'?" She then secured the county executive's approval, and I gratefully accepted the offer. The plethora of documents ran the gamut from Gaffney's personal notes on meetings she had attended to correspondence labeled "confidential."

The second ethical issue was that, through this windfall of documents, I had access to a list of most of the people who had been exposed inside and outside the SOB, each identified by his or her organizational affiliation. Several weeks earlier I had interviewed a health officer for the Civil Service Employees Association (CSEA), who explained that CSEA would like to keep records on its exposed members but could not get the state health department to release the names. The CSEA official assured me that if I ever obtained such a list, a copy would be put to good use. I also wanted to interview some of the people on the list, but these people had not agreed that their identity could be revealed to me. I found no professional guidelines for either of these situations, but I neither sent the list to CSEA nor contacted the workers.[7]

7. I did call some of the presidents of the companies at which exposed workers were employed, asking to talk to some of the workers I knew had been in the building, but I was denied access. In other cases, things worked out differently. For example, in one of my interviews with the guard who was

Finally, I had to resolve the dilemma of whether or not to quote from the many letters for which I lacked the authors' informed consent. I consulted some historians and historical sociologists about what is considered proper in such situations. Most of them had never faced such a problem, because most historical research deals with dead people. But, they said, the usual rule is that if one cannot get both the writer and the receiver of some letter or memorandum to grant permission to use it, the only thing to do is to wait until they die. For me, this was too stringent a requirement, because I researched individuals who might live for another forty years.

I decided I would not use Gaffney's personal notes but I would use official correspondence. When officials wrote these letters and memoranda, they did so in their capacities as public servants, presumably acting in the public interest. I therefore decided that it was not unreasonable to try to decipher how they interpreted what the public interest was. Moreover, institutionalized controls on professional ethics, such as informed consent and peer review of projects involving human subjects, were instituted to protect those who might otherwise lack the power to protect themselves. Thus, I found myself having to decide which groups would receive the most protection. This is not to suggest that people who occupy positions of power are without rights of their own, but I felt that not using the documents would be stretching the intent behind our attempts to define professional ethics.

---

on duty at the time of the accident, I learned of another exposed worker with interesting testimony to relate. The guard offered to give me his name and number, assuring me he would not mind if I called. I declined to take that information and instead arranged for the worker to give explicit permission before I contacted him. I gave a copy of my letter of introduction to the guard, along with my home and office telephone numbers, and asked her to give them to the worker so he could call me. I explained that another way to do this was for the guard to give the letter to the worker, and if he then consented, she could relay that information to me and I would call him. The worker gave the guard permission to give me his name and number, and when I subsequently called him, I again explained the purposes of my research.

References

The references are organized in two categories: first, books and articles, and, second, official correspondence, reports, and studies. The former are cited in the text by author and year. Most of the references in the latter section are cited by author, month, day, and year or by author, month, and year, although several studies that did not carry a specific date are necessarily cited by author and year alone. A List of Interviews follows the References.

Books and Articles

Aldrich, Howard
1979   *Organizations and Environments.* Englewood Cliffs, N.J.: Prentice-Hall.
Aldrich, Howard, and Jeffrey Pfeffer
1976   "Environments of Organizations." *Annual Review of Sociology* 2:79–105.
Aldrich, Howard, and David Whetten
1981   "Organization Sets, Action Sets, and Networks: Making the Most of Simplicity." In *Handbook of Organizational Design,* edited by Paul C. Nystrom and William H. Starbuck, vol. 1, pp. 385–408. New York: Oxford University Press.
Alexander, Ernest R.
1979   "The Design of Alternatives in Organizational Contexts: A Pilot Study." *Administrative Science Quarterly* 24(3): 382–404.
Allison, Graham
1971   *Essence of Decision: Explaining the Cuban Missile Crisis.* Boston: Little, Brown.
Baughman, Robert W.
1974   "TCDD and Industrial Accidents." In "Tetrachlorodibenzo-p-dioxins in the Environment." Ph.D. diss., Harvard University.
Binghamton Evening Press
1981a   "Camping Out Leaves Anderson's Tribe Pining for the Tower." March 26.
1981b   "State Denies Health Official Resigned Over Tainted Tower." October 10.

1982   "Enough PCB Data Compiled." March 29.

Boffey, Philip M.
1983   "PCBs in Buildings Called Wide Peril." *New York Times,* September 1, A15.

Bromet, Evelyn, and Leslie Dunn
1981   "Mental Health of Mothers Nine Months After the Three Mile Island Accident." *Urban and Social Change Review* 14(2): 12–15.

Brown, Michael
1979   *Laying Waste: The Poisoning of America by Toxic Chemicals.* New York: Pantheon.

Brubaker, Rogers
1984   *The Limits of Rationality.* London: George Allen & Unwin.

Calabresi, Guido, and Philip Bobbitt
1978   *Tragic Choices.* New York: Norton.

Campbell, Donald
1975   "Degrees of Freedom and the Case Study." *Comparative Political Studies* 8(2): 178–93.

Campbell, Donald, and Julian Stanley
1966   *Experimental and Quasiexperimental Designs for Research.* Chicago: Rand McNally.

Carson, Rachel
1962   *Silent Spring.* Boston: Houghton Mifflin.

Clark, William
1980   "Witches, Floods, and Wonder Drugs: Historical Perspectives on Risk Management." In *Societal Risk Assessment: How Safe Is Safe Enough?* edited by Richard C. Schwing and Walter A. Albers, Jr., pp. 287–313. New York: Plenum Press.

Clarke, Lee
1988   "Explaining Choices Among Technological Risks." *Social Problems* 35(1): 501–14.

Cohen, Andy
1981   "Young Seeks Consultant on Cleanup." *Binghamton Sun Bulletin,* October 6.

Cohen, Michael, James G. March, and Johan P. Olsen
1972   "A Garbage Can Model of Organizational Choice." *Administrative Science Quarterly* 17(1): 1–25.

Cole, Gerald A., and Stephen B. Withey
1981   "Perspectives on Risk Perceptions." *Risk Analysis* 1:143–63.

Combs, Barbara, and Paul Slovic
1979   "Newspaper Coverage of Causes of Death." *Journalism Quarterly* 56 (Winter): 837–49.

Covello, Vincent T., Joshua Menkes, and Jiri Nehnevajsa
   1982   "Risk Analysis, Philosophy, and the Social and Behavioral Sciences." *Risk Analysis* 2:53–58.

Davis, Fred
   1974   "Stories and Sociology." *Urban Life and Culture* 3(3): 310–16.

Diesing, Paul
   1971   *Patterns of Discovery in the Social Sciences*. Chicago: Aldine.

DiMaggio, Paul, and Walter Powell
   1983   "The Iron Cage Revisited: Institutional Isomorphism and Collective Rationality in Organizational Fields." *American Sociological Review* 48 (2): 147–60.

Douglas, Jack
   1976   *Investigative Social Research*. Beverly Hills, Calif.: Sage.

Douglas, Mary, and Aaron Wildavsky
   1982   *Risk and Culture: An Essay on the Selection of Technological and Environmental Dangers*. Berkeley and Los Angeles: University of California Press.

Dowie, Mark
   1977   "How Ford Put Two Million Firetraps on Wheels." *Business and Society Review* 23 (Fall): 46–55.

Dukes, William F.
   1965   "N = 1." *Psychological Bulletin* 64(1): 74–79.

East, Jim
   1981   "Bill to Clean, Fix, Replace Won't Be Small." *Binghamton Evening Press*, February 6.

Edelman, Murray
   1964   *The Symbolic Uses of Politics*. Urbana: University of Illinois Press.

Egginton, Joyce
   1980   *The Poisoning of Michigan*. New York: Norton.

Einhorn, Hillel J., and Robin M. Hogarth
   1981   "Behavioral Decision Theory: Processes of Judgment and Choice." *Annual Review of Psychology* 32:53–88.

Environmental Health Perspectives
   1973   "Chlorinated Dibenzodioxins and Dibenzofurans." 5 (September).

Erikson, Kai
   1976   *Everything in Its Path: Destruction of Community in the Buffalo Creek Flood*. New York: Simon and Schuster.

Esposito, M. P., Thomas O. Tiernan, and Forrest E. Dryden
    1980   *Dioxins*. Publication no. 600/2–80–197. Cincinnati: U.S. Environmental Protection Agency.

Evan, William
    1966   "The Organization-Set: Toward a Theory of Interorganizational Relations." In *Approaches to Organizational Design,* edited by James Thompson, pp. 175–90. Pittsburgh: University of Pittsburgh Press.

Fairbanks, Phil
    1981   "It's Official: Schecter's Out." *Binghamton Sun Bulletin,* June 25.

Fecteau, Lois
    1981a   "Governments Stay Shut; Costly Cleaning Begins." *Binghamton Evening Press,* February 6.
    1981b   "Tests: Massive Mop-Up a Must." *Binghamton Evening Press,* February 8.
    1981c   "Taint Purge Will Stretch for Months." *Binghamton Evening Press,* February 15.
    1981d   "State Says EPA Tests Welcomed." *Binghamton Evening Press,* February 17.
    1981e   "State May Leave Some PCBs." *Binghamton Sun Bulletin,* February 18.
    1981f   "City Toxin Taint Rivals the Worst." *Binghamton Evening Press,* March 2.
    1981g   "State Muzzles Taint Comment." *Binghamton Evening Press,* March 6.
    1981h   "State Says EPA Tests Welcomed." *Binghamton Evening Press,* March 17.
    1981i   "Experts to Define Toxin Cleanup." *Binghamton Evening Press,* March 26.
    1981j   "State Hires Firm for Cleanup Plan." *Binghamton Evening Press,* April 1.
    1981k   "State Says Tower Will Vent Clean Air." *Binghamton Evening Press,* August 11.
    1981l   "Egan Says Public Relations Only Slip on Tower." *Binghamton Evening Press,* September 10.
    1981m "N.Y. Health Official Resigns over PCBs." *Binghamton Evening Press,* October 8.
    1981n   "Two Exposed to Tower Taint Assail State." *Binghamton Evening Press,* October 12.
    1981o   "PCB Facts Sought." *Binghamton Evening Press,* October 15.

1981p   "Citizens' Group Vows to Watch State Cleanup." *Binghamton Evening Press,* October 22.

Feldman, Martha S., and James G. March
1981   "Information in Organizations as Signal and Symbol." *Administrative Science Quarterly* 26(2): 171–86.

Fischhoff, Baruch
1977   "Cost-Benefit Analysis and the Art of Motorcycle Maintenance." *Policy Sciences* 8:177–202.

Fischhoff, Baruch, Paul Slovic, and Sarah Lichtenstein
1978   "How Safe Is Safe Enough? A Psychometric Study of Attitudes Towards Technological Risks and Benefits." *Policy Sciences* 9:127–52.

Fischkin, Barbara
1982   "The Tainted Tower." *Newsday,* May 10.

Foldes, Mike
1981   "Guard Recalls PCB Night, Scorns Suit." *Binghamton Sun Bulletin,* June 25.

Fox, Jeffrey L.
1983   "Dioxins' Health Effects Remain Puzzling." *Science,* September 16, 1161–62.

Freudenberg, Nicholas
1984   "Citizen Action for Environmental Health: Report on a Survey of Community Organizations." *American Journal of Public Health* 74(5): 444–48.

Gans, Herbert
1979   *Deciding What's News: A Study of CBS Evening News, NBC Nightly News, Newsweek, and Time.* New York: Pantheon.

Geimann, Steve
1981a   "Team of Toxic Waste Experts Begins Downtown Mop-Up." *Binghamton Sun Bulletin,* February 6.
1981b   "Tallon Finds Carey State of Health Message Lacking." *Binghamton Sun Bulletin,* March 5.
1981c   "Carey Says Cleanup's Risks Must Be Tolerated." *Binghamton Sun Bulletin,* March 6.
1981d   "Toronto Faced Toxic Crisis Similar to City's." *Binghamton Sun Bulletin,* March 10.
1981e   "Officials Downplay EPA's Role in Cleanup." *Binghamton Sun Bulletin,* March 16.
1981f   "County Will Do More Tests on Parking Garage." *Binghamton Sun Bulletin,* March 25.
1981g   "Tower Not So Toxic, State Officials Say." *Binghamton Sun Bulletin,* August 11.

1983 "Sore Citizens Second-Guess and Sue State." *Binghamton Evening Press,* February 4.

Goodman, Paul, and Johannes Pennings
1977 *New Perspectives on Organizational Effectiveness.* San Francisco: Jossey-Bass.

Gottfredson, Linda S., and Paul E. White
1981 "Interorganizational Agreements." In *Handbook of Organizational Design,* edited by Paul C. Nystrom and William H. Starbuck, vol. 1, pp. 471–86. New York: Oxford University Press.

Gusfield, Joseph
1981 *The Culture of Public Problems: Drinking-Driving and the Symbolic Order.* Chicago: University of Chicago Press.

Hazardous Materials: Emergency Response Guidebook
1980 Washington, D.C.: U.S. Department of Transportation, 5800.3.

Heimer, Carol A.
1985 *Reactive Risk and Rational Action: Managing Moral Hazard in Insurance Contracts.* Berkeley and Los Angeles: University of California Press.

Hirschman, Albert
1972 *Exit, Voice, and Loyalty.* Cambridge: Harvard University Press.

Hohenemser, Christoph, Roger Kasperson, and Robert Kates
1977 "The Distrust of Nuclear Power." *Science,* April 1, 25–34.

Huffaker, Robert
1983 Letter to the Editor. *Binghamton Evening Press,* March 21.

Jones, Steve
1982 "Money Missing." *Binghamton Evening Press,* February 3.

Jones, Steve, and George Basler
1981 "Fire, Fumes Shut Government Plaza." *Binghamton Evening Press,* February 5.

Kahneman, Daniel, Paul Slovic, and Amos Tversky
1982 *Judgment Under Uncertainty: Heuristics and Biases.* Cambridge: Cambridge University Press.

Kantrowitz, Arthur
1975 "Controlling Technology Democratically." *American Scientist* 63(5): 505–9.

Kates, Robert W.
1977 "Assessing the Assessors: The Art and Ideology of Risk Assessment." *Ambio* 6(5): 247–52.

Katz, Barry
  1981a "Proof Gone." *Binghamton Evening Press,* March 9.
  1981b "Toxic Soot Clogs Work of Offices." *Binghamton Evening Press,* March 22.
Kennedy, Mary M.
  1979 "Generalizing from Single Case Studies." *Evaluation Quarterly* 3(4): 661–78.
Kreps, G. A.
  1984 "Sociological Inquiry and Disaster Research." *Annual Review of Sociology* 10:309–30.
Kruskal, William
  1978 "Statistics: The Field." In *International Encyclopedia of Statistics,* edited by William Kruskal and Judith Tanur, pp. 1071–93. New York: Free Press.
Laumann, Edward O., David Knoke, and Yong-Hak Kim
  1985 "An Organizational Approach to State Policy Formation." *American Sociological Review* 50(1):1–19.
Lave, Lester
  1984 "Regulating Risks." *Risk Analysis* 4(2): 79–80.
Levine, Adeline
  1982 *Love Canal: Science, Politics, and People.* Lexington, Mass.: Lexington Books.
Levine, Sol, and Paul C. White
  1961 "Exchange as a Conceptual Framework for the Study of Interorganizational Relationships." *Administrative Science Quarterly* 5(4): 584–601.
Lichtenstein, Sarah, Paul Slovic, Baruch Fischhoff, Mark Layman, and Barbara Combs
  1978 "Judged Frequency of Lethal Events." *Journal of Experimental Psychology: Human Learning and Memory* 4:551–78.
Lindblom, Charles E.
  1959 "The Science of Muddling Through." *Public Administration Review* 19 (Autumn): 79–88.
  1979 "Still Muddling, Not Yet Through." *Public Administration Review* 39(6): 517–26.
Litwak, Eugene, and Lydia F. Hylton
  1962 "Interorganizational Analysis: A Hypothesis on Co-ordinating Agencies." *Administrative Science Quarterly* 6(4): 395–421.
Long, Norton
  1958 "The Local Community as an Ecology of Games." *American Journal of Sociology* 6(3): 251–61.

Lowrence, William
  1976   *Of Acceptable Risk*. Los Altos, Calif.: Kaufmann.
Lutz, Frank
  1982   "Tightening Up Loose Couplings in Organizations of Higher Education." *Administrative Science Quarterly* 27(4): 653–69.
Lynn, Frank
  1985   "Carey Takes Rare Look Back at Administration." *New York Times,* April 8.
McCullough, Marie
  1981a "He's Taken On Polluted Wells, Contaminated Office Building, and Now He's Taking On the Heat." *Binghamton Evening Press,* March 12.
  1981b "Hey, State Office Workers, Thanks." *Binghamton Evening Press,* March 19.
MacLean, Douglas
  1982   "Risk and Consent." *Risk Analysis* 2:59–67.
March, James G.
  1978   "Bounded Rationality, Ambiguity, and the Engineering of Choice." *Bell Journal of Economics* 9:587–608.
March, James G., and Johan Olsen
  1979   *Ambiguity and Choice*. Bergen, Norway: Universitetsforlaget.
Mazur, Allan
  1973   "Disputes Between Experts." *Minerva* 11(2): 243–62.
  1975   "Opposition to Technological Innovation." *Minerva* 13(1): 58–81.
Metcalfe, Les
  1981   "Designing Precarious Partnerships." In *Handbook of Organizational Design,* edited by Paul C. Nystrom and William H. Starbuck, vol. 1, pp. 503–30. New York: Oxford University Press.
Meyer, John W., and Brian Rowan
  1977   "Formal Structure of Organizations as Myth and Ceremony." *American Journal of Sociology* 83(2): 340–63.
Meyer, John W., and W. Richard Scott, eds.
  1983   *Organizational Environments: Ritual and Rationality.* Beverly Hills, Calif.: Sage.
Meyer, Marshall W., and Kenneth Solomon
  1984   "Risk Management in Local Communities." *Policy Sciences* 16:245–65.

Miles, Matthew
  1979   "Qualitative Data as an Attractive Nuisance: The Problem of Analysis." *Administrative Science Quarterly* 24(4): 590– 601.
Miller, Doug
  1981   "Binghamton Building Haunted by Fear, Doubt After PCB Blaze." *Schenectady Gazette,* February 23.
Milner, Murray
  1980   *Unequal Care: A Case Study of Interorganizational Relations in Health Care.* New York: Columbia University Press.
Mintz, Beth, and Michael Schwartz
  1985   *The Power Structure of American Business.* Chicago: University of Chicago Press.
Mohr, Lawrence
  1982   *Explaining Organizational Behavior.* San Francisco: Jossey-Bass.
Nader, Ralph
  1965   *Unsafe at Any Speed.* New York: Bantam Books.
National Institute of Occupational Safety and Health (NIOSH)
  1977   *Occupational Exposure to Polychlorinated Biphenyls.* Washington, D.C.: U.S. Government Printing Office.
Nelkin, Dorothy, and Michael S. Brown
  1984   *Workers at Risk: Voices from the Workplace.* Chicago: University of Chicago Press.
New York Times
  1983   "Building Is Closed After PCB Spill." December 23.
  1985   "Product Liability: The New Morass." March 10.
Nystrom, Paul C., and William H. Starbuck, eds.
  1981   *Handbook of Organizational Design.* Vol. 1. New York: Oxford University Press.
Otway, Harry, and Kerry Thomas
  1982   "Reflections on Risk Perception and Policy." *Risk Analysis* 2: 69–82.
Pearson, David
  1984   "K.A.L. 007: What the U.S. Knew and When We Knew It." *The Nation,* August 18–25.
Pennings, Johannes M.
  1981   "Strategically Interdependent Organizations." In *Handbook of Organizational Design,* edited by Paul C. Nystrom and William H. Starbuck, vol. 1, pp. 433–55. New York: Oxford University Press.

Perrow, Charles

1983　"The Organizational Context of Human Factors Engineering." *Administrative Science Quarterly* 28(4): 521–41.

1984　*Normal Accidents: Living with High Risk Technologies.* New York: Basic Books.

Pfeffer, Jeffrey, and Gerald Salancik

1978　*The External Control of Organizations.* New York: Harper and Row.

Raiffa, Howard

1980　"Concluding Remarks." In *Societal Risk Assessment: How Safe Is Safe Enough?* edited by Richard C. Schwing and Walter A. Albers, Jr., pp. 339–41. New York: Plenum Press.

Royce, Edward

1985　"The Origins of Southern Sharecropping: Explaining Social Change." *Current Perspectives in Social Theory* 6:279–99.

Sabatier, Paul

1978　"The Acquisition and Utilization of Technical Information by Administrative Agencies." *Administrative Science Quarterly* 23(3): 396–417.

Salancik, Gerald R.

1977　"Commitment and the Control of Organizational Behavior and Belief." In *New Directions in Organizational Behavior,* edited by Barry M. Staw and Gerald R. Salancik, pp. 1–54. Chicago: St. Clair.

Schecter, Arnold, Raymonde Lizotte, Wing Sun, Lawrence Miller, George Gitlitz, Michael Bogdasarian, and Frederick Banting

1985　"Chlorinated Dibenzodioxins and Dibenzofurans in Human Adipose Tissue from Exposed and Control New York State Patients." *Chemosphere* 14(6–7): 933–37.

Schecter, Arnold, and John J. Ryan

1985　"Dioxin and Furan Levels in Human Adipose Tissue from Exposed and Control Populations." Paper presented at the meetings of the American Chemical Society, Miami Beach, Florida, April 28–May 3.

Schecter, Arnold, Fenton Schaffner, Thomas Tiernan, and Michael Taylor

1984　"Ultrastructural Alterations of Liver Mitochondria in Response to Dioxins, Furans, PCBs, and Biphenylenes." *Banbury Report* 18:177–90.

Schecter, Arnold, and Thomas Tiernan

1985　"Occupational Exposure to Polychlorinated Dioxins, Polychlorinated Furans, and Polychlorinated Biphenyls, and

Biphenylenes After an Electrical Panel and Transformer Accident in an Office Building in Binghamton, New York." *Environmental Health Perspectives* 85(60).

Schoenfeld, A. Clay, Robert F. Meier, and Robert J. Griffin.
  1979   "Constructing a Social Problem: The Press and the Environment." *Social Problems* 27(1): 38–61.

Schwing, Richard C., and Walter A. Albers, Jr., eds.
  1980   *Societal Risk Assessment: How Safe Is Safe Enough?* New York: Plenum Press.

Scott, Marvin, and Stanford Lyman
  1968   "Accounts." *American Sociological Review* 33(1): 46–62.

Seely, Hart
  1983   "The Building That Won't Come Clean." *Syracuse Herald American,* August 1 and 3.

Short, James
  1984   "Toward the Social Transformation of Risk Analysis." *American Sociological Review* 49(6): 711–25.

Silbergeld, Ellen
  1983   "Health Effects of PCBs: Occupational Exposure." In *Proceedings, PCB-Seminar,* September 28–30, pp. 136–51. Scheveningen, The Hague: Ministry of Housing, Physical Planning and Environment.

Slovic, Paul, Baruch Fischhoff, and Sarah Lichtenstein
  1979   "Rating the Risks: The Structure of Expert and Lay Perceptions." *Environment* 21 (3): 14–39.
  1980   "Facts and Fears: Understanding Perceived Risk." In *Societal Risk Assessment: How Safe Is Safe Enough?* edited by Richard C. Schwing and Walter A. Albers, Jr., pp. 181–214. New York: Plenum Press.
  1982   "Why Study Risk Perception?" *Risk Analysis* 2:83–93.

Smith, Robert
  1985   "Politics and Science in Public Health Disputes: Two Case Studies of Public Advocacy Research." Ph.D. diss., State University of New York at Stony Brook.

Sproull, Lee, Stephen Weiner, and David Wolf
  1978   *Organizing an Anarchy: Belief, Bureaucracy, and Politics in the National Institute of Education.* Chicago: University of Chicago Press.

Starr, Chauncey
  1969   "Social Benefit Versus Technological Risk." *Science,* September 19, 1232–38.

Staw, Barry M., and J. Ross
    1978   "Commitment to a Policy Decision: A Multi-Theoretical
            Perspective." *Administrative Science Quarterly* 23(1): 40–64.
Tasca, Leo
    1983   "Power and Organization in Organized Anarchies." De-
            partment of Sociology, State University of New York at
            Stony Brook. Typescript.
Taylor, Serge
    1984   *Making Bureaucracies Think: The Environmental Impact State-
            ment Strategy of Administrative Reform.* Stanford: Stanford
            University Press.
Tiernan, Thomas O., John H. Garrett, Joseph G. Solch, Michael L.
    Taylor, Garrett F. VanNess, and Jerry A. Clark
    1981   "Determination of Dibenzo-p-Dioxins and Dibenzofurans
            in Surface Wipes and Related Specimens from Broome
            County Facilities, Binghamton, New York, Contaminated
            as a Result of a Transformer Fire." Brehm Laboratory,
            Wright State University, July 22.
Tiernan, Thomas, Michael Taylor, John Garrett, Garrett VanNess,
    Joseph Solch, Daniel Wagel, Gerald Ferguson, and Arnold Schecter
    1985   "Sources and Fate of Polychlorinated Dibenzodioxins, Di-
            benzofurans, and Related Compounds in Human Envi-
            ronments." *Environmental Health Perspectives* 59:145–58.
Toxic Substances Control Act
    1976   PL 94-469, October. Washington, D.C.: U.S. Government
            Printing Office.
Tversky, Amos, and Daniel Kahneman
    1971   "Belief in the Law of Small Numbers." *Psychological Bulletin*
            76(2): 105–10.
United States Commerce and Trade Code
    1982   "Supplement V, Vol. 2, Title 15." Washington, D.C.: U.S.
            Government Printing Office.
Viscusi, W. Kip
    1979   *Employment Hazards: An Investigation of Market Performance.*
            Cambridge: Harvard University Press.
Walsh, Edward J.
    1981   "Resource Mobilization and Citizen Protest in Communi-
            ties Around Three Mile Island." *Social Problems* 29(1): 1–
            21.
    1985   "On Time, Targets, and Tactics in Social Movements:
            Phases of the TMI Conflict." Paper presented at the East-

ern Sociological Society meetings, Philadelphia, December 1984.

Warren, Roland
1967 "The Interorganizational Field as a Focus for Investigation." *Administrative Science Quarterly* 12 (December): 396–419.

Weber, Max
1978 *Economy and Society.* Edited by Guenther Roth and Claus Wittich. Berkeley and Los Angeles: University of California Press.

Wegars, Don
1983 "Workers Returning to PCB Skyscraper." *San Francisco Chronicle,* May 26.

Weick, Karl
1976 "Educational Organizations as Loosely Coupled Systems." *Administrative Science Quarterly* 21(1): 1–19.
1979 *The Social Psychology of Organizing.* Reading, Mass.: Addison-Wesley.

Whiteside, Thomas
1979 *The Pendulum and the Toxic Cloud: The Dioxin Threat from Vietnam to Seveso.* New Haven: Yale University Press.

Wildavsky, Aaron
1979 "No Risk Is the Highest Risk of All." *American Scientist* 67:32–37.

Woodward, Bob, and Carl Bernstein
1976 *All the President's Men.* New York: Warner Books.

Yin, Robert
1981 "The Case Study Crisis: Some Answers." *Administrative Science Quarterly* 26(1): 58–65.

Official Correspondence, Reports, and Studies

Adler, Norbert
October 19, 1981. Letter to Kathleen Gaffney.
Austin, Roland
February 9, 1981. Memorandum to Arnold Schecter.
Barber, Walter
May 7, 1981. Letter to Daniel Patrick Moynihan.
Broome County Employees
February 18, 1981. Petition to Governor Hugh L. Carey; response by Glenn Haughie.

Broome County Legislature
    May 19, 1981. "Resolution" to authorize $7,200.00 for tests.
Broome County Public Health Committee
    October 15, 1981. Minutes of meeting.
Broome County Public Meeting
    November 30, 1981. Tape transcription.
Buckley, John
    November 23, 1981. Letter to Carl Young.
Citizens' Committee on the Binghamton State Office Building
    October 26, 1981. Transcript of meeting.
City and County Workers
    March 3, 1981. Petition to Arnold Schecter.
D'Amato, Alfonse
    July 13, 1981. Letter to Michael Cardenas.
Drazen, Bruce
    June 5, 1981. Letter to John Burns.
Eadie, John
    April 1, 1981. Letter to David Slaunwhite.
Eadon, George
    February 2, 1982. Memorandum to D. Carpenter.
Eggleston, Judith
    March 2, 1981. Letter to Alfred Libous.
Fitzgerald, Edward F., James M. Melius, Susan J. Standfast,
    Dwight T. Janerich, B. Beckerman, and Lois G. Youngblood
    1984. "Status Report for the Binghamton State Office Building
    Medical Surveillance Program." New York State Department of
    Health Report.
Fitzgerald, Edward F., Aura L. Weinstein, Lois G. Youngblood,
    Susan J. Standfast, and James M. Melius
    August 1985. "The Binghamton State Office Building Medical Sur-
    veillance Program: 1981–1984." New York State Department of
    Health Report.
Fitzgerald, Edward F., Susan J. Standfast, Lois G. Youngblood,
    James M. Melius, and Dwight T. Janerich
    November/December 1986. "Assessing the Health Effects of Poten-
    tial Exposure to PCBs, Dioxins, and Furans from Electrical Trans-
    former Fires: The Binghamton State Office Building Medical Sur-
    veillance Program." *Archives of Environmental Health* 41(6): 368–76.
Gaffney, Kathleen
    March 5, 1981. Memorandum to Edward Mosher.

Haughie, Glenn
  March 4, 1981. Letter to county employees.
  May 12, 1981. Letter to Arnold Schecter.
Hawley, John
  May 1, 1981. Memorandum to Nancy Kim.
Heath, Clark
  October 7, 1981. Letter to Arnold Schecter.
Huffaker, Robert
  February 11, 1981. Memorandum to David Seiffert.
  March 21, 1983. Letter to the editor, *Binghamton Evening Press.*
Jennings, J.
  August 4, 1981. Telegram to Governor Hugh L. Carey.
Lafornara, Joseph
  March 20, 1981. Memorandum to Kenneth Stoller.
Landrigan, Philip
  May 20, 1981. Letter to Arnold Schecter.
  August 24, 1981. Letter to Arnold Schecter.
Lee, James
  August 5, 1981. Memorandum to Arnold Schecter.
Moynihan, Daniel Patrick
  April 14, 1981. Letter to Walter Barber.
New York Department of Health
  February 24, 1981. "Laboratory Test Results." Report.
New York Office of General Services (OGS)
  February 26, 1981. "Cleaning Operations at the Binghamton State
  Office Building Suspended." Press release.
  August 4, 1981. "General Health and Safety Plan for Cleanup of
  Binghamton State Office Building."
  August 28, 1981. "Negative Declaration to Department of Environ-
  mental Conservation."
  1982. "Binghamton: A Chronicle."
O'Keefe, Patrick
  February 8, 1981. "Soot, Transformer Fire." New York Department
  of Health internal report.
Panel Packet
  April 3, 1981. Collection of materials distributed to expert panel,
  media, and the public.
Public Meeting Transcript
  December 2, 1981. Binghamton, New York.
Rappe, Christoffer
  June 1, 1981. Report to Glenn Haughie on chemical levels.

Schecter, Arnold

February 25, 1981. Memorandum to Carl Young.

February 26, 1981. "Commissioner's Order" to close the SOB; never issued.

March 2, 1981. Memorandum to James Wahl.

March 4, 1981. "Commissioner's Order" for the return of all material removed from SOB.

March 4, 1981. Memorandum to Edward Mosher.

March 24, 1981a. Letter to Carl Young.

March 24, 1981b. Memorandum to Carl Young.

April 1, 1981. Letter to Carl Young.

May 5, 1981. Letter to Glenn Haughie.

May 14, 1981. Letter to Patrick Mullins.

May 15, 1981. Letter to Glenn Haughie.

May 15, 1981. Letter to Philip Landrigan.

May 18, 1981. Memorandum to Carl Young and James Lee.

Smith, R. M., P. W. O'Keefe, D. L. Hilker, B. L. Jelus-Tyror, and K. Aldous

February 20, 1981. "Analysis of 2,3,7,8 Tetrachlorodibenzofuran and 2,3,7,8 Tetrachlorodibenzo-p-dioxin in a Soot Sample from a Transformer Explosion in Binghamton, New York." New York State Department of Health Report.

Stalling, David

March 31, 1981. "Chlorinated Dibenzofurans and Related Compounds in Soot Formed in a Transformer Fire, in Binghamton, NY." Report to New York State Health Department.

August 18, 1981. Letter to Arnold Schecter.

Tardiff, Robert

September 8, 1981. Letter to Arnold Schecter.

Taylor, Philip

February 13, 1981. Memoranda to David Axelrod.

April 1, 1981. Letter to five Binghamton physicians.

Testani, James

March 2, 1981. Press release.

March 2, 1981. Letter to Arnold Schecter.

Tumasonis, Casimir, and Laurence Kaminsky

N.d. "Preliminary Report: Chick Embryos as a Probe of the Relative Toxicities of Soot Samples from a Polychlorinated Biphenyl-Containing Transformer." Internal report, New York State Department of Health.

Upton, Arthur

August 21, 1981. Letter to Arnold Schecter.

Wiegert, Wallace
  February 26, 1981. Letter to David Seiffert.
Young, Alvin
  May 7, 1981. Letter to Glenn Haughie.
Young, Carl
  February 24, 1981. Memorandum to Arnold Schecter.
  November 25, 1981. Memorandum to county employees.
Youngblood, Lois G., and Aura L. Weinstein
  1986. "The Binghamton State Office Building Medical Surveillance Program." Status Report for Expert Advisory Panel.

List of Interviews

All interviews were conducted by the author unless otherwise noted.
This list includes only interviews actually cited.

Anderson, Warren
    August 20, 1981. Telephone interview.
Barber, Cleon
    August 12, 1981. Binghamton, New York.
Beaudoin, Arthur
    October 6, 1981. Albany, New York.
Briganti, Vincent
    July 17, 1981. Telephone interview.
Brown, Paul
    May 3, 1982. Telephone interview.
Byrne, Owen
    August 13, 1981. Binghamton, New York.
Drazen, Bruce
    February 15, 1983. Telephone interview.
    July 2, 1983. Binghamton, New York.
Engineer (anonymity requested)
    February 22, 1982. Telephone interview.
Faughnan, Donald
    August 13, 1981. Binghamton, New York.
Gaffney, Kathleen
    August 12, 1981. Binghamton, New York.
Haughie, Glenn
    October 8, 1981. Albany, New York.
Health nurse (anonymity requested)
    December 1981. Binghamton, New York.
Hudacs, John
    October 8, 1981. Albany, New York.
Huffaker, Robert
    October 6, 1981. Albany, New York.
Kimbrough, Renate
    July 15, 1981. Telephone interview.

Lanahan, Peter
  October 7, 1981. Albany, New York.
Landrigan, Philip
  September 1, 1981. Telephone interview.
Libous, Alfred
  November 30, 1981. Binghamton, New York.
Mesite, Jacklyn
  June 14, 1981. New York, New York.
Peterson, Gary
  July 27, 1981. Telephone interview.
Rings, David
  December 4, 1984. Telephone interview.
Schecter, Arnold
  August 10, 1981. Binghamton, New York.
  January 21, 1982. Binghamton, New York.
  October 3, 1983. Binghamton, New York.
Seiffert, David
  October 8, 1981. Albany, New York.
Slaunwhite, David
  December 24, 1981. Telephone interview.
Stuckart, Cathy
  April 29, 1982. Telephone interview.
Svoboda, Joseph
  December 3, 1981. Binghamton, New York.
Tallon, James
  August 10, 1981. Binghamton, New York.
Taylor, Philip
  July 8, 1981. Telephone interview.
  August 4, 1981. Telephone interview.
  August 8, 1981. Telephone interview.
  December 11, 1981. Telephone interview.
Thompson, James
  October 28, 1981. Telephone interview.
Whittemore, Lois
  August 11, 1981. Binghamton, New York.
Young, Carl
  May 20, 1981. Interview by Steven Geimann.
  Binghamton, New York.
  December 2, 1981. Binghamton, New York.

Index

Acceptable risk, defining of, 11–12, 28, 60, 75–77; agencies responsible for, 30–31; and blunting of dissent, 131–32, 170; and domain consensus, 137–38; individual behavior and, 154; and interorganizational garbage can, 162–64; media and, 167–68; and organizational environment, 56, 57–58; and organizational and political interests, 81–83; organizations and, 4, 12, 13, 65, 81–83, 138; preconditions of, 56; public and, 151–56; rational choice and, 181; reduction of actors and, 132; science and, 11; and struggle among organizations, 118–19. *See also* Risk analysis

Access structures, 164–65

Accountability, 114, 118, 130n.7, 151, 164, 168

Action set, 169–71

Administrative Science Quarterly, 173

Agent Orange, 121

Air: ambient levels of, 134; federal standard for PCBs in, 61; toxin levels in, 115–16n.1, 116

Albany, N.Y., transformer leak in, 8

Aldrich, Howard, 169

Alexander, Ernest R., 82

All the President's Men (Woodward and Bernstein), 189n.2

Allwash, Inc., 142, 142n.4, 147–48

Alternative solutions: and access structures, 164–65; and authority, 169; collecting, 121; defeating, 82–83; establishing premises of, 123–24; narrowing agenda of, 137; ordering, 60, 71–75; power and, 176; risk analysis and, 181

Ambiguity: and authority, 31; and business, 40; and cleanup, 115; and control of information, 106–7; individual vs. organizational behavior and, 147; and interorganizational decision making, 12, 14, 26–27, 83; and medical surveillance, 11, 95–96, 100; and organizational behavior, 158, 174; rationality and, 180; and

social constraints on officials, 25; sociopolitical, 160; technical, 160. *See also* Uncertainty

"Analysis of 2,3,7,8 Tetrachlorodibenzofuran and 2,3,7,8 Tetrachlorodibenzo-p-dioxin in a Soot Sample . . ." (Smith et al.), 124–25

Anderson, Warren, 47

Authority, 31, 85, 160, 168, 180; centralization of, 169–71; and cleanup, 118–19, 131; domain consensus on, 137; and garbage can theory, 174; and medical surveillance, 88–89; within organizations, 173

Average toxic levels, 116, 124

Axelrod, David, 10, 16, 18, 20, 64, 89, 119, 120, 152; and EPA, 53; and Schecter, 18, 86, 93

Bernstein, Carl, 189n.2

Bhopal, India, toxic chemical leak in, 2, 11, 20, 21, 24, 58, 114, 159n.2, 178

Bias: of decision makers, 101, 123; of study, 191

Binghamton, N.Y.: city building in, 31–32; city council of, 16, 34–35; city employees of, 31–32, 146–47; city government in, 31–35, 40, 57, 58, 119, 135; City Hall incident in, 45, 45n.5; population of, 121, 139, 139n.1

Binghamton Evening Press, 98n.10

Binghamton General Hospital, 18–19, 86, 104–6

Binghamton Municipal and Public Affairs Committee, 34

Binghamton State Office Building (SOB): and callous-bureaucracy theory, 20–24; chemical levels in, 115–17, 115–16n.1, 124–27; and cleanup company warning, 22, 23; closed, 143; constricting field of organizations involved with, 30–58; contaminated garage under, 12–13, 41, 59–83; destruction of, considered, 118, 118n.2, 121, 132, 134–37, 138, 169; and disruption of rou-

221

Compositor: Graphic Composition, Inc.
Printer: Braun-Brumfield, Inc.
Binder: Braun-Brumfield, Inc.
Text: 11/13 Baskerville
Display: Baskerville